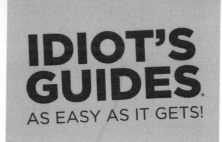

IDIOT'S GUIDES.
AS EASY AS IT GETS!

Raspberry Pi™

by Thorin Klosowski

ALPHA
A member of Penguin Random House LLC

ALPHA BOOKS

Published by Penguin Random House LLC

Penguin Random House LLC, 375 Hudson Street, New York, New York 10014, USA • Penguin Random House LLC (Canada), 90 Eglinton Avenue East, Suite 700, Toronto, Ontario M4P 2Y3, Canada (a division of Pearson Penguin Canada Inc.) • Penguin Books Ltd., 80 Strand, London WC2R 0RL, England • Penguin Ireland, 25 St. Stephen's Green, Dublin 2, Ireland (a division of Penguin Books Ltd.) • Penguin Random House LLC (Australia), 250 Camberwell Road, Camberwell, Victoria 3124, Australia (a division of Pearson Australia Group Pty. Ltd.) • Penguin Books India Pvt. Ltd., 11 Community Centre, Panchsheel Park, New Delhi—110 017, India • Penguin Random House LLC (NZ), 67 Apollo Drive, Rosedale, North Shore, Auckland 1311, New Zealand (a division of Pearson New Zealand Ltd.) • Penguin Books (South Africa) (Pty.) Ltd., 24 Sturdee Avenue, Rosebank, Johannesburg 2196, South Africa • Penguin Books Ltd., Registered Offices: 80 Strand, London WC2R 0RL, England

IDIOT'S GUIDES and Design are trademarks of Penguin Random House LLC

International Standard Book Number: 978-1-61564-778-1
Library of Congress Catalog Card Number: 2014957361

17 16 15   8 7 6 5 4 3 2 1

Interpretation of the printing code: The rightmost number of the first series of numbers is the year of the book's printing; the rightmost number of the second series of numbers is the number of the book's printing. For example, a printing code of 15-1 shows that the first printing occurred in 2015.

Printed in the United States of America

Note: This publication contains the opinions and ideas of its author. It is intended to provide helpful and informative material on the subject matter covered. It is sold with the understanding that the author and publisher are not engaged in rendering professional services in the book. If the reader requires personal assistance or advice, a competent professional should be consulted. The author and publisher specifically disclaim any responsibility for any liability, loss, or risk, personal or otherwise, which is incurred as a consequence, directly or indirectly, of the use and application of any of the contents of this book.

Most Alpha books are available at special quantity discounts for bulk purchases for sales promotions, premiums, fund-raising, or educational use. Special books, or book excerpts, can also be created to fit specific needs. For details, write: Special Markets, Alpha Books, 375 Hudson Street, New York, NY 10014.

Publisher: *Mike Sanders*
Associate Publisher: *Billy Fields*
Senior Acquisitions Editor: *Brook Farling*
Development Editorial Supervisor: *Christy Wagner*
Production Editor: *Jana M. Stefanciosa*

Cover Designer: *Laura Merriman*
Book Designer: *William Thomas*
Indexer: *Brad Herriman*
Layout: *Brian Massey*
Proofreader: *Laura Caddell*

Contents

Appendixes

Introduction

For such a small computer, the Raspberry Pi has made a big impact since its initial release in 2012. Priced at just $35 ($20 for the Model A+), the credit card–sized computer is an easily customizable, affordable computer and also has been used for countless creative projects by do-it-yourselfers. The Raspberry Pi is simple to use, it's open source, and it can be manipulated to do all sorts of different things. At a glance, it's just an inexpensive computer that runs an operating system based on Linux, but it's truly so much more.

The Raspberry Pi was initially created as a fun and inexpensive educational tool to get kids interested in computer programming. The setup process alone—getting this basic computer hooked up to peripherals, the internet, and power—teaches you a bit of programming, and the fact that it's a little difficult to use at first means you learn some basic computer-related skills by just getting it to turn on. Over time, the most popular operating system for the Raspberry Pi, Raspbian, has expanded to include a massive toolkit of software that helps further teach programming and a basic understanding of computer science.

The Raspberry Pi still meets its initial goal of education, but its popularity has expanded far beyond just children as adults are getting a ton of use out of it as well. In fact, the DIY electronics movement latched on to the Raspberry Pi when it was first released, resulting in the little device being nearly impossible to purchase for the first few months because it was sold out everywhere.

Since the initial release, we've seen a few models of the Raspberry Pi. The Model A+ is a simple, affordable version great for low-power projects, while Models B and B+ add a few extra USB ports and more RAM. The Raspberry Pi 2 ups the processing power and RAM of the B+ while maintaining the design and USB ports.

The DIY movement loves the Raspberry Pi for myriad reasons, but the big one is familiarity. Unlike other similar computer boards released before, the Raspberry Pi is capable of running Linux, an operating system that's familiar to many people. Sure, Linux isn't Windows or Apple's OS X, but you can boot it up and understand how it works within a few moments, especially if you have prior experience with the other systems. This is a far cry from other boards like the Arduino that require a much more hands-on programming approach to use.

In this book, you learn everything there is to know about the Raspberry Pi, starting with its history and creation and including a wide variety of projects that aim to teach you how to use your Raspberry Pi in different ways. Throughout the course of these projects, you explore how to use and manipulate Linux, compile software, do some light programming, and build everything from a home security system to a private music streaming device.

For example, one of the most popular Raspberry Pi projects is a media center. With just a little bit of setup, you can use your Raspberry Pi to watch live video, stream movies, and do just about everything else a set-top box like a Roku or Apple TV can do. In fact, media centers are such a popular use for the Raspberry Pi, you can find numerous different operating systems to run it.

Likewise, you have alternatives for basic operating systems to run if you're looking for a straight-forward computer to use. Raspbian is the most popular operating system—and it was built just for the Raspberry Pi—but it's not your only choice. You can search for other builds of Linux or even find versions of Raspbian created for specific projects. Examples include an operating system built for people who want to control robots, lightweight distributions that get rid of all the fluff, and just about anything you can think of. And if you're really interested in messing around, you can even emulate old operating systems like the Commodore 64 or MS-DOS.

Choice is a big part of the Raspberry Pi's success. Because the software is open source, you tend to have a lot of flexibility in what you can do with it. In this book, you learn one way to turn your Raspberry Pi into a music streaming device, but it's certainly not the only way to do it. In fact, you almost always have several other possibilities available.

The Raspberry Pi runs Linux, so that means any software built for Linux can work on the Raspberry Pi. You can opt for just what you want to use for software and customize your Raspberry Pi however you like.

That flexibility extends to other facets of the Raspberry Pi as well. Pretty much any Wi-Fi adapter will work with this device, as will just about any keyboard. You can even skip all that and access your Raspberry Pi remotely if you want. It's really up to you, and unlike software like Windows or OS X, nothing is closed off. You have access to every single little thing the Raspberry Pi can do at all points, and you can tinker with it as you see fit.

In this book, you're going to do a lot of different projects, and sometimes you're probably going to mess things up a little. Unlike Windows or OS X, making mistakes is okay. The Raspberry Pi is built so the operating system runs off an inexpensive SD card, so if you make a significant goof-up, all you need to do to start over from scratch is make another copy of the SD card. This is great for beginners and advanced tinkerers alike because the cost of failure isn't that high.

If you follow the lessons in this book closely, you'll complete a project, but individual set-ups, changes to small amounts of code, or even just a quirk in your own home network will give you the opportunity to explore beyond the pages of this book to discover more things you can do with the Raspberry Pi. That's part of this device's appeal. There's not necessarily one right way to do things, so you'll constantly be learning about different methods and other tricks.

What's more, you have a huge community of people to talk to about any problems that come up as you get creative with your Raspberry Pi. Countless websites, forums, and news stories are available to guide you through any troubles you might have. You'll even be able to talk with Linux experts for help. You have a pretty big resource in the community of people who love the Raspberry Pi, and by the end of this book, you'll be a contributing member to that community as well.

It's easy to discount the Raspberry Pi as a hobbyist's play toy, or just a fun little gimmick. However, once you get into it and start building things for yourself, you'll realize just how much you can do with it. The Raspberry Pi is great for a lot of projects, but things will really start to get interesting once you have an understanding of how it works and you start developing your own uses for it. Every day, someone out there is coming up with a clever new use for their Raspberry Pi. Hopefully, by the end of this book, you'll be an active member in the Raspberry Pi community, making all types of projects on your own and sharing them with people across the world.

Collaboration is a big part of the Raspberry Pi, and you'll likely be doing a lot of it moving forward. You can tackle everything in this book on your own, but it's a lot more fun when you're working with others to solve problems and expand on the projects included here. You'll get a lot more out of the Raspberry Pi when you share and work with other people.

The Raspberry Pi is about fun. Sure, its main goal is to provide an inexpensive computer to anyone in the world, but you can do so much more than that with it.

How This Book Is Organized

This book is divided into four parts. Each part is meant to familiarize you with different aspects of the Raspberry Pi:

Part 1, Getting Started with Your Raspberry Pi, covers the inception of the device, introduces you to the foundation that created it, explains what the device is typically used for, and shares other basics about its history and creation alongside its technical details. This part provides the foundation for everything you'll learn in subsequent parts.

Once you get through the history, you move on to getting your Raspberry Pi up and running. In **Part 2, Setting Up Your Raspberry Pi,** you learn how Linux works, how to use the command line, and how to install operating systems on your Raspberry Pi. The Raspberry Pi is pretty easy to use, but it does require some basic computer know-how. By the end of this part, you'll have the skills you need to move forward.

Once you get your Raspberry Pi set up, it's time to start actually making things with it. **Part 3, Raspberry Pi Projects,** is all about projects you can complete with your Raspberry Pi. In these chapters, you use your Raspberry Pi to build projects ranging from a set-top media box to a home security system. With each project, you learn something new about programming, Linux, DIY culture, and the Raspberry Pi itself. By the time you finish the projects, you'll be well on your way to creating and defining your own.

Finally, **Part 4, Going Further with Your Raspberry Pi,** shows you a number of ways to really push your Raspberry Pi beyond what's covered here. The Raspberry Pi can be used for countless projects, and it's impossible to cover them all in one book. Beyond simply running a copy of Linux, you can attach your Raspberry Pi to other peripherals, robots, and more. Chances are, once you finish the projects in Part 3, you'll want to do more. This final part gives you the toolkit for doing just that.

Extras

Throughout this book, you'll come across a number of different sidebars. These are meant to further your understanding of the Raspberry Pi or the project you're working on. Here's what to look for:

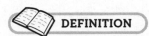

DEFINITION

Definitions help clarify a complicated term or phrase.

HARDWARE HELPER

In these sidebars, I share more information about the various accessories you can attach to your Raspberry Pi.

PI POINTER

Pi Pointers give you additional tips and tricks or helpful workarounds.

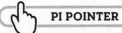

SOFTWARE SOLUTION

These sidebars share some notes on software you might want to try on your Raspberry Pi.

 ## Online Bonus

Throughout the book, I share code you can type in at the command line to get your Raspberry Pi to do different things. Some of these code excerpts are rather long, so as a bonus to the book, we've included the longer bits of code (3 lines or more) you're asked to type in on our website. When you see this icon in the book, point your browser to idiotsguides.com/raspberrypi, and copy and paste the appropriate code.

Acknowledgments

I'd like to thank everyone who directly or indirectly contributed to my finishing this book, fed me when I was too busy to eat, patted my back at the right time, or forced me to take breaks when I was pulling out my hair trying to get my Raspberry Pi to do what I wanted: my parents, Joe Flores, Bryan Danknich, Jen Betterly, Brian Ernst, and Tuyet Nguyen. Likewise, I couldn't have done it without my co-workers, Whitson Gordon, Alan Henry, and the rest of the staff at Lifehacker.

Special Thanks to the Technical Reviewer

Idiot's Guides: Raspberry Pi was reviewed by an expert who double-checked the accuracy of what you'll learn here, to help us ensure this book gives you everything you need to know about making the most of your Raspberry Pi. Special thanks are extended to Kyle Prier.

Trademarks

All terms mentioned in this book that are known to be or are suspected of being trademarks or service marks have been appropriately capitalized. Alpha Books and Penguin Random House LLC cannot attest to the accuracy of this information. Use of a term in this book should not be regarded as affecting the validity of any trademark or service mark.

Getting Started with Your Raspberry Pi

In Part 1, you meet the Raspberry Pi and read about how it came to be. From conception to release, this little computer was designed by a very small team of engineers who had a lot of problems to solve to make the Raspberry Pi everything they wanted it to be.

In addition, you learn about the various components in the Raspberry Pi, why they were chosen, and how they work. The Raspberry Pi isn't quite as straightforward as a traditional computer, so familiarizing yourself with its components is helpful.

A few models of the Raspberry Pi are available, and they're each a little different. Picking the right one for you is really about the types of projects you want to use the computer for, so in this part, you also discover the key differences among the models and explore a few uses for each.

Introducing the Raspberry Pi

The Raspberry Pi is a tiny, single-board computer. It's inexpensive, easy to work with, and adaptable to a variety of fun and creative projects. Originally released in 2012, the Raspberry Pi was created by a nonprofit, the Raspberry Pi Foundation, looking to get computers into the hands of young students. But electronics hobbyists have since latched on too because it's so simple to use and flexible in its capabilities.

At just $20 for the Model A+ and $35 for B, B+, and 2, the Raspberry Pi is one of the most economical computers available. It's about the size of a credit card; runs free, *open-source software;* and can be set up in a matter of minutes. It's so inexpensive because you don't get a case, a monitor, or even a keyboard, but you can probably use the accessories you already own with it.

The Raspberry Pi is built and priced so it's affordable and pliable enough for use with all kinds of single-purpose projects. We're going to look at a lot of those projects throughout this book. But first, we need to learn the basics of the Raspberry Pi's hardware and how it came to be.

In This Chapter

- Getting to know the Raspberry Pi

- The Raspberry Pi architecture

- The mission of the Raspberry Pi Foundation

- The Raspberry Pi's history and launch

The Single-Board Computer

A single-board computer (SBC) is a computer built on one circuit board. It has a *microprocessor,* memory, inputs, outputs, and everything else it needs to work all built onto a single board. This differs from a traditional desktop personal computer, in which all those components are separate pieces.

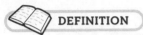 **DEFINITION**

> **Open-source software** is computer software whose source code is available to the public. This means multiple people can develop the software collaboratively. Typically, open-source software is free and without regional restrictions so anyone can use it anywhere in the world. A **microprocessor** includes all the functions of a central processing unit (CPU; the "brains" of a computer) on a single circuit. This means one processor can have multiple functions. It works a lot like your laptop or desktop computer, but it's smaller and a little slower.

The Raspberry Pi is built so the processor, graphics processor, and memory are all on the single, credit card–size board. Because everything is condensed in such a small space, it's not super powerful, but it is inexpensive to manufacture.

The Raspberry Pi is a single-board computer about the size of a credit card that has myriad options for customization.

The lack of processing power also means it doesn't take a lot of electricity to run the Raspberry Pi. All you need to turn it on is an inexpensive, 5-volt mobile phone power cord. Unlike a traditional computer, the Raspberry Pi doesn't use that much energy when it's running, so it's a good way to keep power consumption down in the home.

In addition to the Raspberry Pi, other popular single-board computers include the Arduino Intel Galileo, BeagleBoard, and other computers used to power systems like video poker and digital kiosks. These computers work very similar to the Raspberry Pi, although they typically have different components and run other operating systems. It'd be wrong to say they directly compete with each other, but they certainly exist in the same space and are used for similar types of projects.

Single-board systems are popular with electronics hobbyists—especially the do-it-yourselfers—because they're an affordable way to prototype ideas and don't require a ton of technical skill to use. Almost anyone can create a simple electronics system with a single-board computer because they're easy to develop for and cost-efficient to experiment with. Even better, it's almost impossible to mess up the operating system because the code and software are rarely stored on the device itself.

Raspberry Pi Hardware

A few different versions of the Raspberry Pi are available as of this writing, the Model A+ (which replaced the Model A), the Model B, the Model B+, and the Model 2. The basics of the hardware are pretty much the same across all four models:

A Broadcom BCM2835 system on a chip (SoC): This is your Pi's main processor, or brain. It includes a 700MHz ARM-based processor that handles all the actual computing done on the Pi. Its initial purpose was for mobile products. The Model 2 has a new chip, the BCM2836 ARMv7, which runs at 900MHz—significantly faster than previous models.

VideoCore IV GPU: This is your Raspberry Pi's graphics processing unit (GPU). It's integrated into the SoC and works with the processor to display graphics, including 1080p HD video.

256 to 1GB RAM: The original Raspberry Pi (the Model A) launched with 256MB RAM (random access memory), which is also what the Model A+ has, but subsequent versions (Models B and B+) have 512MB. The Model 2 doubles that with 1GB RAM. The extra RAM makes it possible for the newer Raspberry Pis to display better graphics, process higher-quality video, and run more advanced applications.

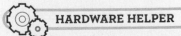

HARDWARE HELPER

It might not seem like much, but combined, the Raspberry Pi's processor and graphics processor are about as powerful as the original 2001 Xbox.

That's a brief look at the Raspberry Pi hardware for now. We'll dig into the specifics of the hardware for each different model more in the next chapter.

The Raspberry Pi Foundation

Established in 2009 in the United Kingdom, the Raspberry Pi Foundation is a charity designed to encourage computer science in schools and ensure people all over the world can have access to cheap computers and learn computer science at a young age. According to the foundation's website, its mission is to "promote the study of computer science and related topics, especially at school level, and to put the fun back in learning computing."

The foundation also is responsible for the production of the Raspberry Pi as well as the nonprofit programs that helped create the computer. The organization itself is actually two parts: the charity portion and the engineering portion. The engineering portion handles the actual manufacturing and distribution of the Raspberry Pi.

Eben Upton, Rob Mullins, Jack Lang, Alan Mycroft, Pete Lomas, and David Braben founded the Raspberry Pi Foundation. Upton was the main face of the Raspberry Pi during its production and launch, and he also was responsible for the software and hardware architecture. As a co-founder of the foundation, he, along with the other co-founders, worked to get the Raspberry Pi into the hands of as many people as possible at launch.

Currently, the foundation's website (raspberrypi.org) hosts resources for students and teachers to learn the basics of computer science, as well as most of the files necessary to get the Raspberry Pi up and running. The foundation also does outreach to schools in both the United Kingdom and the United States to provide related resources for students.

Most of the lessons and resources for teachers are open source. The Foundation has also worked with Cambridge University Press to create a free, massive open online course (MOOC) that teaches basic computer science with the Raspberry Pi.

Although the Raspberry Pi has gone on to be used in many different ways beyond enabling students to learn about computers, the Raspberry Pi Foundation's main purpose is still to support teaching computer science to young people.

On top of that, it's also about getting a computer into the hands of as many people as possible. The Raspberry Pi Foundation wants to ensure every person can have a personal computer without spending hundreds of dollars for it. From there, the Foundation hopes to bring more people into computer science as well as provide a good foundation for learning the basic computer skills necessary to work in the future.

How the Raspberry Pi Came to Be

A small team of people from the University of Cambridge's Computer Laboratory initially created the Raspberry Pi. The team noticed a decline in the number of students enrolling in the computer science program, and their solution was to create a small, inexpensive computer to get more people, especially children, interested in computing.

In 2008, the team started to work with Pete Lomas of Norcott Technologies and David Braben, co-author of the video game *Elite*. Together, they began working on what would become the Raspberry Pi by prototyping a number of different boards.

In 2011, the team started working with the RISC OS Open Ltd. (ROOL) community to create a version of the operating system Linux that would work well on the Raspberry Pi. This would eventually be replaced with Raspbian, the most popular operating system for the Raspberry Pi. (I show you how to install and get Raspbian running in Chapter 8.)

In 2012, as they got closer to production, the founders partnered with Premier Farnell, Allied Electronics, and Sony's Technology Package in Wales to create the Raspberry Pi.

 PI POINTER

Where did the name *Raspberry Pi* come from? In a 2012 interview, Raspberry Pi Foundation co-founder Eben Upton explained:

> Raspberry is a reference to a fruit naming tradition in the old days of microcomputers. A lot of computer companies were named after fruit. There's Tangerine Computer Systems, Apricot Computers, and the old British company Acorn, which is a family of fruit.

> Pi is because originally we were going to produce a computer that could only really run Python. So the Pi in there is for Python. Now you can run Python on the Raspberry Pi but the design we ended up going with is much more capable than the original we thought of, so it's kind of outlived its name a little bit.

The Pi's Original Purpose

The original purpose of the Raspberry Pi was to make available a cheap computer anyone could afford. To further that goal, it supports a number of free, Linux-based operating systems, so there's no cost of purchasing an operating system to worry about. Because of this, you can choose between wide varieties of operating systems for your Raspberry Pi. The most popular operating system is Raspbian. If you're not familiar with Linux, the way it works is a bit confusing, but I talk more about this in Chapter 7.

 PI POINTER

> The Linux thing can be confusing. The Raspberry Pi does run Linux, but *Linux* is just a blanket term for operating system distributions built on Linux. So Raspbian is an operating system that uses the core of Linux (mostly just the kernel) but is otherwise its own thing. (I explain this more in-depth in Chapter 7.)

But there's a little more to it than just that.

In the 1980s, computers weren't as user friendly as they are today, so people had to learn basic programming just to use a computer. As a result, some of those folks grew up and became interested in computer science.

Nowadays, however, most tasks on computers are so much easier, and that spark isn't quite as strong as it once was. The Raspberry Pi hopes to change this. The creators made the Raspberry Pi easy enough to use that children can learn programming and other computer tricks with it. However, it's not as simple to use as more advanced operating systems like Windows or Apple's OS X. Therefore, it's nearly impossible to complete a project with the Raspberry Pi without learning something, which was a design intention from the start.

Throughout this book, you'll explore many different projects for the Raspberry Pi, and each will teach you a little something about computer science along the way. In some cases, this is as simple as learning how your Wi-Fi adapter works on your computer. In others, you'll dig into basic programming to get everything working. Don't let any of that scare you though. It might sound difficult now, but you'll have a pretty good grasp of it all by the end.

After all, the original goal of the Raspberry Pi remains the same today: to show people how computers really work, how they can use them to manipulate the world around them, and how to program.

Initial Technology and Design

The Raspberry Pi's initial designs were based both on the Raspberry Pi's mission statement and a single goal: to release a $25 model as well as a $35 model. These target prices helped shape the design of the Pi. The designers wanted the Raspberry Pi to run Linux initially, along with programming software like *Scratch* and *Python*—another factor that influenced the final design.

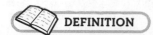 **DEFINITION**

> **Scratch** is a programming language for kids that uses flowcharts and animations to teach basic programming skills. Unlike most programming languages, it doesn't require a lot of text input and instead relies on graphics to make programs. **Python** is a much more complicated programming language and is used to create all kinds of software. The goal of Python is simplicity, so it tends to use less lines of code than other programming languages. This makes it a good fit for the Raspberry Pi because it's great for beginners.

The design of the Raspberry Pi was all about subtraction. The creators had two unavoidable costs: the RAM and the processor. From there, they had to add and remove different functions until they got something working at the price point they wanted. Because of this, the Raspberry Pi lacks a few modern conveniences. For example, a 5-volt USB socket handles the power. Not having an internal power supply keeps the cost down, but it also means there's no power switch. The Pi is missing other common features, too, like flash memory, Wi-Fi, and a traditional hard drive. An SD card handles all the storage.

It's not just the big stuff; the Raspberry Pi cuts all kinds of corners to keep the price down. It doesn't have a battery-based clock, for instance, so it has to grab the time and date from a network or from the user every time it's powered on.

All that work resulted in a computer that's useable right out of the box for $35 or less. You can add most functions (like Wi-Fi) to suit your needs with the USB ports for just a few dollars more.

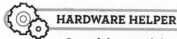 **HARDWARE HELPER**

> One of the initial designs of the Raspberry Pi used a 22.1MHz processor and could only generate a 320×240 video signal. The final version has a 700MHz processor and can output a full HD-quality signal.

The Launch of the Raspberry Pi

From conception to launch, it took 7 years to bring the Raspberry Pi to market. In late 2011, the early alpha versions of the Raspberry Pi were being tested, and by January 2012, the beta versions were auctioned off to raise money for the charity.

By April 2012, the first Raspberry Pis began shipping with a limit of one per customer. Those restrictions were lifted by July of the same year as production increased to keep up with demand.

In November, the Model B of the Raspberry Pi was announced and released. It was the same basic board as the first version, but it had 512MB RAM, an additional USB port (two total), and an Ethernet port, all for a cost of $35. As a result, the Model A dropped to $25.

By October, 2 million Raspberry Pi units had been sold, and by June 2014, they hit the 3 million mark.

In July 2014, the Raspberry Pi Model B+ was released. In this model, the design was overhauled with more headers, two more USB ports (four total), a micro SD card slot, better audio, and a new design. The Model B+ and Model B both took on the $35 price tag.

In November 2014, the Model A+ was announced as a replacement for the original Model A. Like the B+, it features more GPIO pins, a micro SD card slot, and better audio. It retails for $20.

In February 2015, the Model 2 was announced and released. This model keeps the same design, USB ports, and micro SD card slot of the B+ but doubles the RAM and features a new, faster processor.

 PI POINTER

The Raspberry Pi was always intended as an education device, but the creators figured out early on that hobbyists would be the driving force financially. The initial launch of the Pi marketed the device to these hobbyists, and it quickly became a go-to device for all kinds of do-it-yourself projects.

What's Next for the Raspberry Pi

As of this writing, no immediate plans are in the works for an updated model, according to the Raspberry Pi Foundation's website, which states:

> … [A] new model may be released in 2–3 years, but this is not a firm schedule. A new model would inherently undo much of the community work that has been done to date on the Raspberry Pi, which would be counter-productive to our educational aims. We concentrate our engineering effort on making the software that runs on the Raspberry Pi faster and better all the time.

So dig in and feel confident that the work you're doing to learn the ins and outs of the Raspberry Pi now won't quickly be outdated with a new model release.

The Least You Need to Know

- Originally, the Raspberry Pi was created to provide a low-cost computer to young students.

- The Raspberry Pi Foundation is the nonprofit responsible for getting the Raspberry Pi into the hands of students.

- The Raspberry Pi's most popular operating system is Raspbian, a Linux-based operating system that's free and has a distribution maintained by the Raspberry Pi Foundation.

- To keep the cost low, the engineers who created the Raspberry Pi had to get creative and cut out common features.

Choosing a Raspberry Pi

As of this writing, four versions of the Raspberry Pi are available—the Model A+, the Model B, the Model B+, and the Model 2. Each is slightly different from the others, and each has its pros and cons, depending on your intended use.

For most DIY projects, it's usually best to get the newest model so you have the most up-to-date equipment and software, but the older models still have their charm and usefulness.

Which is right for you depends on what you want to use your Raspberry Pi for. If you're interested in multimedia projects, the B+ is your model. If you'd prefer to just run a small, out-of-the-way automation system, the Model A+ will do the trick. Whichever model you choose, you can do plenty of projects with it.

In this chapter, we take an in-depth look at the four models, the hardware of each, and ways to pick the right one for your needs.

In This Chapter

- Raspberry Pi models available

- Differences among the models

- Choosing your model

- Buying your Raspberry Pi

The Different Models

Let's start by looking at some of the very basic details about each model. It might surprise you that the actual chip and processor are quite similar on each model. The latest model has gained some processing power, with more memory and USB ports added as new models launched.

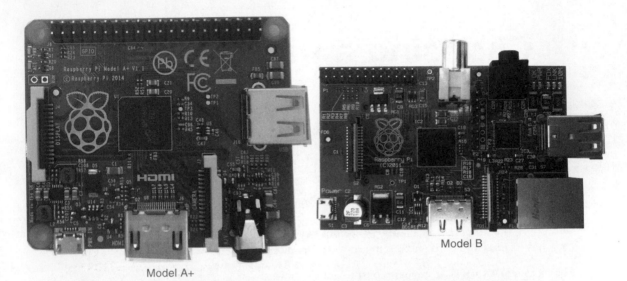

Model A+

Model B

Model B+

Model 2

All the Raspberry Pi models look mostly the same but have a few upgrades.

The following table offers a breakdown of the key points of each model.

	Model A+	Model B	Model B+	Model 2
Chip	Broadcom BMC2835 SoC multimedia processor	Broadcom BMC2835 SoC multimedia processor	Broadcom BMC2835 SoC multimedia processor	Broadcom BMC2836 SoC quad-core processor
RAM	256MB *SDRAM*	512MB SDRAM	512MB SDRAM	1GB SDRAM
Storage	micro SD card	SD card	micro SD	micro SD
USB ports	1	2	4	4
GPIO pins	40	26	40	40
Price*	$20	$35	$35	$35
Ethernet	0	1	1	1

Price as of this writing.

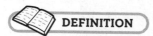 **DEFINITION**

Random access memory (RAM) is a form of computer storage from which programs can temporarily read and write data. Nearly every computer has RAM these days, including your smartphone. **Synchronous dynamic random access memory (SDRAM)** is RAM that can run at higher clock speeds than other types of RAM. The speed is synchronized with the system speed. **GPIO,** or **general-purpose input/output,** is a connector that enables you to connect your Raspberry Pi to other computers for more advanced projects.

Each iteration of the Raspberry Pi is an improvement on the previous version. The Model B got an upgrade in RAM from the Model A to increase its speed, while the B+ was an overhaul of the whole thing, with additional USB ports, a different type of SD card, and more. The B+ has a totally different setup and is much larger than the other models. The Model 2 keeps the design of the B+ while swapping out the processor and RAM. Still, each is about the size of a credit card and only weighs a few ounces. And regardless of which model you get, you'll be able to complete every project in this book. You'll definitely notice some speed improvements with video- and graphic-intensive programs with the B and B+ though.

Let's start by taking a look at its hardware.

The Model A+

Unlike its older brothers, the Raspberry Pi Model A+ only has one USB port, no Ethernet port, and only 256MB RAM. It consumes about a third of the power the Model B does, so it's great for low-power projects.

The Model A+ Raspberry Pi.

Model A+ Hardware Specifications

The Raspberry Pi Model A+ is designed specifically to run small, portable equipment that doesn't need internet access. Because of that, it's even more stripped down than the B, B+, and 2 models. It's also physically smaller than the other two, coming in at about an inch less in length. Here's an overview of what's on the board:

256MB RAM: The small amount of RAM means this model isn't as powerful as the others, but it also means it consumes less power.

Broadcom BCM2835 SoC with 700MHz low-power ARM1176JZF-S applications process: The processor is the Raspberry Pi's main brain, and it's the same for all three of the bottom-tier models. It was originally designed for mobile phones, but it's powerful enough for the Raspberry Pi to run full desktop software.

Dual-core VideoCore IV multimedia co-processor: This graphics processor is the same for all four models. It's integrated into the SoC, but it's a separate piece of hardware and enables the Raspberry Pi to power all kinds of graphically intense games and applications.

Micro SD slot: This is for the micro SD card. The Raspberry Pi doesn't have a regular hard drive. Instead, you install the operating systems on an SD card using your home computer. (I cover this process in Chapter 8.)

5-volt micro USB power slot: This is where you plug in your Raspberry Pi for power. (I walk you through getting a power supply that works with the Pi in the next chapter.)

That's it for the Raspberry Pi's main hardware. The key differences between the Model A+ and the other models are the ports.

 HARDWARE HELPER

> The Raspberry Pi only has a handful of USB slots, but you can always add more using a powered USB hub. Nonpowered USB hubs won't work because the Pi doesn't have enough power to share. You can find powered USB hubs at almost any electronics retailer.

Model A+ Ports and Connectors

The price, size, and power consumption of the Model A+ are what set it apart from the other models, but it comes at the cost of ports. Here are the ports you get on the Model A+:

Single USB connector: You can only connect one USB device to the Raspberry Pi Model A+ at a time. That means if you want to use both a keyboard and a mouse, you need an external USB hub.

HDMI port: You can output video from the Raspberry Pi Model A+ using the HDMI port, which also outputs audio. The HDMI output gives you a clearer HD picture and works best with modern monitors or televisions.

3.5mm audio jack: This audio-plus-video jack does double-duty. For audio, you need a 3.5mm audio cable, but if you want to send out composite video, you also need a 3.5mm-to-3 RCA adapter cable. The Model A+ also improves on previous versions (Models A, B, and B+) by adding a dedicated low-noise power supply so it can send a better signal.

GPIO (general-purpose input/output) connector: The GPIO connector enables you to hardwire the Raspberry Pi into other components for more advanced DIY projects. (If this sounds a bit scary, don't worry. I cover this in Chapter 6.) The Model A+ has a 40-pin GPIO header.

Camera connector: This allows you to connect the official Raspberry Pi camera.

Display connector: The display connector is great if you want to hardwire your Raspberry Pi to a screen instead of going through the HDMI port.

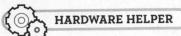

HARDWARE HELPER

The Raspberry Pi Model A+ does not have an Ethernet jack, which means you can't get connected to the internet with it unless you use the one USB connector for a Wi-Fi adapter.

That's it. As mentioned, the Raspberry Pi Model A+ is the minimalist of the bunch. It still gets the job done, but it's not the best for beginners looking to play around with a lot of different types of projects.

The Model B

The Raspberry Pi Model B is a step up from the Model A+, but the two have the same basic blueprint. The Model B has a bit more power in the form of more RAM and more ports to work with.

The Model B Raspberry Pi.

Model B Hardware Specifications

With the exception of the on-board RAM, the hardware in the Model B is similar to the Model A+'s:

512MB RAM: The Model B has double the RAM the Model A had (256MB), so it can run a lot more advanced software. It also means it's a lot better at doing anything with video, including encoding and outputting in HD.

Broadcom BCM2835 SoC with 700MHz low-power ARM1176JZF-S applications process: This processor is the same for all three models.

Dual-core VideoCore IV multimedia co-processor: This graphics processor is the same for all three models.

SD, MMC, SDIO card slot: The Model B is the only currently available model of the Raspberry Pi that uses a standard-size SD card slot.

5-volt micro USB power slot: This is where you plug in your Raspberry Pi for power. All four models have this slot.

 HARDWARE HELPER

The upgrade from 256MB RAM in the Model A to 512MB in Model B (and the B+) adds a significant boost to the Raspberry Pi's multimedia power. 256MB RAM is just enough to run a media server, but 512MB makes the Raspberry Pi much more suited for games and video. The Model 2's 1GB is even faster, and you can run a lot more complicated programs with it.

The Model B has a few more ports that make it a lot easier to work with.

Model B Ports and Connectors

The Model B has a similar set of ports and connectors to the Model A+, with an additional USB port and Ethernet jack.

Two USB connectors: You can connect two different USB devices to the Raspberry Pi Model B at once, or more if you get a powered USB hub.

10/100 Ethernet RJ45 jack: The Ethernet jack enables you to connect your Pi to the internet via an Ethernet cable.

HDMI port and composite RCA output: These are the same as the Model A+.

3.5mm audio jack: The Model B has a 3.5mm audio jack output.

GPIO (general-purpose input/output) connector: The Model B has a 26-pin GPIO header.

Camera connector: This is the same for all four models.

Display connector: This is the same for all four models.

The Model B manages to get most of what you need onto the board, but although it's perfectly good for nearly any DIY project, it's not as powerful as the B+ or the 2.

The Model B+

The Raspberry Pi Model B+ marks the first big advancement in the Raspberry Pi hardware line. Unlike the leap from the original Raspberry Pi to the Model B, the Model B+ changes the overall architecture and adds a ton of improvements.

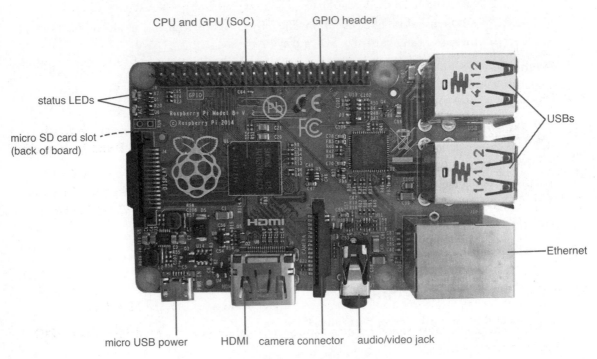

The Model B+ Raspberry Pi.

Model B+ Hardware Specifications

With the exception of a new micro SD card slot, all the improvements to the B+ come in the form of new ports. So for the most part, the specifications are basically the same as the Model B:

512MB RAM: The Model B+ has the same amount of RAM as the B.

Broadcom BCM2835 SoC with 700 MHz low-power ARM1176JZF-S applications process: This processor is the same for all three of the bottom-tier models.

Dual-core VideoCore IV multimedia co-processor: This graphics processor is the same for all four models.

SDIO card slot: This is for the micro SD card.

5-volt micro USB power slot: This is where you plug in your Raspberry Pi for power. All four models have this slot.

HARDWARE HELPER

The Model B+ is a nice upgrade to the B that really makes it easier to use and a bit more powerful. The audio jack in particular features an upgrade that makes output audio sound a lot better than the older models.

The big difference with the Model B+ is the ports, so let's take a look at how it changes things up.

Model B+ Ports and Connectors

Like any computer, the Raspberry Pi has a variety of ports and connectors so you can attach accessories, screens, and other cables. The Model B+ differs from the Model B and A+ in that it has more USB connectors. Both the A+ and B+ have more GPIO pins as well.

Four USB connectors: The Model B+ doubles the USB connectors the Model B has for a total of four. This makes it a lot easier to use as a computer with a keyboard, mouse, Wi-Fi adapter, and whatever else you need to plug into it.

10/100 Ethernet RJ45 jack: This is the same as the Model B.

HDMI: The HDMI port is the same as the Model B.

3.5mm audio/video jack: This is the same as the audio/video jack on the Model A+.

GPIO (general-purpose input/output) connector: The B+ (and the Model A+) has a GPIO header with 40 pins.

Camera connector: This is the same for all four models.

Display connector: This is the same for all four models.

The Model 2

The Model 2 improves on the previous models by adding in a new CPU and more RAM.

The Model 2 Raspberry Pi.

Model 2 Hardware Specifications

The Model 2 has a few updates to be happy about:

1GB RAM: The Model 2 has 1GB RAM—twice that of Models B and B+.

Broadcom BCM2836 quad-core 900Mhz ARMv7 processor: The Model 2 gets a brand-new processor that's about six times faster than the ones on previous models.

Dual-core VideoCore IV multimedia co-processor: This graphics processor is the same for all four models.

SDIO card slot: This is for the micro SD card.

5-volt micro USB power slot: This is where you plug in your Raspberry Pi for power. All four models have this slot.

Other than the speed, the Model 2 is about the same as the B+ with everything else.

Model 2 Ports and Connectors

The Raspberry Pi has several ports and connectors. The Model 2 is pretty much the same as the Model B+ in this respect.

Four USB connectors: The Model 2 has four USB ports.

10/100 Ethernet RJ45 jack: This is the same as the Model B+.

HDMI: The HDMI port is the same as the Model B+.

3.5mm audio/video jack: This is the same as the audio/video jack on Models A+ and B+.

GPIO (general-purpose input/output) connector: The Model 2 (and Models B+ and A+) has a GPIO header with 40 pins.

Camera connector: This is the same for all four models.

Display connector: This is the same for all four models.

That's it for technical details. Let's move on to picking the right Raspberry Pi for your specific needs.

Which Model Is for You?

Each Raspberry Pi model is suitable for different projects. Because of that, it's a good idea to know what you want to do with your Raspberry Pi before you purchase one.

There's no real wrong choice here. Among the four models, each can do almost everything the others can, although the newer B, B+, and 2 models are much better suited to multimedia work.

What Do You Want to Do?

Which model is best for you depends on what you want to start making.

The Model A+ is aimed toward more advanced users who want to make low-power DIY projects that don't require a lot of external components. Because the Model A+ only has one USB, it's not as well suited for running Linux or doing anything where you need a keyboard and mouse.

In addition, the lack of Ethernet makes it a poor choice for most beginners who'll need to download and install a lot of new software on their Pi to complete the more popular projects.

However, the Model A+ is great for projects like making a DIY camera because it doesn't consume much power and you won't need the USB ports for the camera.

The B, B+, and 2 models are all equally good for just about everything else. If you want to use the Raspberry Pi as a full computer, the B, B+, and 2 models have all the USB ports you'll need.

Because the B, B+, and 2 models have more RAM, they're also better suited for multimedia projects and games. If you really want to do some work with your Raspberry Pi, the Model 2 is powerful enough to handle all kinds of modern applications and is your best choice.

If you're not sure which is best for you, the B+ or 2 is the likely the one to go with because it's the newest model and it'll have everything you could possibly need.

 PI POINTER

Besides the currently available models of the Raspberry Pi, different revisions existed as well. These are no longer available to purchase, but this is how they differed from current models:

Model A: The original Model A was the same size as the Model B, had a standard SD card slot, and cost $25.

Model B Rev 1: The original Model B, known as *revision 1*, only had 256MB RAM. Otherwise, it was the same as the currently available Model B (known as *revision 2*).

Pros and Cons of Models B, B+, and 2

For the time being, the B, B+, and 2 models are all still available, but the Model 2 is clearly meant as a replacement for Models B and B+. Because they're all available, the main pros and cons are really a matter of which accessories you already own.

The big difference between the B and the 2 (and B+) is the SD card slot. The B uses a standard SD card, whereas the Model 2 uses a micro SD. If you already have a Raspberry Pi and have made a lot of SD cards with all your different operating systems, you'll basically have to start over from scratch to use Models B+ or 2. Likewise, the standard SD card pokes out from the board, whereas the micro SD is flush.

Similarly, if you already purchased or made a case for an earlier model, you'll have to get a new one. (I talk more about cases in Chapter 4.)

If you're starting from scratch though, the Model 2 is definitely the way to go. It's more powerful, has more ports, and is going to be a better system all around.

Price and Availability

As of this writing, the Raspberry Pi has a set price structure for the models, and all are generally only available through a few authorized dealers.

The pricing structure for the Raspberry Pi is intentionally set in stone:

Model A+: $25

Model B: $35

Model B+: $35

Model 2: $35

For the most part, these prices shouldn't fluctuate for any reason, unless, perhaps, a new model is released. If you go through an unauthorized seller, you might end up paying a little more for your Raspberry Pi.

PI POINTER

The prices of the Raspberry Pi are set at $20 and $35, so if anyone's ever trying to charge you more than that, look elsewhere. They're widely available, so you shouldn't have trouble finding an authorized seller and lower price.

Every region has authorized Raspberry Pi sellers, but in the United States, the official seller is element14 (element14.com).

You also can find a Raspberry Pi at a number of resellers, including larger sites like Amazon, but most of them are getting their Raspberry Pis from element14. These other resellers might charge more than the set $25 and $35 price points, too.

The Least You Need to Know

- A few different models of Raspberry Pi exist as of this writing—the Model A+, the Model B, the Model B+, and the Model 2.

- The main difference among the four models is the number of ports they have and their overall power.

- Each model has its strengths and weaknesses, but you'll be able to do most of the projects in this book on any model.

- Depending on your region, you'll need to buy your Raspberry Pi from an authorized retailer. But you should be able to pay the same price from any authorized retailer.

Required Accessories

To keep the cost of the Raspberry Pi so low, you have to do a bit of work and accessorizing to get it up and running. You don't get everything you need in the box, for example, so you have to find the additional components you need on your own. For people who like to customize their computers, this is great. If you're not one of those people, don't worry. In this chapter, you learn what accessories you need to work with your Raspberry Pi.

To start, you'll need a power supply, an SD card for storage, and a few other cables to get your Raspberry Pi hooked up to a screen and to the internet. Chances are, you probably have most of this stuff already, and even if you don't, many of these parts are inexpensive. The Raspberry Pi is made to be as affordable as possible, so that means it has universal plugs and a wide range of support for accessories.

With that in mind, let's go through the list of what you need to get your Raspberry Pi outfitted.

In This Chapter

- Getting power to your Raspberry Pi
- Picking the right SD card
- Choosing a keyboard and mouse
- Working with video and audio output
- Getting your Raspberry Pi online

Powering Your Raspberry Pi

The Raspberry Pi uses a 5-volt micro USB power supply. This is similar to what you get with a mobile phone. Each version of the Raspberry Pi needs a different amount of power, but you can generally use the same power adapter for each model. Power adapters are tricky business, so you'll want to be sure you get the right one.

Amperage and Voltage Requirements

The power adapter requirements for the Raspberry Pi are surprisingly confusing, but thankfully, you only need to know a few different numbers.

The Raspberry Pi requires a 5-volt (5V) power adapter that connects with a micro USB. A ton of different mobile devices already come with these kinds of power adapters, including Kindles, Android phones, and many other devices. If you look at a power adapter, you'll usually see the voltage listed on the adapter itself.

You'll need a power supply with an *amperage* rating of at least 1.2 amps for Models A+ and B, and 2.5 amps for Models B+ and 2. The number is the amperage you need to provide enough juice to the Raspberry Pi. *Amps* (often abbreviated *A*) are the current that supply power to your device. You can go over in amps, but you can't be under. Models B+ and 2 have more USB ports, so they need more power to send to the accessories you connect.

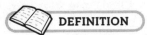 **DEFINITION**

Amperage is the amount of ampere (usually shortened to *amp* or abbreviated *A*), which is the unit used to measure electric current. For power adapters, it's used to gauge the maximum number of power the adapter can send from an outlet to the device. If it's too high, the power adapter will adjust downward to avoid overloading the device, but if it's too low, the device simply won't power on.

If this all sounds confusing, don't worry. Purchasing a Raspberry Pi power supply is really easy.

Finding a Power Adapter

When shopping for a power supply for your Raspberry Pi, look for something that will work with the model you have. If you have a Model A+ or B, look for a 5V micro USB power supply with a current rating of 1.2A. If you have a Model B+ or 2, you want a 5V micro USB power supply with a current rating of 2.5A. Typically, you can search for these online and find what you need, but you can also take a look at any power adapters you already have around the house.

Look at a power adapter, and you'll find a lot of different numbers and symbols. Most of them don't matter to you right now. What you want to look for is the output voltage (that's the 5V) and the current in amps (that's the 1.2A or 2.5A). If you have a power adapter that meets those ratings and connects to a micro USB cord, you can use it with your Raspberry Pi.

Otherwise, you need to find a power adapter in a store or online. The Raspberry Pi doesn't have an official power adapter, so any adapter you find that meets the voltage and amperage requirements should work.

SD Cards

Unlike a traditional computer, the Raspberry Pi doesn't have a hard drive of any kind. Instead, it uses an SD card, like you find in digital cameras, for all its storage. You'll eventually install your operating system on the SD card (or micro SD in the case of Models B+, A+, and 2), and you'll keep all your files there as well. This might sound like a hassle, but it's actually an advantage.

The "Hard Drive" for Your Pi

On the Raspberry Pi, the SD card works just like a hard drive on your laptop or desktop computer. You install your operating system onto it, you store your files on it, and you can use it just like you would a regular hard drive.

This ends up being pretty handy because chances are, you'll want to experiment with a lot of different projects on the Raspberry Pi. SD cards are rather inexpensive, so it's easy to just swap them for different projects instead of switching to a different Raspberry Pi.

Recommended SD Cards

For the most part, almost any SD card will work as long as it's listed as a class 4, but it's recommended you get one with at least 8 gigabytes (GB) of storage. This gives you enough space to install the operating system and any additional programs you need.

Almost any SD card should work with the Raspberry Pi, but some exceptions exist. The eLinux page has a breakdown of every SD card tested with the Raspberry Pi at elinux.org/RPi_SD_cards. Before you order an SD card, check this list to be sure the one you're looking at will work.

The same goes for Models A+, B+, and 2, but you'll need a micro SD card instead of a standard-size SD card.

PI POINTER

You have a lot of operating system options on the Raspberry Pi. The nice thing about using SD cards to hold your operating system is that you can swap operating systems and setups as often as you like, just by changing the SD card.

The Raspberry Pi is equipped with both HDMI and composite ports for video output.

Composite and HDMI Options

What you're connecting to your Raspberry Pi dictates which type of video output you use. If you're connecting an older TV, you're probably going to be stuck with a composite cable— the yellow cable used with pre-HD televisions. If you're using an HD TV or a newer PC monitor, you'll probably use HDMI.

On whatever screen you're connecting your Raspberry Pi to, you'll find either a composite or HDMI input, or both. HDMI is the flat connector found in most modern screens that outputs both audio and video in one signal. The composite video input is almost always yellow, and all you'll need is a RCA cord to connect it.

On Models A+, B+, and 2, the RCA composite jack has been replaced with a 3.5mm RCA jack, which outputs both audio and video, but to use it, you'll need a 3.5mm-to-3 RCA adapter cable, similar to the cables you'd use with a camcorder. The HDMI port is flat and a bit square, and you'll need a HDMI cable to use it.

 HARDWARE HELPER

> If you want to output in HD to a widescreen television or monitor, pick up an HDMI cable. With it, you can easily hook up your Raspberry Pi to just about any modern screen.

For the most part, it doesn't really matter what brand of cable you use for your Raspberry Pi. Any HDMI or RCA composite cable will work; just be sure it's long enough for your needs.

Connecting to PC Monitors Versus HD TVs

You can use either a PC monitor or an HD television with your Raspberry Pi if you want an HD signal. The Raspberry Pi doesn't support VGA (video graphics array), so if you still have an old monitor left over from the 1990s, it won't work.

Choosing between a PC monitor and an HD television is really about your planned usage. If you plan on using your Raspberry Pi to watch movies, play games, or do any other multimedia activities, an HD television is probably the best option. If you plan on using it as an actual computer and will be typing on it a lot, you might be better off with a small PC monitor.

Sound Output

The Raspberry Pi has two different sound outputs: HDMI audio and the 3.5mm audio jack. Which option is best is partially based on which model of Raspberry Pi you have and what you plan on doing with it.

Like HDMI video, the HDMI audio signal is a crisp HD signal, and using the HDMI cable means you'll get high-quality sound from your Raspberry Pi. It only works through the HDMI cable, so you'll likely be running your audio through your computer monitor or television.

Your other option is to send your audio through the 3.5mm stereo audio jack. This is the jack on your Raspberry Pi that looks similar to the headphone jack you'll find on a smartphone. Model B outputs a grainy signal through the stereo jack, so it's not recommended for use if you really care about your audio quality. Models A+, B+, and 2 improved on this though, and the audio quality is a lot better.

3.5mm audio jack

HDMI audio/video port

*The Raspberry Pi has two options for audio output: an HDMI audio/video port and a
3.5mm audio jack.*

 HARDWARE HELPER

If your computer monitor doesn't support HDMI, you can use a DVI-to-HDMI cable to
hook up your Raspberry Pi to it. These cables usually cost around $5 and enable you
to easily connect your Raspberry Pi to older monitors.

Connecting to the Internet

Finally, the last key accessory and connection you'll need to get your Raspberry Pi up and
running is an internet connection. You can connect to the internet by either the built-in Ethernet
adapter or by installing your own Wi-Fi adapter through a USB connection.

Nearly every project in this book requires an internet connection from either your personal
computer or the Raspberry Pi itself. If you don't have one, it's still possible to use the Raspberry
Pi, but it's considerably more difficult.

On-Board Ethernet

Out of the box, you'll likely want to connect your Raspberry Pi to the internet through the
Ethernet port. You can then connect your Raspberry Pi directly to a modem or a router.

Wi-Fi Adapters

If you'd prefer your Raspberry Pi be a bit more mobile than wired Ethernet allows, you can connect it to a USB Wi-Fi adapter.

You can use the Raspberry Pi's Ethernet or USB ports to get online.

However, you'll need to download some drivers and run a few setup procedures before you do that, so Ethernet is recommended for at least the first portion of the setup process. Don't worry if this sounds complicated. I walk you through setting up Wi-Fi in Chapter 11.

The Least You Need to Know

- The Raspberry Pi costs only $35 at the upper end of the price scale, but you'll still need to purchase a few accessories to actually get it working.

- You need to purchase a compatible power adapter for your Raspberry Pi, but most mobile phone chargers will do the job.

- The SD card is where you'll store all your files as well as the operating system you use to run your Raspberry Pi.

- The Raspberry Pi has several options for audio and video output, depending on what you need.

Picking a Case

One of the first things you'll notice when you open up the box your Raspberry Pi came in is that it's a bit, well, naked. To keep cost down, the Raspberry Pi doesn't come with a case, so when you first open it up, you're greeted with a bare-bones circuit board.

Thankfully, cases for the Raspberry Pi are plentiful online—and often inexpensive. The size of the Raspberry Pi makes it so you can enclose it in just about anything, so it's very easy to find cases. Even better, you can make your own case very easily with stuff you probably have sitting around the house already.

Because the Raspberry Pi has been embraced by the DIY community, you can find all kinds of options for cases you can make. If you're into woodworking, you can make a wood case. If you're into LEGOs, you even can make a LEGO case. Make your Raspberry Pi your own. After all, you're basically building a computer from scratch here, so gussy it up with a case you like.

In This Chapter

- Why you need a case
- The best cases for your project
- Make your own Raspberry Pi case

In this chapter, we take a look at a few of the many different styles of cases available and help you pick the right one for whatever type of project you're working on. In addition, I share a few great DIY options if you'd prefer to make your own Raspberry Pi case.

PI POINTER

No official case for the Raspberry Pi exists because the creators wanted to keep the Raspberry Pi as open as possible. That means you have a ton of different options when it comes to cases.

Project-Based Cases

Every Raspberry Pi project is a little different. As a result, oftentimes, the style of case you need depends on what you plan on building.

In some instances, a simple plastic case will do the job, while other projects might require something more rugged and appropriate for outdoor use. Often, you won't actually touch the Raspberry Pi after you set it up, so a simple little cardboard case does the trick.

You'll likely have a few different cases you use for different projects, so let's take a look at some of the best options.

With all these cases, keep in mind the model of Raspberry Pi you have. The size and shape of each is a little different, so these cases aren't universal. Always double-check which model of the Raspberry Pi a case is made for before you purchase it.

The Best All-Purpose Cases

Many of the Raspberry Pi cases you find online are just fine for general use, but a few tend to get better reviews than others. For the most part, if you're just looking for a generic case, it's just about aesthetics, so pick whichever case you think looks best. That said, let's run through a few of the more popular cases to give you an idea where to start.

The Pibow is a Raspberry Pi case designed by Paul Beech—the same person who designed the official Raspberry Pi logo. While there isn't an official Raspberry Pi case, this is probably the closest option.

The Pibow comes in a few color variations, but each is essentially a block of acrylic plastic that tightly houses the Raspberry Pi while still giving you access to its components. This means your Raspberry Pi is protected, but you can still plug in all your accessories. The Pibow tends to retail for around $19.95.

The Pibow Raspberry Pi case.

If $20 is a little steep for you, DIY website Adafruit (adafruit.com) offers a simple plastic case for $10. The Raspberry Pi securely snaps into the bottom portion of the case, and a clear plastic enclosure snaps onto the top. This is similar to most generic plastic cases you'll find online but is built a little better than most.

HARDWARE HELPER

The Pibow, Adafruit Pi case/enclosure, and most other cases are available in multiple sizes to fit the different Raspberry Pi models so you can choose the correct version for your Raspberry Pi.

All-in-One Computer Cases

If you want to use your Raspberry Pi as an all-in-one computer, there are cases built just for that purpose.

If you're looking to snap your Raspberry Pi onto the back of a computer monitor, opt for a VESA mount case. These tend to retail for around $10 and include screws so you can mount it to the back of a monitor for an all-in-one computer.

If you're feeling adventurous, you can get a case that also adds a touch screen to the Raspberry Pi. The PiTFT Pibow kit is a case that also includes a place to snap on a small, 2.8-inch touchscreen display so you can use the Raspberry Pi as a tiny handheld machine.

Cases for Outdoor Use

If you plan on using your Raspberry Pi outdoors, you'll want a more rugged and weatherproof case. You have a couple good options here, depending on what you need.

Waterproofing is a big part of using a Raspberry Pi outdoors, but you don't need to spend too much to do so. The 2000 Series Waterproof and Crushproof Case made by Calculator Source is technically made for a calculator, but fits the Raspberry Pi perfectly and only costs $15.

PI POINTER

Regardless of what type of case you're looking for, it's a good idea to buy from the same authorized retailers who sell the Raspberry Pi instead of buying a generic case from a major retailer. The generic cases sometimes fit poorly, which makes them pretty useless. And remember to always read the reviews before you buy a case.

If rugged is more your style, the UniPi Unibody case is made of solid aluminum and can withstand a heavy beating—including a car backing over it. It's costly at $50, but its durability makes it worth it if you need it.

DIY Cases

When all is said and done, the Raspberry Pi is all about DIY, so it shouldn't be surprising that making your own case is pretty easy to do. You can make these cases out of just about anything you want.

And with the Raspberry Pi's small footprint, you can put it inside just about anything. People have made Raspberry Pi cases out of old Nintendos, old computers, and even old stereos.

Let's take a look at three of the easier cases you can build at home.

LEGO Cases

Making a Raspberry Pi case from LEGOs is a fan-favorite option and was one of the first real DIY case solutions to come about. Cases made of LEGOs can be customized in all sorts of ways. All you need to do is grab some LEGOs and build a structure the Raspberry Pi can sit inside of.

You'll need your own LEGOs to make one of these cases, but otherwise, these cases tend to be built from readily available parts. Far too many variations of these cases exist to list, but if you're looking for inspiration, the DIY website Instructables (instructables.com) features several. User darrennie, in particular, has made one of the more popular cases. You can find the instructions at instructables.com/id/Lego-Raspberry-Pi-Case.

Wood Cases

LEGOs are great, but they're not for everyone. If you're a bit of a woodworker, you can put your skills to use making a wood case for your Raspberry Pi.

You don't need expert-level woodworking skills to do this, though. One of the more popular wooden case designs just uses two pieces of wood mounted together with four nuts and bolts. This creates a solid enclosure and only costs about $10 to make. It also doesn't require advanced skills or tools. You can get the whole guide to make it for yourself on Instructables at instructables.com/id/Oak-Raspberry-Pi-case-for-under-10.

Cardboard Cases

Finally, if you really don't feel like building anything, you can make a Raspberry Pi case from either humble cardboard or cardstock by simply printing out folding instructions and making some folds.

PI POINTER

The Raspberry Pi doesn't output much heat, so you don't need to worry about enclosing the board in a case. Still, if you decide to build your own case, be careful to leave some room for airflow so your Raspberry Pi remains cool.

A few different variations of cardboard cases exist, but one of the more popular ones is the Punnet case Mk 1. Download a printable PDF file with folding instructions from squareitround.co.uk/Resources/Punnet_net_Mk1.pdf, and print it onto a sheet of cardboard or card stock. Cut out the case diagram, fold it as directed, and you have a quick and easy case for your Raspberry Pi. You can also use a sheet of thin plastic if you prefer.

If you're not a fan of the design of the Punnet, authorized Raspberry Pi retailer MCM also has a cardboard option available at s3.amazonaws.com/mcmelectronics/misc/Build-A-Raspberry-Pi-Case.pdf. Like the Punnet case, all you need to do is print it out on a piece of cardstock paper, cut it out, and fold it up. Easy.

Really, what you end up using for a case is completely up to you. The Raspberry Pi is all about DIYing and ingenuity, so if you can come up with a case design that works for you and your needs, then go with it!

The Least You Need to Know

- The Raspberry Pi doesn't include a case, so you need to make or purchase one for yourself.

- You can get a solid case for under $10, or you can spend more if you need something durable.

- The Raspberry Pi is all about DIY, so people often make their own cases with whatever materials they have sitting around.

- Cases are sized differently for each model of the Raspberry Pi, so be sure you pick up (or make) the right one for your particular model.

Setting Up Your Raspberry Pi

The Raspberry Pi isn't as easy to set up as most computers. In fact, the setup process is meant to teach you all types of tricks for using the Raspberry Pi.

In Part 2, you get your Raspberry Pi set up with software and additional hardware, and you learn about picking an operating system to use with your Raspberry Pi. Some of this stuff is pretty obvious, like plugging in your Raspberry Pi to a monitor. Other facets of the setup process, like choosing the right kind of power adapter, are a lot more complicated. You explore all this and more in Part 2.

What You Need for Setup

As you've learned in previous chapters, one way the Raspberry Pi's cost stays so low—just $20 for Model A+ and $35 for Models B, B+, and 2—is because it excludes a lot of accessories other computers come standard with. That means you need to do a bit of work before you can actually use your Raspberry Pi. Thankfully, you probably have everything you need already, and what you don't have, you can purchase pretty inexpensively.

The Raspberry Pi uses common computer accessories like a USB keyboard and mouse and Ethernet cable for the internet. It has two options for connecting your Pi to a screen, as you read in Chapter 3. In this chapter, we review everything you need to get your Raspberry Pi set up and ready to go.

In This Chapter

- Necessary computer equipment for setup
- Essential cards and card readers
- All the cables and connectors you need

Personal Computer

It might sound a little silly that you need a personal computer to set up your Raspberry Pi computer, but it's true. In order to download and install the necessary operating systems and put them onto SD cards so your Raspberry Pi can utilize them, you'll need a computer to help with this setup process.

Pretty much any computer—PC or Mac—will do. If you don't have a personal computer, don't worry. I share a few alternative ideas for getting operating systems in this chapter, too.

> **PI POINTER**
>
> Throughout this book, I walk you through the setup process using both Windows and Mac computers. Both types of computers work perfectly fine and require about the same amount of work on your part.

HDMI or Composite-Enabled Monitor or TV

Many computers need monitors, and the Raspberry Pi is no different. Because you need to see what you're doing on the Raspberry Pi, you need a television or monitor to connect it to. You have two options for connecting the Pi to a screen: HDMI, which is usually found on newer HD monitors and televisions, or composite, which is usually found on older TVs.

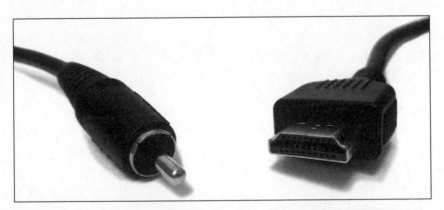

HDMI (right) and composite cables (left) are two options for connecting your Raspberry Pi to a display.

HDMI is typically the preferred method because the Raspberry Pi can output an HD signal, but if you only have an older composite cable–compatible TV sitting around, that will work fine.

The Raspberry Pi can be run without a monitor at all, but that's typically reserved for more advanced users. Even if you don't have it connected all the time, a screen is useful during the setup process because you go through a lot of menus and options.

The Raspberry Pi is small enough that you can attach it to a TV or monitor without it getting in the way, so don't worry if you have to unplug other equipment you're currently using to use the Raspberry Pi. If you have a monitor or TV right now, it should be perfectly capable of working with the Pi, at least temporarily during setup.

USB Keyboard and Mouse

You also need a keyboard to do most of the setup on your Raspberry Pi. Some of the projects in this book won't require the keyboard after you're all set up, but one is required for the initial installation.

And if you plan on using an operating system like Raspbian, you'll probably also want a mouse.

Pretty much any USB mouse and keyboard should work with the Raspberry Pi. Like most accessories in this chapter, you don't need to go out and buy anything new. You can use the keyboard and mouse you already have with your Raspberry Pi and move them back to your computer when you're finished.

Internet Connectivity

The internet is incredibly helpful when setting up your Raspberry Pi for two main reasons:

- You need to download your operating system from the internet.
- You need to download software onto your Raspberry Pi.

Technically, it is possible to do a lot of different projects with the Raspberry Pi without the internet, but it's much more difficult.

With most models, you can connect your Raspberry Pi to the internet via the Ethernet port with an Ethernet cable. For the Model A+, you need a Wi-Fi adapter (more on this in Chapter 11). But even for that, you'll need a wired connection via USB.

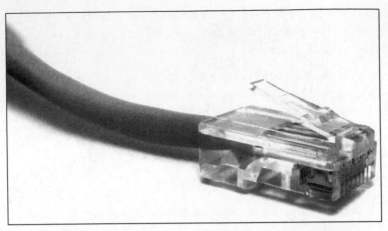

You'll need an Ethernet cable to get your Raspberry Pi online.

PI POINTER

If you don't have internet access, you can still get your Raspberry Pi up and running, but you'll need to purchase an SD card with an *image*, or a copy of all the software you need, already saved on it.

For now, just be sure you have some way to connect your Raspberry Pi and your personal computer to the internet.

SD Cards and Readers

Finally, you need an SD card. The Model B uses a standard SD card, while Models A+, B+, and 2 use a micro SD.

SD cards are small memory cards often used in digital cameras. The Raspberry Pi supports most SD cards, but be sure you get one with at least 8GB of memory. You can get more than that if you like, but it's not required. The more memory you have, the more storage you'll get on the Raspberry Pi.

Depending on what model Raspberry Pi you have, you might need a micro SD card (left, center) or a standard-size version (right).

If you plan on doing a few different projects, it's good to have multiple SD cards. The Raspberry Pi's operating system is entirely housed on the SD card, and because the card is removable, you can swap out different cards—and, therefore, different operating systems—as often as you like. For example, you might want to have one that contains Raspbian and another that holds a media center. Essentially, one Raspberry Pi can do multiple things if you have multiple SD cards. It's like being able to toggle between Windows and OS X by just swapping hard drives.

I walk you through setting up your SD card in Chapter 8, but if you don't have a personal computer, you can purchase preloaded SD cards from the Raspberry Pi website at swag.raspberrypi.org/collections/frontpage/products/noobs-8gb-sd-card. These preloaded cards are great if you don't have access to a computer or the internet, but they're a bit more costly than a typical SD card.

Finally, be sure your personal computer has an SD card reader. If it doesn't, you can usually get a USB reader when you purchase your SD card. This enables you to plug an SD card into the reader and then into a USB port on your personal computer.

And that's all the essential equipment you need—besides your Raspberry Pi—to get your Pi set up. In the next chapter, I guide you through the next steps in the setup process.

The Least You Need to Know

- The Raspberry Pi is, itself, a computer, but you still need some external accessories to actually use it.

- You have two options for hooking up your Raspberry Pi to a screen: HDMI and composite. This should allow you to hook up your Raspberry Pi to a TV or monitor you already own.

- You need a USB keyboard and mouse to help with the setup and use of your Raspberry Pi, but many projects don't require them after the initial setup.

- The Raspberry Pi uses SD cards instead of hard drives, so it's easy to swap between operating systems.

Ports, Pins, and Plug-Ins

We've had a quick look at the basics of everything on the Raspberry Pi, but it's time to dig a little deeper into its different ports and pinouts.

When you look at your Raspberry Pi, you probably recognize ports like the HDMI or USB plugs. But you'll also notice some strange pins sticking out of it. These are the GPIO pins. These GPIO plugins aren't as obvious to use as something like a USB port, so they require a bit more in the way of explanation.

After you understand the GPIO pins, it's time to connect your Raspberry Pi to the peripheral equipment you want to use with it. From there, it's almost time to boot up your Raspberry Pi for the first time.

In this chapter, I demystify all the ports on your Raspberry Pi and explain what each is used for.

In This Chapter

- The Raspberry Pi's ports and pinouts
- Connecting various equipment
- The Raspberry Pi's component

Ports and Pinouts

The Raspberry Pi has a few easy to recognize ports, like USB, HDMI, and Ethernet, but it also has a pinout section that might be a bit confusing to look at. Thankfully, these pinouts are pretty easy to understand once you see a diagram showing what they connect to. First, let's take a look at all the ports.

 HARDWARE HELPER

The Raspberry Pi has all kinds of extra peripherals you can attach to it, including a camera and a display. Both of these types of peripherals get their own port on the board. (I talk about these more in-depth in Chapter 21.)

Raspberry Pi Ports

Your Raspberry Pi has a number of different ports you can use to connect various components to it. Here's a rundown of each of these ports:

USB ports: The USB ports on your Raspberry Pi are where you connect accessories like a keyboard, mouse, Wi-Fi adapter, and more. The Model A+ has one, the Model B has two, and Models B+ and 2 have four.

Ethernet port: The Ethernet port is where you connect an Ethernet cable to access the internet. The Model A+ does not have an Ethernet port.

HDMI port: You connect an HDMI cable here to output a HD video and audio signal to a monitor or television.

Composite video port (Models A+ and B): You can use an RCA cable here to connect your Raspberry Pi to a composite TV or monitor.

Audio jack/3.5mm video port (Models A+, B+, and 2): On Models A and B, you use this jack or port to output audio through a 3.5mm cable. On Models A+, B+, and 2, it's used for both audio and video.

Digital Serial Interface (DSI): This is another video output port, made for direct connections. This is a bit more advanced. If you were to use a small LCD screen with your Raspberry Pi instead of a monitor, you could use this port.

Camera Serial Interface (CSI): This interface is for the Raspberry Pi camera. The camera has a cable that connects directly to this port.

Joint Test Action Group (JTAG) Headers: This port is for connecting your Raspberry Pi to a debugger. This is only for advanced users, so I won't be covering it in much detail here.

That's it for your ports. Now let's take a closer look at the GPIO pins.

Raspberry Pi Pinouts

Pinouts are the little pins you see on your Raspberry Pi. These are GPIO (general-purpose input/output) pins that enable you to connect your Raspberry Pi to more devices than just the ones listed in the preceding section.

On all Raspberry Pi models, the GPIO header (the black bar), holds the GPIO pins.

GPIO pins connect your Raspberry Pi to various hardware components, enabling you to send inputs and outputs from the Raspberry Pi. Essentially, the GPIO pins make it so you can directly connect your Raspberry Pi external hardware.

Typically, you'll do this with a *solderless breadboard*. A breadboard features a board of terminal strips upon which you can link two wires together without soldering or tying the cables together. They're often used to prototype electronics.

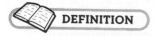 **DEFINITION**

A **solderless breadboard** is a prototyping device that enables you to connect two wires without soldering or tying them together. You can purchase a solderless breadboard for around $5 from many electronics shops.

Each section of the GPIO pins does a different thing. Some are for inputs, and other are for outputs. Some are powered, and others are not. You'll only need the latter if you're programming external hardware (which we won't be doing in this book), but it's good to know what they're used for and where they are if you decide to do any advanced projects. The GPIO layout is a little different between Models B+ and 2 and older versions.

Before we get to that, let's define some of the shorthand used in the pin charts:

SDA (serial data line) and **SCL** (serial clock line) are inter-integrated circuits. They're simple, two-wire interfaces. The SCL, the clock line, is used to synchronize data transfers on a timer. SDA is the data line that does the same thing.

UART stands for *universal asynchronous receiver/transmitter.* This means it takes individual bits sequentially. Basically, one bit is sent over at a time in a long row.

Ground is the reference point for the electric circuit. Think of it as 0. It works the same way as the ground on your car's battery or in your household wiring.

MOSI stands for *master out, slave in.* This sends a master signal out of your Raspberry Pi and receives data from the slave. A slave could be a hard drive, a robotic controller, or pretty much anything else with an output.

MISO stands for *master in, slave out.* It works the opposite way as MOSI.

SCLK (serial clock) is a clock line. It's generated by the master and drives communication in both directions.

This can be a bit complicated, but don't worry. Although it's important for you to know, you won't really need to use it very often.

GPIO Pin Locations

Now let's take a look at which pin does what on the Raspberry Pi. Here's a chart to get a handle on what each does.

PI POINTER

The GPIO pins are arranged in two columns and numbered from the top left, across to the right, down to the left, and so on. The "Pin" columns in following tables mimic the layout of the pins in the GPIO header on your Raspberry Pi.

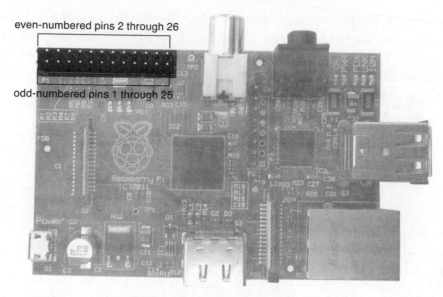

The GPIO pins on the Model B.

Model B GPIO Pin Uses

Pin	Use	Pin	Use
1	3.3V	2	5V
3	I2C1 SDA	4	5V
5	I2C1 SCL	6	Ground
7	GPIO 4	8	UART TXD (transmit)
9	Ground	10	UART RXD (receive)
11	GPIO 17	12	GPIO 18
13	GPIO 27	14	Ground
15	GPIO 22	16	GPIO 23
17	3.3V	18	GPIO 24
19	MOSI	20	Ground
21	MISO	22	GPIO 25
23	SCLK	24	GPIO 8
25	Ground	26	GPIO 7

The Model B+ is a little different because it has more GPIO pins. Still, the setup is basically the same as what's on the Model B.

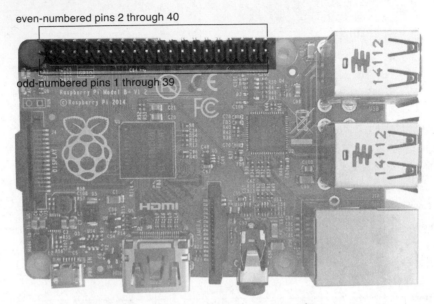

The GPIO pins on Models A+, B+, and 2.

Models A+, B+, and 2 GPIO Pin Uses

Pin	Use	Pin	Use
1	3.3V	2	5V
3	I2C1 SDA	4	5V
5	I2C1 SCL	6	Ground
7	GPIO 4	8	UART TXT
9	Ground	10	UART RXD
11	GPIO 17	12	GPIO 18
13	GPIO 27	14	Ground
15	GPIO 22	16	GPIO 23
17	3.3V	18	GPIO 24
19	MOSI	20	Ground
21	MISO	22	GPIO 25
23	SCLK	24	GPIO 8

Pin	Use	Pin	Use
25	Ground	26	GPIO 7
27	DNC (do not connect)	28	DNC
29	GPIO 5	30	Ground
31	GPIO 6	32	GPIO 12
33	GPIO 13	34	Ground
35	GPIO 19	36	GPIO 16
37	GPIO 26	38	GPIO 20
39	Ground	40	GPIO 21

That's it for GPIO. It can be a bit confusing and difficult to really understand until you actually need it. Don't worry though, if you do end up using these pins for a project, it becomes a lot less confusing when you start working with them.

Connecting Equipment

Now that you've got a basic understanding of how everything on the Raspberry Pi works, it's time to start plugging in components. This part's pretty self-explanatory, but let's walk through the process so you know what you're doing.

Adding Accessories

If you happened to get a dedicated display for your Raspberry Pi or the camera connection kit (I talk about these more in Chapter 21), you can connect them to your Raspberry Pi now.

The camera attaches to the camera connection, the CSI, using the ribbon cable that came with it. Just line it up and clip the ribbon on the Raspberry Pi. Plug the end into your camera, and you're good to go.

Likewise, if you're using a dedicated display, you can connect the ribbon cable from the display into the display connection, the DSI, the same way.

If you're not using either, you can skip ahead and plug in your other cables.

Plugging In

Now it's time to get your Raspberry Pi plugged in and running. Here's what you need to do:

1. Plug your USB keyboard and USB mouse into the USB slots. If you're using the Model A+, you'll need to either use a USB hub or a keyboard that has an extra USB input on it.

2. Connect the HDMI cable to the HDMI input or the composite cable to the RCA input. If you have a Model A+, B+, or 2, connect your 3.5mm to RCA converter into the 3.5mm jack.

3. Connect your video cable into your TV or monitor.

4. Plug the Ethernet cable into the Ethernet jack on your Raspberry Pi and then the Ethernet port on your modem or router. If you're using the Model A+, you'll need a USB Wi-Fi adapter for internet access.

You have two more items to plug in—the SD card and the power adapter.

PI POINTER

Don't worry too much about the order you plug in your accessories. The only thing that really matters is that the power cable gets plugged in last. The Raspberry Pi doesn't have a power switch, so plugging in the power supply turns it on automatically. You don't want to do this until everything is set up and ready to go.

Connecting the SD Card

Plug your SD card into the slot on the bottom of the Raspberry Pi. Just slide the card in until it clicks into place.

However, before you do that, you'll need to set up the SD card with an operating system. We take a look at the various options in the next chapter.

Powering On

Last but not least—and after you've outfitted your SD card with your desired operating system—it's time to power up your Raspberry Pi. Simply attach the power cord to your Raspberry Pi and then plug the other end into an electric outlet.

The Least You Need to Know

- The Raspberry Pi has myriad different kinds of inputs and outputs for connecting various devices.

- The GPIO pins are great for connecting your Raspberry Pi to external hardware, but you won't need to use them for most beginner projects.

- To connect your Raspberry Pi to your accessories, you need a USB mouse, a USB keyboard, a TV or monitor that supports either HDMI or composite video, and a modem with an Ethernet port.

- The SD card port is located on the bottom side of your Raspberry Pi.

Selecting an Operating System

One of the best things about working with the Raspberry Pi is that you can pick your operating system. Because all the operating systems available for the Raspberry Pi are based on Linux, you have a wide variety of options to choose from, and each has advantages and disadvantages.

It's not just about picking an operating system to do regular computer work with either. Custom operating systems exist to turn your Raspberry Pi into a media center, a learn-to-code machine, and so much more.

In this chapter, we explore a few of the most popular operating systems available for the Raspberry Pi, and I explain a bit more about why the Raspberry Pi uses Linux instead of any other operating system.

In This Chapter

- Why Linux?
- Versions of Linux for the Raspberry Pi
- Media center options

An Introduction to Linux

Linux (linux.com) is a free and open-source operating system originally released in 1991 by software engineer Linus Torvalds. Because it's open source, it's available in many different variations and can work on everything from mobile phones to personal computers, all without any licensing. For example, the smartphone operating system Android is based on Linux.

Linux is meant to be a free, fully customizable alternative to the Windows and OS X operating systems. It works essentially the same way as these operating systems, although it certainly has its own set of quirks. It isn't as polished or fancy as the newest version of Windows, but it does what it needs to do.

Unlike in Windows or OS X, a lot of the work you do in Linux takes place at the *command line,* where you type in specific commands instead of using a mouse to click buttons or menus. Subsequently, it's a bit harder to use than something like Windows.

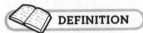 **DEFINITION**

The **command line** is a way to interact with a computer program using typed commands as text instead of a mouse. Instead of clicking on something with your mouse, you tell your computer to perform an action using a simple string of text. Working with the command line might sound intimidating, but it's actually very easy once you get the hang of it. (I talk more about the command line in Chapter 9.)

Linux is based on UNIX, which is the same operating system OS X was built on. These days, Linux is primarily used for servers, but plenty of people use it as the operating system for their personal computing needs as well.

Linux comes in many variations, called *distributions.* Raspbian (Raspbian.org), Mint (linuxmint.com), Ubuntu (ubuntu.com), Debian (debian.org), and Fedora (getfedora.org) are some of the more popular versions. Each distribution looks and handles things a little differently.

Anyone can make a distribution of Linux, so it's also popular for home theater PCs. For example, OpenELEC (openelec.tv) is an operating system built on Linux that's meant to turn your computer (or Raspberry Pi) into a media center.

 PI POINTER

Remember, with the Raspberry Pi, you install your operating system on an SD card. This means you can download as many operating systems on different SD cards as you like and swap among them.

Why the Raspberry Pi Uses Linux

It's natural to assume that the Raspberry Pi uses Linux as its operating system because it's free, but that's not the only reason. Free means you don't have to pay any licensing fees to use it, like you would with Windows. It also means anyone in the world can use a Raspberry Pi without jumping through any hoops to get a license.

Because Linux is open source, you can make customized versions of Linux for the Raspberry Pi for your own unique projects. For example, the operating system arkOS (arkos.io) is just for email hosting, and Mozilla, the team behind the web browser Firefox, is making an operating system called Firefox OS (mozilla.org/en-US/firefox/os) that will work on the Raspberry Pi.

Besides Linux, other popular open-source software includes the web browser Chromium (chromium.org) and the office suite LibreOffice (libreoffice.org).

Open-Source Ideology

The Raspberry Pi itself is open source, as are most of the materials the Raspberry Pi Foundation releases for it. This means people are usually free to license, reuse, and remix the software or hardware any way they like. It also means the source code (or schematics) are available for everyone to see.

Typically, open source also means collaboration. Because everyone out there can see the source code, everyone can work on it together. In the case of the Raspberry Pi, this was an important factor in how the creators wanted the device to work.

The primary purpose of the Raspberry Pi is to teach children to code at a young age, so the designers needed an operating system that could do that. Linux is a perfect fit. Most of the software available on Linux is open source as well.

The Raspberry Pi Foundation wants to get kids tinkering with electronics, and the best way to do that is to give them open access to any software they want. Linux makes it easy to tinker with the core of the system, and that's a great way to learn how it works.

Why Windows and OS X Don't Work

Simply put, Windows and OS X won't work on the Raspberry Pi because the device isn't powerful enough to run any modern version of these operating systems.

It's also because of the type of processor the Raspberry Pi has. It's an *ARM processor,* and no versions of Windows support ARM. ARM is a completely different type of system architecture typically meant for smartphones.

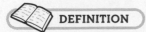 **DEFINITION**

An **ARM processor** is a type of processor architecture made to use fewer transistors than other processors. This means they're usually cheaper, use less power, and don't create as much heat. They're often the choice for processors in smartphones, tablets, laptops, and set-top boxes. The Raspberry Pi uses an ARM processor to keep costs down and power consumption low.

Linux Distributions for the Raspberry Pi

The Raspberry Pi can work with many different Linux distributions, but in this book, we'll stick to just the more popular ones. These include Raspbian, Arch Linux, and Debian, along with a few more specialized distributions. Each distribution can also have several variants, which usually just slightly alter the bundled software inside a distribution.

So many versions of Linux exist because each distribution is a little different, and typically one is better at a specific task than another is. Sometimes it's just cosmetic, but for the most part, you can determine which version of Linux is best for you based on what you plan on doing with it.

Let's take a look at some of the most popular options.

Raspbian

Raspbian (Raspbian.org) is the most popular version of Linux built for the Raspberry Pi. It was the first one available, and it remains the most actively developed version.

Raspbian is based on the popular Linux distribution Debian, but it's optimized to work with the Raspberry Pi's hardware. Raspbian is appealing because it includes a ton of software right from the start so you don't need to go out and download stuff on your own. Pretty much everything you need to get started is included—a web browser, notepad, setup tools, and more. Whatever isn't included can easily be downloaded from the Pi Store (store.raspberrypi.com).

What's more, the settings for all the software included in Raspbian are adjusted to work with the Raspberry PI CPU. That means almost everything works smoothly on the Raspberry Pi and you don't have to worry much about changing settings to get hardware working properly.

Raspbian isn't actually affiliated with the Raspberry Pi Foundation in any way. It was created by, and continues to be developed by, a small team of developers who believe in the foundation's goals. That said, the Raspberry Pi Foundation has its own distribution of Raspbian that's packed with software the foundation recommends. You can download other variations of Raspbian, including a minimalist image, an image built specifically for education, and more from the Raspbian website (raspbian.org). (I show you how to install and use Raspbian in the next chapter.)

PI POINTER

The operating systems mentioned in this section aren't the only options for your Raspberry Pi. Many variations on Linux exist—and even variations on those variations. For example, there are at least seven other versions of Raspbian out there. Anyone can make a Linux distribution, so be sure to always download from trusted sources.

Arch Linux

Arch Linux (archlinux.org) takes the opposite approach Raspbian takes. Instead of including as many pieces of software as possible, it includes as few. Arch Linux is a much more minimalist operating system.

Unlike Raspbian, Arch Linux features mostly command line tools instead of a graphical interface. Subsequently, Arch Linux tends to be the preferred operating system for more advanced users who don't need the point-and-click simplicity of Raspbian. Arch Linux still has a graphical frontend, but you don't rely on it nearly as much you would with something like Raspbian.

Arch Linux was originally released in 2002 and is currently developed by programmer/developer Aaron Griffin and a small team. The Raspberry Pi version, also known as Arch Linux ARM (named for the CPU), was developed by a small team of four developers. Arch Linux ARM (archlinuxarm.org) works on any computer running an ARM CPU.

Arch Linux ARM is targeted more toward experienced Linux users who are familiar with the system. It's a small, unobtrusive operating system, tends to be a little faster than something like Raspbian, but is considerably harder to use. Arch Linux is a great operating system to use once you're familiar with your Raspberry Pi, but skip it for something easier for your first few projects.

Debian

Debian (debian.org) is another of the more popular distributions of Linux and is used as the base of Raspbian. Because Debian is open source, the developers of Raspbian adapted Debian so it could be optimized to work on the Raspberry Pi.

Debian was originally released in 1993, with the first stable release in 1996. As one of the earliest Linux distributions, it remains the base for many other versions of Linux, and it's still one of the most popular Linux distributions for personal computers.

Like Raspbian, the default installation of Debian includes free software that enables you to edit photos, play media files, and browse the web.

You can still install Debian on your Raspberry Pi, but it's not well supported and will take a lot of work to get everything running smoothly. Instead, it's typically recommended that you use Raspbian because it's based on the Debian and is optimized to work well with the Raspberry Pi.

Raspbmc, XBian, and OpenELEC

Many Raspberry Pi users turn the device into a *media center.* Media centers allow you to play movies you own, stream content from sites online, play music, and even browse photos. If you've never used a media center before, think of it like a DIY version of Roku, Apple TV, or another similar set-top box. In the case of the Raspberry Pi, you provide the hardware and then download and install the software you want.

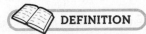 **DEFINITION**

> **Media center** is really just a fancy phrase for a computer that hosts your media. You can set up a media center to stream content from an external hard drive, from another computer in your house, or from sources online. They're basically a DIY set-top box you make yourself.

Several different media center distributions are available, but Raspbmc, XBian, and OpenELEC are the most widely used. All three are based on the Linux-based open-source media center software XBMC (kodi.tv). Popular for personal computers, XBMC was originally released in 2002 as a means to add media center functionality to the Xbox but has since grown into software that works on Windows, OS X, Android, iOS, Linux, and more. In the case of the Raspberry Pi, most media centers are their own distributions.

Which media center is best is really up to your preferences. They're easy enough to install, it might be worth you checking out all three before you make your decision. Let's look at each in a bit more detail to help you decide:

Raspbmc: Raspbmc (raspbmc.com) is the most complete of all three options. It's built on XBMC, and everything works right out of the box so you don't have to go search for extra stuff to install. Raspbmc runs as a full Linux build, so it's a little slow to boot and takes up a big chunk of space on your SD card. That said, the fact that it includes everything on the SD card means you don't really need to do much to set it up. Once you install Raspbmc onto your SD card, you can boot it up and start using all its features right away.

XBian: Whereas Raspbmc is packed full of features, XBian (xbian.org) prides itself on getting those features *first.* XBian is all about the cutting edge, and it constantly updates with new features, regardless of whether they've been tested for bugs. So although XBian is often feature-packed, it's also usually a little wonky.

XBian is built on Raspbian, so it can do just about everything Raspbian can. XBian is also incredibly configurable. You can set it up with a ton of different software and extend its functionality with more features than Raspbmc. Even with the potential bugs, XBian is pretty easy to use and good for beginners who don't like Raspbmc.

OpenELEC: Raspbmc and XBian strive to include a ton of features, but OpenELEC (openelec.tv) tries to include as few as possible. OpenElec is essentially Raspbmc stripped down to just the essentials. Therefore, it's incredibly quick and boots a lot faster than XBian or Raspbmc. It also loads media faster.

Unfortunately, the speed comes at the cost of features. If you want to add special drivers, you have to reinstall OpenELEC from scratch. It also takes a little more technical know-how to get OpenELEC working because the installation process isn't as easy as something like Raspbmc.

This might feel like a lot to process, but you can relax. We look at media center operating systems more in depth in Chapter 12.

Specialized Distributions

Besides media centers, several other specialized operating system distributions exist for the Raspberry Pi. These distributions might not be built on Linux, but they are designed specifically for the Raspberry Pi. Here are some of the more well-liked ones:

RISC OS: RISC OS (riscosopen.org) was initially released in 1987 as an operating system built for the ARM chipset. That's the same chip the Raspberry Pi uses, which makes RISC OS great for the Raspberry Pi.

RISC OS isn't built on anything else; it's entirely its own operating system, so it's not as familiar to use. For example, applications don't get their own executable programs. Instead, they're just folders with a ! in front of them. It also makes heavy use of the mouse, so if you want to experiment with this operating system, be sure you have a mouse handy. And although RISC OS is similar to Linux in the way it looks, it handles certain operations differently, like multitasking.

RISC OS isn't as widely supported as Linux by any means, but even with a lack of hardware, it does work well on the Raspberry Pi.

RetroPie: The operating system RetroPie (blog.petrockblock.com/retropie) turns your Raspberry Pi into a dedicated gaming machine. Out of the box, it includes dozens of video game emulators, and you can use it to play old-school games from Nintendo, Sega, and more. RetroPie also supports controllers if you want to add a USB controller instead of using a keyboard and mouse.

OpenWrt: OpenWrt (openwrt.org) is an open-source router operating system. You might not realize it, but your home Wi-Fi router runs its own operating system. OpenWrt is essentially Linux for your router. Once you get it installed, you get a ton of new features for your router, including the ability to set bandwidth caps, add security, and more.

Google Coder: Google Coder (googlecreativelab.github.io/coder) turns your Raspberry Pi into a server you can access from your computer and learn how to do basic coding. It's all about teaching you basic HTML, JavaScript, and CSS web coding work. (I talk about this a lot more in Chapter 18.)

PI POINTER

Anyone can make a unique distribution of an image for the Raspberry Pi, so plenty of different variations exist. Most are built on an existing version of Linux, but many are specially made just for the Raspberry Pi. So if you're looking for something in particular, it's worth searching online to see if someone has made what you need.

Why Raspbian Is Best

With all these options, you might be wondering why Raspbian tends to be the go-to choice for beginners and advanced users alike. The main reason is pretty simple: Raspbian has the most software available on it. Out of the box, it's already packed with a ton of software you can start using right away.

Similar to making the choice between Windows and OS X, or Android and iPhone, software is the driving choice for most operating systems. On the Raspberry Pi, Raspbian is constantly updated, and most Linux software works on it. So when you boot up Raspbian, you get to run a bunch of software without needing to customize the settings.

It's also the most full-featured of the operating systems, and it's built for people who might not be familiar with Linux. It's also relatively easy to use if you're familiar with Windows or Mac computers.

If you've never used Linux before, Raspbian makes that transition simple by giving you many utilities not always included in Linux. This includes software to set up a Wi-Fi card, an email client, and terminal app so you can use the command line. There's even an app store to help you find software that works on Raspbian.

There's a good chance that even if you're completely unfamiliar with Linux, you'll understand how to use Raspbian pretty quickly. Its library of software also makes it great for anyone looking to use their Raspberry Pi as a full-blown computer

The Least You Need to Know

- You have a lot of options when it comes to operating systems for your Raspberry Pi.

- Most of the popular Raspberry Pi operating systems are built on Linux.

- You can turn your Raspberry Pi into a media center using one of three different operating systems made specifically for media centers.

- Raspbian is the most popular operating system because it supports a lot of different software and is relatively easy to use.

Installing Linux

You have many options for operating systems with your Raspberry Pi, but Raspbian, a variant of Linux, is the most widely supported and optimized operating system available. It gives you a lot of compatible software, and installation is easy.

Raspbian also is going to be the most familiar operating system to you if you're a Windows or Mac user. Although it does do some things differently, the overall interface is easy to understand. For the most part, you can do almost everything you need to do with just a mouse, but I'll show you some command line tricks as well.

The installation process is the same for every operating system that works on the Raspberry Pi, so once you get Raspbian installed and running, you'll know how to install any others you might want to try.

In this chapter, you learn how to download Raspbian, install it on your SD card, get Raspbian configured correctly, and launch your Raspberry Pi for the first time. This is a little complicated at first, but follow along and you'll be fine. And once you get the hang of it, you'll be loading up new operating systems all the time.

In This Chapter

- Downloading the Linux variant Raspbian

- Saving Raspbian on your SD card

- Customizing Raspbian

- Getting more software

Downloading Raspbian

Raspbian is a free operating system that's constantly being updated with new features. You can always find the newest version on the Raspberry Pi site. Here's how:

1. Point your computer's web browser to raspberrypi.org/downloads.

2. Click the **Download ZIP** button in the Raspbian section. It's a big file, so it might take a little while to download.

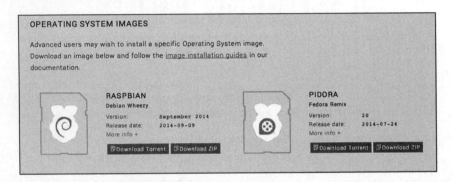

3. When it's finished downloading, double-click the .zip file to unzip it. This creates a new folder that includes an image (IMG) file of the Raspbian operating system. That's what you'll install on your SD card.

    SOFTWARE SOLUTION

If you're not sure which operating system you want to use, you can download the most popular options all at once with NOOBS (new out of the box software). NOOBS lets you install different operating systems using your SD card and the Raspberry Pi itself. Download NOOBS at raspberrypi.org/downloads.

Installing Raspbian on Your SD Card

Your SD card is going to become your Raspberry Pi's main hard drive. You'll install Raspbian onto the SD card using your personal computer. The process is a little different, depending on whether you're on a Windows or Mac machine.

Windows:

Getting Raspbian installed on your Windows PC takes one piece of external software (Win32 Disk Imager, which enables you to write an image to your SD card), so you'll need an internet connection to download it. Be sure your SD card is installed in your SD card reader and it's hooked up to your computer.

Here's what to do:

1. Download Win32 Disk Imager from sourceforge.net/projects/win32diskimager.

2. Double-click the downloaded file to unzip it. This creates a new folder.

3. Inside that folder is an application called **Win32DiskImager.exe**; double-click it to open it. If you're on Windows 7 or 8, right-click and choose **Run as Administrator**.

4. Win32 Disk Imager should automatically choose your SD card, but if it doesn't, click on the drop-down menu and choose your SD card from the list. Be sure to choose your SD card and not your hard drive.

5. Click the folder icon, and select the Raspbian IMG file you downloaded in the earlier "Downloading Raspbian" section.

6. Click the **Write** button, and wait for Win32 Disk Imager to run. When it's complete, you can eject your SD card.

Now your SD card has Raspbian installed on it. It's time to get started playing with your Raspberry Pi.

Mac:

You'll need one extra piece of software (RPi-sd card builder) to get Raspbian onto your SD card using your Mac. The process only takes a few minutes—be sure your SD card is connected to your Mac:

1. Download RPi-sd card builder from alltheware.wordpress.com/2012/12/11/easiest-way-sd-card-setup.

2. Double-click the downloaded file to unzip it, and double-click the **RPi-sd card reader** application inside that folder.

3. You'll be asked for your Raspbian image. Select the IMG file you downloaded in the earlier "Downloading Raspbian" section.

4. You'll be asked to verify your SD card. Be sure it's the correct drive, and click **OK**.

5. Enter your computer's password, and click **OK**.

6. You'll get a prompt saying your SD card was ejected. Do not remove the SD card, but check that it's no longer visible on your desktop. If the SD card isn't visible, select **Continue**.

7. Sit back and relax while RPi-sd card builder does its job. When it's finished, it'll display a note saying it's complete.

That's it. Now you can boot up and start configuring your Raspberry Pi.

Booting Up

Now you have your Raspberry Pi's operating system ready to go. Plug the SD card that contains Raspbian into your Raspberry Pi. If you haven't already, plug in your keyboard and mouse, and connect your Raspberry Pi to your display. Finally, connect your Raspberry Pi to your power adapter. Your Raspberry Pi will now boot up on its own.

If everything goes properly, you're greeted with the Raspberry Pi boot screen. After a few seconds, you're shown the Raspberry Pi configuration screen.

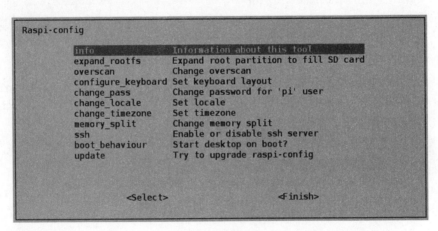

When you start your Raspberry Pi, you should see this configuration screen.

Now you need to set up some specifics with the Raspberry Pi.

Configuring Raspbian

The first screen you'll see on your Raspberry Pi is the Raspi-config menu. This is where you'll set up some of the basics of your Pi. You can navigate the menu with your keyboard; hit **Enter** to select a highlighted item.

Configuring Raspbian for Full Storage

When you create your SD card image, the image takes up space on the entire card. This means you can't install new software because the SD thinks it's full. You can expand the SD card so you get more space. Select the **expand_rootfs** option, and let the software do its thing.

Configuring Raspbian for Full-Screen

Depending on the type of display you're using, you might need to change the overscan option. Older TVs used overscan to properly display an image full-screen, but most new models don't need it.

If you're using a monitor or HD TV, you can most likely turn off overscan so the operating system takes up the full screen. If this is the case, select the **overscan** option, and disable it.

Establishing Keyboard Layout

The Raspberry Pi is originally from the United Kingdom, so the initial keyboard configuration is based on the UK layout. If you're not in the UK, select the **configure_keyboard** option, and pick your region.

Changing Your Password

By default, the Raspberry Pi's password for the main user ("pi"), is "raspberry." This isn't very secure, so now is a good time to change your password.

Select the **change_pass** option, and type in a password of your choice.

Setting Your Time Zone

So your clock is correct, let's set your time zone. Select the **change_timezone** option, and pick your local time zone.

Configuring Raspbian for Boot-to-Desktop

If you want your Raspberry Pi to boot straight into Raspbian (instead of the command prompt), select the **boot_behaviour** option. This way, when you turn on your Pi, it'll load Raspbian automatically.

When you're done with these settings, select **<Finish>**, and your Raspberry Pi will reboot.

Logging In for the First Time

Now to boot into the Raspbian operating system. If you selected the boot-to-desktop option, Raspbian will automatically load when you turn on your Raspberry Pi.

Depending on the settings you chose in the preceding section, you might need to type in your username and password to log in. If you didn't set one, the default username is **pi** and the password is **raspberry**.

Accessing the Raspi-Config Tool

If you want to change any of the settings you adjusted in the preceding section, you can do so at any time. From the command prompt, type in `raspi-config` to load the configuration menu.

You can get to the command prompt from Raspbian by selecting the **Logout** option from the bottom-left corner menu in Raspbian or by opening LXTerminal in Raspbian. I cover what all this means more in the next chapter, but it's worth mentioning briefly here.

Launching Raspbian Manually

If you didn't set your Pi to boot to desktop, you'll get a command prompt when you turn on your Raspberry Pi. Type `startx` to boot into the desktop environment.

Getting Acquainted with Raspbian

Raspbian is the main operating system for your Raspberry Pi, so spend a little time familiarizing yourself with how it works. The graphical front end is going to be similar to Windows or OS X, but how you actually use it differs in a few subtle ways.

Similar to Windows or OS X, Raspbian comes with all kinds of preinstalled applications and utilities to get you started. You also can download third-party applications, mess around with system settings, and more.

Raspbian shares many visual similarities with Windows.

 PI POINTER

Raspbian isn't all that different from Windows. You can find a folder with all your applications in the bottom-left corner, all your applications are divided into different categories so they're easy to find, and applications that are running show up in the bottom menu so you can quickly access them. Installing new applications is a very different process from something like Windows, but otherwise, you should have no problem getting used to Raspbian.

Learning the Raspbian Interface

If you've never used Linux before, Raspbian might be a bit confusing at first. However, if you can navigate Windows, Raspbian won't be completely foreign-looking from the start. Let's go through a few of the basics so you can start using it:

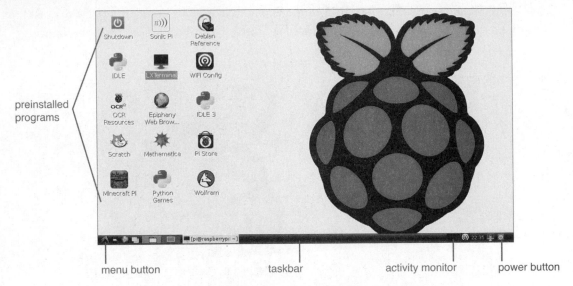

Raspbian is pretty user friendly.

The menu button in the bottom left-corner works just like the Start menu in Windows. Click it, and you're shown a list of applications.

The desktop works the same as Windows as well. Depending on which version of Raspbian you have installed, different applications will already be on your desktop. Just double-click an icon to launch the preinstalled program.

In the bottom-right corner of the screen, you'll see an activity monitor that displays how much CPU Raspbian is currently using as well as a power button. The activity monitor shows how many resources you're currently using. When you're running a lot of software it'll show green spikes. Click the power button when you want to shut down or reboot.

When you open an app, you'll see a shortcut to it appears in the taskbar at the bottom of the screen. You can reopen apps from here, minimize them, or maximize them.

You'll also find a file manager option in your programs. This works just like Explorer on Windows. You can browse files on your Raspberry Pi and open them with a double-click of the mouse.

Otherwise, Raspbian tends to work the same way as the personal computers you're probably already used to. It has its quirks, but don't be afraid to poke around a little bit to get to know it when you first launch it.

Preinstalled Applications

Raspbian comes packed with a lot of different applications you need to get started right away. Much like Windows, you can pull up your installed applications by clicking on the menu button in the bottom-right corner of the screen and selecting what you want.

We're not going to go through every single program installed on Raspbian here, but the following are the most notable applications you'll find yourself using:

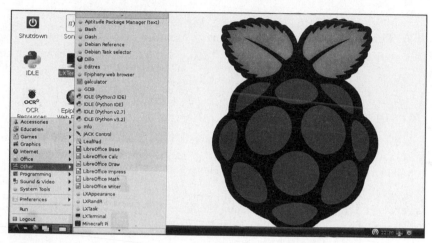

Depending on your version of Raspbian and from where you downloaded it, you have a suite of programs already installed.

Scratch: Scratch is a coding program that teaches children how to program. It's simple to use and utilizes a lot of images and diagrams instead of complex coding to teach the basics of computer science.

Epiphany Web Browser: This is your web browser. Like Chrome, Safari, or Firefox, you simply type in the URL of the website you want to visit, and off you go. It's not as powerful as any of those browsers though, so you might notice that it's a bit slow and struggles to load complicated pages.

LeafPad: This is your notepad. It works just like you'd expect.

Mathematica: Mathematica is a program that teaches computer science and mathematics in relation to computers. It's built by the technical search engine Wolfram|Alpha.

The list of installed applications varies depending on which version of Raspbian you have installed and from where you download it. The Raspberry Pi Foundation loads up their image with a lot of programming utilities, while other distributions might have a different suite of software. The preceding applications are usually included in builds of Raspbian from the foundation, but that might change over time.

Desktop Utilities

There's more than just applications to play around with. Raspbian is also packed with just about every utility you'll need to use your Raspberry Pi. These include tools to access the terminal from inside Raspbian, configure a Wi-Fi USB adapter, and more.

Here's a taste of what you'll actually use:

WiFi Config: This is the setup utility for your wireless internet. (I go more in depth into how to set this up in Chapter 11.)

LXTerminal: This is the terminal program that gives you access to the Linux Shell and allows you to access your command line at any time. (I talk all about the command line in the next chapter.)

 PI POINTER

Linux Shell is a program that takes commands from your keyboard and gives them to the operating system to perform. Basically, it gives you access to the command line, where you can type in commands instead of clicking around the graphical user interface.

File Manager: Like Explorer on Windows or Finder in OS X, you'll use File Manager to search for files, browser folders, and move things around.

Xarchiver: This is your archive program. It can zip and unzip files you download from the internet. Generally speaking, you'll only need this if you download a program as a zipped file.

IDLE: IDLE is a Python shell. Like LXTerminal, it allows you to type commands directly into the Raspberry Pi using Python. We won't be covering Python much in this book, but it's a good advanced project to pursue if you're interested in programming.

Unlike Windows, these utilities aren't included in every Linux-based operating system, so it's nice to have them with Raspbian so you don't have to go search for simple things like a file manager program.

Getting and Installing New Applications

Although it comes with a lot, Raspbian doesn't come with absolutely everything you could possibly need. Chances are that at some point, you'll want or need to track down some more software so you can use Raspbian exactly how you want.

Because Raspbian is built on Linux, you actually have two different ways to do this: through the Pi Store or manually through the command line.

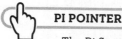

> **PI POINTER**
>
> The Pi Store launched in 2012 with just 23 titles. Now, it includes more than 100 games, tools, and other applications made by Raspberry Pi users just like you.

Linux doesn't install programs the same way as Windows or OS X. You can't simply download a file anywhere online and install it. With the exception of the Pi Store, you'll need to do a little bit of command line work.

Shopping the Pi Store

The Pi Store is the easiest place to find and install software for your Raspberry Pi. You can find the Pi Store on Raspbian's desktop; just double-click the Pi Store icon to launch it. Much like the app store on your smartphone, it's a quick, one-stop shop where you can find all the software you need.

The store is divided into sections for Games, Apps (applications), Tutorials, Dev (developer) Tools, and Media.

Games and **Apps** are both pretty self-explanatory.

Tutorials include video guides, downloadable programming lessons, and PDF guides for different projects.

Dev tools are typically for advanced users who aren't satisfied with the development tools included in Raspbian. These are usually alternative programs to access the terminal or other coding programs.

Media is where you'll find all types of video guides and digital magazines filled with more information about Raspbian. If you're still yearning for more after you finish this book, the Media tab in the Pi Store is a great place to find more project ideas.

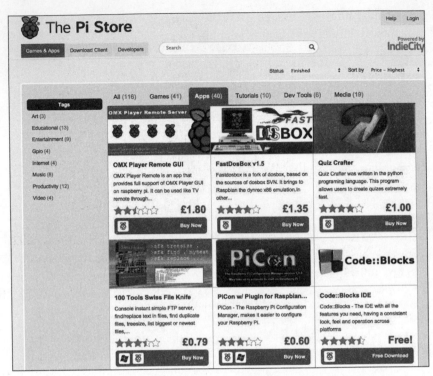

You can find all sorts of software for your Raspberry Pi at the Pi Store.

Finding Applications Manually

Most applications are installed manually in Linux. This means you pull up the terminal, type in a command, and the program you want is downloaded and installed from an online repository.

You can download software using the command line a number of ways, and if you're browsing on a website, you'll usually find specific instructions for how to download software directly from the developer. If you just want to download a program directly, it's pretty easy.

You can find and install more applications for your Raspberry Pi through the command line.

You can do this from LXTerminal in Raspbian or from the command line when you exit out of Raspbian. Here's how to search for and download a program:

 PI POINTER

You'll need internet access to do this, so be sure you're connected to your router or modem through your Ethernet cable.

1. At the command line, type in `apt-cache search` along with the type of program you're looking for. For example, if you're looking for games, type in `apt-cache search games`. If it's word processors you're after, type in `apt-cache search word processors`. You'll get a list of all the programs that match that genre.

2. Navigate the list with the arrow keys on your keyboard until you find something you want to download. Make a note of the first word on the list—this is the name of the program.

3. To download and install the program, type in `sudo apt-get install` and the program name. For example, if you want to download the office suite LibreOffice, type in `sudo apt-get install libreoffice`.

Your Raspberry Pi will download all the files it needs to run the program you want to download.

In the next chapter, we're going to explore the command line more in-depth and learn what each command means.

The Least You Need to Know

- You'll need a computer with an SD card reader and the internet to download and install Raspbian.

- Once you get Raspbian onto your SD card, you can set up some basic settings in the Raspi-config menu.

- Raspbian includes a handful of preinstalled applications to get you started with programming, browsing the web, and more.

- Downloading and installing programs on Raspbian works a little differently from Windows or OS X. You'll need to type in commands into the command line to download most software.

Working with the Command Line

In addition to Raspbian's graphic interface, a lot of what you do in this book requires you to type commands into your Raspberry Pi. You do this through the *command line interface*. This is essentially a blank screen with a text cursor where you use your keyboard to type in commands that make your Raspberry Pi do specific actions.

For many people, working with the command line can be strange or even a bit intimidating at first. It can feel archaic to type in commands to a computer these days, but in reality, it's a helpful task in getting to know how your Raspberry Pi works. And when you get the hang of it, you'll find that the command line is actually a lot easier to use than a graphic interface. It's also far faster because you can just type in one line to make something happen instead of clicking a bunch of checkboxes.

It's really important to remember that the command line is nothing to be scared of. At its core, it works just like your mouse, but instead of clicking on something, you type the command, information, etc., with your keyboard. It's going to feel a little strange and confusing initially, so be sure you practice a bit and take the time to familiarize yourself with all the settings.

In This Chapter

- Getting comfortable with the command line

- The command line tools you need for your Raspberry Pi

- Tips for editing files from the command line

Throughout this chapter, I cover some of the most common commands, show you how to move files around, explain how to download files, and more. First, though, we have to get a solid understanding of what the command line is and how it works.

Getting to Know the Command Line

The command line interface enables you to interact with your Raspberry Pi by typing in specific commands. You're essentially keying instructions for the operating system. The command line was the original way people interacted with computers before graphical user interfaces like Windows came around.

It might seem like an antiquated way of working on such a high-tech device as a computer, but the command line is used more than you might think. It's especially useful for programmers and coders because it provides access to the finer details of a computer. Even casual users can make use of the command line to explore various settings in their operating system.

Linux makes heavy use of the command line, and some distributions are more reliant on it than others. Raspbian gives you two direct ways to access the command line: by exiting the graphical user interface or through a command line shell called LXTerminal. (A *shell* is a program that runs inside a graphical user interface but still gives you access to the command line.) This isn't specific to Linux, though. You can find these types of shells on both Windows and OS X.

PI POINTER

You can download any Linux shell program you want to use on your Raspberry Pi. LXTerminal is included with Raspbian, but it's not your only option. Other popular terminal shells include Terminator (gnometerminator.blogspot.com/p/introduction.html), GNOME Terminal (wiki.gnome.org/Apps/Terminal), and Konsole (konsole.kde.org).

Although it's a bit complicated at first, the beauty of the command line lies in its simplicity. Because the Raspberry Pi doesn't have a lot of resources, the command line is actually easier to use than the graphic interface. We use it quite a bit throughout this book, so you'll get the hang of it pretty quickly.

The Command Line and Raspbian

Linux works a bit differently from other operating systems, so even just basic use requires the command line. The graphical interface in Raspbian is fine, but it doesn't give you access to everything you need.

Much of the basic work you need to do throughout the lessons in this book requires using the command line. In fact, most projects you'll do with your Raspberry Pi call for you to type in at least a few commands. Even the simplest stuff, like setting up a Wi-Fi adapter, is easier to do from the command line than the graphical interface.

In addition to the Pi Store, you can download files using the command line. In the projects in this book, you learn how to compile programs, edit text files, check for updates, set up your hardware, and even create a few small programs yourself.

Accessing the Command Line in Raspbian

You can access the command line directly on your Raspberry Pi with Raspbian in one of two ways: through a shell program or by exiting the graphical interface. Either method works well.

In Raspbian, you use a shell program called LXTerminal. Here's how to open it:

1. Click the menu button in the bottom-left corner of the screen in Raspbian.

2. Select **Utilities > LXTerminal**.

You can also exit the Raspbian interface completely to get to the command line. Here's how:

1. Click the menu button in the bottom-left corner of the screen.

2. Select **Exit desktop**.

When you get to the command line, you're greeted with a black screen with the following prompt:

```
pi@raspberrypi ~ $
```

This is the command prompt. It shows the host name, raspberrypi, and the username, pi, of your Raspberry Pi.

Basic Command Line Tools You Need to Know

Unlike with a graphical interface, with the command line, you can't blindly click around on things until you find what you're looking for. Instead, to get anything done, you have to type in very specific commands. You'll need to get used to this because mistyping even just a single character incorrectly can cause the entire line to produce an error.

PI POINTER

To help you avoid problematic typos, the longer sections of commands and code you need to type in throughout the lessons in this book are available at idiotsguides.com. See the book's introduction for more information.

A variety of commands exist for the command line and do all kinds of interesting things. But for now, let's cover a few of the basics so you can get an understanding of how the command line works and what you'll use it for.

Sudo

Sudo, which stands for *superuser do*, is one of the most important commands you can type into the command line. This gives you administrative access to your Raspberry Pi and allows you to run as a *root user*. This means that whatever changes you make will also affect any other users who have accounts on that Raspberry Pi.

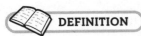

DEFINITION

Sudo stands for *superuser* do and means you're running a command as a *root user*. This is essentially the same as running a command as an administrator. As a superuser, you can access files that wouldn't normally be available to all users and delete system files you might need, so be careful when you run anything as sudo.

If you need to do anything permanent in the system—like move around hidden files, download software to specific folders, or even compile software—you need to run those commands as a superuser. To do this, start your command with sudo before typing anything else.

Sudo comes with its own set of cautions. For example, you're permanently altering files, and if you do something wrong, it'll mess up everything on your Raspberry Pi. Don't let this scare you though. Remember, part of the beauty of the Raspberry Pi is the SD card that houses the operating system. If something goes wrong, it's very easy to start again from scratch.

Navigating Files and Folders from the Command Line

With Linux, even basic use requires a little extra work than other operating systems might require. Let's start by learning a few commands you can use to navigate folders on your Raspberry Pi.

For starters, at the command line, type the following:

```
pwd
```

This stands for *present working directory*. When you type it in, you should get the output /home/pi. This is the directory you're currently in. When you run commands, you're often executing them from the directory you're presently in.

Don't worry if you accidentally run a command from the wrong folder. You can move files around pretty easily, thanks to the cp (copy) and mv (move) commands. So if you want to move a file from one folder to another, you'd type something like the following:

```
mv file.txt /username
```

This moves the file.txt file to the /username directory.

If you want to delete a file, use the rm command. To delete the file you just moved, type this:

```
rm file.txt
```

This works with more than just files. You can move and delete directories the same way. Likewise, you can create a new directory with the mkdir command. For example:

```
mkdir newdirectory
```

This command makes a new directory called newdirectory.

To see exactly what's in a directory at any point, use the ls command to list the contents of the directory:

```
ls -la
```

The -la command is called a *flag*. Flags modify the command you're trying to run. In this case, l results in a list display, and a shows all the files.

You also can navigate to different folders using the command line using cd. For example, if you want to navigate to the newdirectory folder you just created, type this:

```
cd newdirectory
```

This changes the current directory to the new directory. To get back to the first directory, type in cd.

PI POINTER

If you ever need to type in a command you've already typed, you can use the history function with the arrow keys. Just tap the up and down arrows on your keyboard to pull up a history of the commands you've entered.

Downloading and Installing Programs from the Command Line

We briefly explored how to install programs from the command line in the last chapter, but let's take a closer look at what exactly you're doing when you're typing in those commands.

Unlike on Windows or Mac computers, Linux downloads programs as a package. This means that if you download a program, at the same time, you also download any other software you might need to run it. To download software, use the apt-get command. *Apt* stands for *advanced package tool*. This downloads all the necessary software. For example, if you want to download the office suite LibreOffice, type in this:

```
sudo apt-get install libreoffice
```

Hit **Enter**, and the software will download and install.

PI POINTER

If you're not sure the exact name of the software you want to install, you can search for it using the *apt-cache search* option. Just type in apt-cache search at the command line followed by the type of software you're looking for. This works even if you're looking for something specific and just want to be sure you download the right software. For example, apt-cache search spotify returns the exact download name for the Spotify music software.

You can also use this command to update all the software on your Raspberry Pi at once using the get upgrade command. You'll first need to see if any updates are available. To do this, type the following:

```
sudo apt-get update
```

You'll get an output saying whether or not updates are available. If updates are available, type:

```
sudo apt-get upgrade
```

This command updates all the software on your Raspberry Pi to the newest version, including any updates to Raspbian itself.

You also can delete software this way using the `remove` command. Let's delete the version of LibreOffice we just downloaded but keep the configuration settings:

```
sudo apt-get remove libreoffice
```

When you're downloading, installing, and removing software, you have to use the `sudo` command because you need to be an administrator to install software on your system.

Other Common Commands

You'll likely never need to use the bulk of the commands available for Linux, but here are a few more that will prove helpful as you work through the various tutorials in this book, and as you start to work on your own projects:

`man`: Short for *manual*. If you type `man` before any other command, you can learn exactly what that command does and how to properly use it.

`help`: Similar to `man`, `help` can teach you how a command is used. Just type it in before any other command.

`tar/zip/gzip`: These three commands extract or archive files. You'll often need to do this after downloading a software suite.

`cal/date`: Need to get a quick look at the month's calendar? Type `cal` at any point. Prefer to get a look at the exact date? Type `date`.

`top`: When you type the `top` command, you get a list of the programs currently running on your system. This can be helpful when you're troubleshooting.

Ctrl+C: If you tap Ctrl+C on your keyboard at any time, you'll stop the current process. This is handy if you make a mistake or if something is taking too long.

Essentially, if you can do a task with the mouse, you can probably do it from the command line. Conservatively, there are hundreds of different commands that do hundreds of different things. What's covered in this chapter is plenty to get you through this book.

Editing Text Files from the Command Line

The command line isn't just about moving around files, though. You can also edit files from the command line. Typically, you'll only do this with TXT (text) files, but it's also useful for editing several kinds of settings.

You can edit files with the nano command.

Loading a Text File

To load a text file, use the nano command. This brings up Linux's text editor program.

If you want to manually edit the configuration file raspi-config created, for example, type the following:

```
sudo nano /boot/config.txt
```

You're greeted with a text file with all the configuration settings (and more) you changed in raspi-config in Chapter 8. You can navigate this text editor with the arrow keys on your keyboard.

PI POINTER

You'll notice that many lines in the config.txt file start with a #. This means they're commented out. When you want to leave a comment in a text file like this, you can start a line with a # to tell the system not to run that command. If you delete the #, it will try to load that line.

Navigating, Editing, and Saving Files

Navigating around a text file is easy with your keyboard's arrow keys. This changes the location of the cursor, and you can type anywhere the cursor is. To delete any text, use the **Delete** key on your keyboard.

A handful of keyboard shortcuts are available in the editor, as shown in the following table.

Keystroke	Task
Ctrl+X	Exit the editor. When you do this, you'll be asked if you want to save the file or not.
Ctrl+R	Add text from another file you've previously copied to the clipboard.
Ctrl+C	Display the cursor position.
Ctrl+K	Cut texts.
Ctrl+U	Paste text you just cut.
Ctrl+O	Save the file you're working on.
Ctrl+T	Check the spelling of your text file.
Ctrl+W	Search the text. You can set it to search for any word or phrase you like.
Ctrl+A	Go to the beginning of the line you're currently on.
Ctrl+E	Go to the end of the line you're currently on.
Ctrl+G	Pull up the help menu.

These are the basic commands you'll need to know to use the text editor. You'll use these often to edit configuration files when you're troubleshooting or adding small lines of code to programs.

Get to know, and feel comfortable with, the command line. Remember, it's not all that different from a text editor you'd find on Windows or Mac. With the command line, you just don't have a mouse cursor to move around.

The Least You Need to Know

- The command line takes some getting used to, but once you learn all the commands, it's actually faster than using a mouse.
- You can access the command line in Raspbian using a shell program called LXTerminal.
- The command line might look archaic, but you can use it with modern operating systems like Windows and OS X. (In fact, most Linux commands do the same thing on Macs.)
- It's faster to download and install programs from the command line in Linux.

Raspberry Pi Projects

What makes the Raspberry Pi truly amazing is what you can do with it. Out of the box, it's a pretty boring little device, but you can create myriad different things with it. In this part, you discover some of what you can do with your Raspberry Pi.

The projects in the following chapters range from beginner projects, like setting up your Raspberry Pi as a computer, to more advanced projects, such as using your Raspberry Pi to power a home security system. Some can be done in a few minutes, while others take hours, but every one teaches you something new about your Raspberry Pi.

Some of these projects might be more interesting to you than others, so feel free to skip around if a particular project doesn't grab you. You have plenty to choose from.

Building a Useable PC

The Raspberry Pi isn't the fastest nor the most powerful computer, but that shouldn't stop you from using it as your personal computer. It's not going to rival the newest machine from Dell or Apple, but it'll certainly be powerful enough to run word processors, video players, email, and everything else you actually need.

A Raspbian-powered computer is handy for all kinds of things. If you have kids, it makes a great little kids-only computer they can use to do homework and safely browse the web. It also makes a great addition to a guestroom if you want to provide guests access to the internet without handing over your own computer.

A Raspberry Pi PC also is handy if you need help focusing. Trying to write a report but keep getting distracted by all the great stuff on your full-size PC? The Raspberry Pi, outfitted with an office suite, makes an ideal little writing machine running just a word processor. The Raspberry Pi is super for any other single-purpose tasks you might need to do.

In This Chapter

- The Raspberry Pi as a full-time computer
- Setting up Raspbian to mimic Windows
- Installing necessary software

In this chapter, you learn to set up your Raspberry Pi as a useable PC and install different software. You also discover how to make Raspbian a bit more of a familiar place to work by giving it some Windows-like traits.

Making Raspbian More Windows-Like

Most people probably aren't familiar with Linux, and Raspbian (a Linux variant) feels a bit harder to use because of that. It doesn't look familiar to what many people see when they sit down to their computers, and it takes a little bit of getting used to before you can really do anything productive with it.

You can change the Raspbian interface in subtle ways to make it a little more similar to what you're comfortable with by using Windows skins.

If you're not a regular Raspbian user, the interface might feel a bit foreign to you. You can fix that.

Simple Adjustments

The easiest thing you can do is adjust the user interface to make it more your style. Here's how to do it:

1. Click the menu button in the bottom-left corner of the Raspbian screen.

2. Select **Preferences** > **Openbox Configuration Manager**.

This loads the Openbox Configuration Manager. Here, you can change the theme (colors), appearance (window outlines and fonts), windows (changes how windows act), and more. You can change these settings to suit your needs and style.

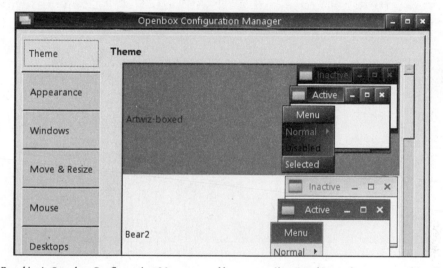

Raspbian's Openbox Configuration Manager enables you to adjust Raspbian to be more user friendly.

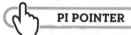 **PI POINTER**

It's natural to want to make Raspbian look a little more familiar to you, but don't discount it right away. Give the interface a few days to see if you like it before switching over to something else. Not only will this familiarize you with how Raspbian works, but it'll also enable you to find a theme that really suits your style. Of course, if you like Windows, there's nothing wrong with loading a solid Windows theme, either.

Windows 7 or 8

If simple user interface adjustments aren't enough for you to feel comfortable with Raspbian, you can change things even more, including the taskbar and dock.

With a theme called WinAte, you can make Raspbian look and act like Windows 7 or 8. This changes the windows, the fonts, and even the icons to look more like Windows.

WinAte makes your Raspbian screen mimic a Windows setup.

The installation process takes just a few steps:

1. Open **LXTerminal**.

2. Type in the following:

    ```
    git clone https://github.com/nhermosilla14/WinAte.git
    ```

    This downloads the WinAte files you need to install the theme.

3. When the theme has finished downloading, type in this:

    ```
    cd WinAte
    ```

4. Then, to install the files, type this:

    ```
    bash install.sh -force
    ```

5. Press **Enter** when prompted.

6. Type 2 for English, and press **Enter**.

7. When asked for your distribution, type Debian and press **Enter**.

8. Type 7 or 8 for the version of Windows you want Raspbian to mimic, and press **Enter**.

9. When asked if you want transparent windows, type N and press **Enter**.

10. When asked if you want to change the wallpaper, type N and press **Enter**. (You do that manually in the next section.)

11. When it's finished running, exit out of LXTerminal.

12. Click the **power button** in the bottom-right corner of the Raspbian screen, and select **Reboot**.

Your system needs to reboot so the changes can take effect. After it reboots, it should look like the version of Windows you selected. You can change this at any time by clicking the menu button in the bottom-left corner and selecting **Preferences > Openbox Configuration Manager**. For now, you've got a version of Raspbian that looks a lot like Windows and should be less intimidating to use.

If Windows isn't your thing, you have other options. Using Openbox themes, you can customize the look of Raspbian in any number of combinations. To take a look at other people's themes available for download, head to openbox.org/download-themes.php.

Changing the Wallpaper

Changing your screen's wallpaper is a quick and easy way to make your desktop feel like your own. It's also very easy to do. Here's how:

1. Right-click anywhere on your desktop.

2. Select **Desktop Preferences**.

3. Click the box marked **Wallpaper**, and select the image file you'd like to use.

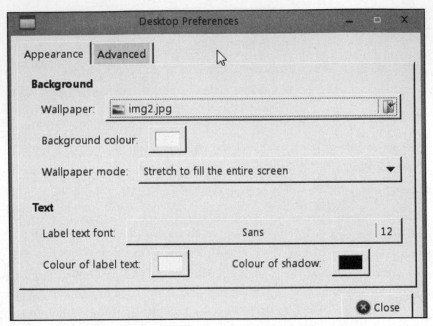

Raspbian makes it simple for you to change your desktop image.

4. Click **Open** to use that wallpaper as your desktop images.

You can use any wallpaper you like that's already included with Raspbian (or the WinAte theme), or you can download wallpapers from websites to use here. It's really up to you, so customize your wallpaper as you see fit.

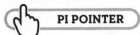

PI POINTER

If you're hunting for a new wallpaper, countless options are available online. If you're not sure where to start, try InterfaceLIFT (interfacelift.com), Simple Desktops (simpledesktops.com), or DeviantArt (deviantart.com) for high-resolution images that make attractive wallpaper.

Popular Software You Need

Of course, an operating system isn't just about looks. It's mostly about software. You'll need to download a lot of programs to get your Raspberry Pi up and running with something akin to Windows.

In this section, I share some recommended software, a bit about what it does, and the command to type into LXTerminal to download it. Remember, these commands have to be typed exactly as they're printed here, so pay close attention as you type. When the programs are finished downloading, you can launch them from the menu button in the bottom-left corner of your Raspbian screen.

Web Browsers

The default web browsers included with Raspbian work great in Raspbian, but new users aren't very familiar with them. Both Google Chrome and Mozilla Firefox have browsers that work in Linux, and they both work on the Raspberry Pi, so they're best bets for many users.

Google Chrome: Google Chrome's Linux web browser is called Chromium, and it works just like Google Chrome on Windows or OS X. To download it, type the following into LXTerminal:

```
sudo apt-get install google-chromium
```

Mozilla Firefox: Firefox doesn't exist on Linux, but a web browser called Iceweasel is based on Firefox and works exactly the same. To download it, type the following into LXTerminal:

```
sudo apt-get install iceweasel
```

Other browsers are available for Linux, but Chromium and Iceweasel are the most popular and familiar for Windows and OS X users.

Office Productivity Tools

No computer is complete without some good productivity tools, and you have a few fantastic options for Raspbian. This is the software you need to use your Raspberry Pi like a full computer, such as an office suite, mail client, and more.

LibreOffice: LibreOffice is the premier office suite on Linux, and it's a terrific replacement for software like Microsoft Office. With it, you'll get a word processor, spreadsheet program, presentation tool, a drawing application, and database software. If you want to use your Raspberry Pi to just get some work done, LibreOffice is required. To download it, type the following into LXTerminal:

```
sudo apt-get install libreoffice
```

It's a big file, so it'll take a few minutes to download.

Claws: If you need an email client, Claws is fast and easy to use. It doesn't have a ton of features, but it's simple and it works really well on the Raspberry Pi. To download it, type the following into LXTerminal:

```
sudo apt-get install claws-mail
```

Once it's installed, follow the setup instructions to get it working with your email provider.

Dropbox: If you use Dropbox on your home computers to synchronize your files, you'll also want to get it onto your Raspberry Pi. If you're not familiar with it, Dropbox is a service that stores your files online so you can access them from any computer or device with an internet connection. For example, Dropbox makes it easy to write a paper on one computer and finish it on another. To install it, type the following into LXTerminal:

```
sudo apt-get install dropbox
```

When it's installed, follow the setup directions to get it working on your Raspberry Pi.

GIMP: GIMP is a free, open-source photo-editing tool similar to Photoshop. It's a pretty powerful program, and the Raspberry Pi isn't quite powerful enough to run it at full speed, but if you need to do some photo editing now and then, it's nice to have. Just be sure you're not running any other apps at the same time. To install it, type the following into LXTerminal:

```
sudo apt-get install gimp
```

It's a big file, so give it lots of time to download.

Pidgin: Pidgin is an instant-message (IM) client. With it, you can message friends on a variety of services, including Google Hangouts, AIM, and others. If you chat over IM, it's nice to have Pidgin on your Raspberry Pi. To install it, type the following into LXTerminal:

```
sudo apt-get install pidgin
```

SOFTWARE SOLUTION

Almost any software that runs on Linux can run on your Raspberry Pi, but it might be incredibly slow. It's still worth trying though. You might be surprised at how many Windows and OS X programs are available on Linux or have Linux equivalents. Search around online, and give some new software a try.

These apps give you a good starting point to begin your work with your Raspberry Pi, but don't be afraid to try out new programs you hear about or find online. Some won't work really well on the Raspberry Pi, but it's always worth a try to check.

Video and Music Players

Raspbian doesn't have much in the way of software for playing music or videos, so you need to track these down yourself. With the following, you can watch and listen to just about anything.

VLC: VLC is a popular video player on both Windows and OS X. It's also one of the best video players for Linux, and it works great on the Raspberry Pi. With it, you can play videos in about any format on your Raspberry Pi. For example, if you have camcorder home videos on a USB drive, you can plug it into your Raspberry Pi and play the movies saved there with VLC. To install it, type the following into LXTerminal:

```
sudo apt-get install vlc
```

Spotify: Spotify is a streaming music service with software available for Windows, OS X, iPhone, and Android. You also can install it on your Raspberry Pi. When you do, you'll have access to thousands of songs and albums. To install it, type the following into LXTerminal:

```
sudo apt-get install spotify-client
```

Clementine: Clementine is a music player similar to iTunes. If you plan on playing MP3 files on your Raspberry Pi, Clementine is a must have. To install it, type the following into LXTerminal:

```
sudo apt-get install clementine
```

That's enough to get you started. You should be able to play just about any kind of media you could possibly imagine when you have these programs on your Raspberry Pi.

Antivirus Tools

Antivirus tools are not nearly as important on Raspbian as they are on Windows because Linux is less susceptible to viruses, but if you're going to use your Raspberry Pi as a full-time computer, it's a good idea to set up some kind of protection for it. For the Raspberry Pi, ClamAV is a solid antivirus option.

To install it, type the following into LXTerminal:

```
sudo apt-get install clamav
```

When it's finished installing, type in the following:

```
sudo freshclam
```

This updates all the virus databases to ensure ClamAV is up to date and ready to tackle any problems.

Once you get all that software installed, you can start using it just like you would any other computer. With the Raspberry Pi, you don't want to have a lot of software running at once, but it can handle everything you downloaded nearly as well as a more expensive computer.

The Least You Need to Know

- With a little work, you can make Raspbian look more like Windows. It won't work identically, but it'll be a bit easier to use if that's the operating system you're familiar with.

- Even if you don't want to make your Raspberry Pi look exactly like Windows, you can tweak the appearance in a variety of ways.

- You can install all kinds of software on your Raspberry Pi, including a full-blown office suite, media player, MP3 player, and more.

- You can download software quickly by using the apt-get command.

Adding Wi-Fi

The one built-in feature the Raspberry Pi lacks is wireless internet. And that's rather inconvenient these days, when Wi-Fi is available on just about every other device you own, from your phone to your video game systems—even some kitchen and laundry room appliances have wireless built in. Yet to keep costs down, the Raspberry Pi only includes a *wired* network adapter.

Don't worry though. Although this might sound like a big pain, it's actually very easy to set up wireless on your Raspberry Pi using an inexpensive Wi-Fi USB adapter. (You can usually get a Wi-Fi USB adapter for under $10.)

In this chapter, I show you how to choose a Wi-Fi adapter that works with your Raspberry Pi, install it, and set it up so it works every time you boot up your Raspberry Pi. As you learn throughout this book, not everything is perfect with the Raspberry Pi, so I also share some common testing and troubleshooting tips that enable you to handle any issues you might have with Wi-Fi.

In This Chapter

- Installing a Wi-Fi USB adapter

- Configuring the adapter to work on startup

- Accessing the internet with your Raspberry Pi

- Avoiding—or correcting— common problems

The Convenience of Wi-Fi

When was the last time you actually used a *wired* internet connection for your computers? Unless you can't have Wi-Fi in your home, chances are, you use it for pretty much all of your devices.

With your Raspberry Pi, having wireless is incredibly helpful because you're not always going to have access to a wired connection. This is especially the case when you're using your Raspberry Pi for projects you want to keep mobile. But without a built-in wireless adapter, you have to add an external, third-party wireless adapter to your Raspberry Pi. A USB adapter is just what you need to add wireless to your Raspberry Pi.

It's important to note here that if you have a Model A+, the USB adapter will take up the only USB slot available on your specific model. And even on the Model B, you only have two ports, so you might not be able to connect a USB Wi-Fi adapter, a keyboard, and a mouse all at once. The solution is a powered USB hub, or a hub with its own power adapter. A powered hub provides the power to your USB devices so your Raspberry Pi doesn't have to. You can find USB hubs at most electronics stores for under $10.

 HARDWARE HELPER

> A powered USB hub is handy if you want to connect several peripherals to your Raspberry Pi. With a powered hub, you can connect as many USB devices as it supports, which is nice if you want to plug in a keyboard, mouse, and Wi-Fi adapter.

A Wi-Fi adapter won't work unless it has something to connect to. To set up a wireless network in your home, you'll need either a router or a built-in router and modem combination unit from your internet provider.

Now let's pick out a Wi-Fi adapter to work with your Raspberry Pi.

USB Wi-Fi Adapters

Walk into an electronics store, and you'll find a variety of options for USB Wi-Fi adapters. These range in price based on speed, software support, and compatibility. On almost all of them, you'll see a bunch of different text and numbers, so let's take a second to demystify exactly what it all means.

802.11b/g/n/ac: *802.11* is a wireless standard that makes it possible for computers to communicate with each other in the same language. The *b/g/n/ac* part refers to a version and a data transfer speed.

Mbps: *Mpbs* stands for "megabits per second." A *megabit* is the unit of measurement used for digital information. It's the standard used for most wireless transfer protocols and the same number you'll see from your internet provider. The higher the number, the faster the data transfer rate—or the faster you can access websites online. For wireless, you'll see these letters and numbers on both your Wi-Fi adapter and your router. B is 11 Mbit/s, G is 54 Mbit/s, N is 600 Mbit/s, and AC is 1 gigabit per second. That said, the speed is still limited by your internet connection speed.

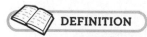 **DEFINITION**

> A **megabit** is 1 million bits, or 1,000 kilobits, which is the equivalent of about 100 pages of plain text. This measurement is usually used when talking about data transfer, so you'll see it places like your internet service provider bills. For context, a *megabyte*—the word we use to describe data storage—is 8 megabits combined.

Wireless operating frequency: This refers to the wireless channels in which the adapter can operate. In most cases, this is 2.4 gigahertz (Ghz), which means it can operate in channels 1 through 11. Channels 12 through 14 are restricted by the Federal Communications Commission (FCC) in the United States, but they are allowed in some other countries, including Japan. Canada allows channels 1 through 12, while the UK allows channels 1 through 13. Typically, all this isn't anything to worry too much about. It just refers to the frequencies at which your router operates. All wireless adapters operate in the same range as your router, so you can typically ignore this setting when you're buying an adapter.

 PI POINTER

> It can be useful to change the frequency to get a stronger signal when you're in an area with a lot of other wireless networks. Think of it like tuning your television by moving or turning the antenna around a little.

Support for WPA-PSK/WPA2-PSK, and WEP Security: These are three different security protocols for your wireless network. When you set up your router, you'll usually also set up a password or passcode to authenticate certain users so everyone can't get into your network. *WPA* stands for "wireless protected access," and *WEP* stands for "wired equivalent privacy."

Nowadays, WPA-PSK isn't used much and instead, WPA2-PSK is the most commonly used security method. WEP should be avoided because it's unsecure and prone to unauthorized access. Which system you use depends on your router, but every Wi-Fi adapter is compatible with whichever you use.

Now that we've got all the technical language sorted out, it's time to pick up an adapter to pair with your Raspberry Pi.

Choosing the Right Adapter

The Raspberry Pi is compatible with hundreds of different Wi-Fi adapters, but unlike Windows and OS X, you won't find a note about compatibility on the adapter's box. Instead, you'll need to do some research yourself to find an adapter that works with your Raspberry Pi.

Thankfully, most of that research has already been done for you. You can find a massive list of compatible USB Wi-Fi adapters at elinux.org/RPi_USB_Wi-Fi_Adapters.

If you don't feel like sorting through that entire list, you can follow the crowd. Many Raspberry Pi users have opted for the Edimax EW-7811Un 150Mbps wireless 11n nano-size USB adapter. This adapter works out of the box with Raspbian and typically costs under $10 at most retailers. You basically can just plug it in and it'll work right away without an additional setup process.

Where to Buy Your Adapter

You can purchase a Wi-Fi adapter from pretty much any retailer that sells them, but if you want to be certain it will work well with your Raspberry Pi, a few different retailers cater to that. Here are a few worth checking out:

Adafruit: Adafruit (adafruit.com) is a DIY electronics store packed full of all kinds of Raspberry Pi accessories. Everything Adafruit sells is verified to work with the Raspberry Pi.

MCM Electronics: Like Adafruit, MCM Electronics (mcmelectronics.com) offers a ton of Raspberry Pi accessories and verifies that they work with the Raspberry Pi.

element14: element14 (element14.com) is not just an electronics retailer; it's also a landing spot for all kinds of Raspberry Pi content. You can order just about everything you need from them, including a selection of Wi-Fi adapters guaranteed to work with the Raspberry Pi.

Once you have your Wi-Fi adapter in hand, it's time to set it up.

 **HARDWARE HELPER**

Don't spend a lot of money on an adapter. Any inexpensive adapter will do what you need, and any benefits of a more expensive adapter won't be useful on the Raspberry Pi because it's such a low-powered device.

Getting Online

You have to do some minor setup for your Wi-Fi adapter before you can access the internet wirelessly. First, you need to connect your Wi-Fi adapter to your Raspberry Pi's USB port. Then boot up your Raspberry Pi.

You can use Raspbian's graphical interface or the command line to set up Wi-Fi for your Raspberry Pi, and it works in both places. So if you set it up with the graphical interface and then exit out to the command line, your wireless connection will continue to work.

Setting Up Wi-Fi with Raspbian's Graphical Interface

Most modern versions of Raspbian include drivers for Wi-Fi adapters, so it's actually very easy to set up. Here's how:

1. Double-click the **WiFi Config** app on your desktop.

2. Click the **Scan** button.

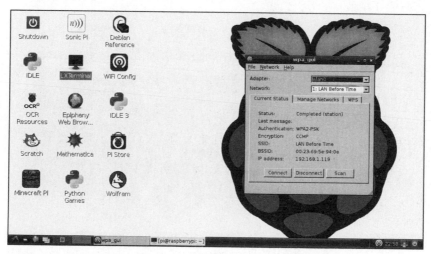

Setting up your Wi-Fi adapter with Raspbain's graphical interface takes just a few clicks of your mouse.

3. Find your router's name on the list, and double-click it.

4. Enter your router password in the **PSK** field.

5. Click **Add**.

You should now have wireless internet access on your Raspberry Pi.

Setting Up Wi-Fi with the Command Line

If you're not using Raspbian, or if you just want to get a little more familiar with the command line, you can set up your Wi-Fi adapter right from the command line. In this case, you'll just need to edit a few lines of code:

1. Open LXTerminal in Raspbian, or log out to command line as described in Chapter 9.

2. At the command line, type the following:

   ```
   sudo nano /etc/network/interfaces
   ```

   This opens an editor screen of your Wi-Fi configuration file.

3. Near the bottom of the configuration file, there are two lines you need to edit. Using your keyboard's arrow keys, move the text cursor to the line **wpa-ssid "my-network-ssid"** and delete **my-network-ssid**. Then type your router's name between the quotation marks.

4. Move the text cursor down one line to **wpa-psk "my-wifi-password"** and delete **my-wifi-password**. Replace it with your router's password.

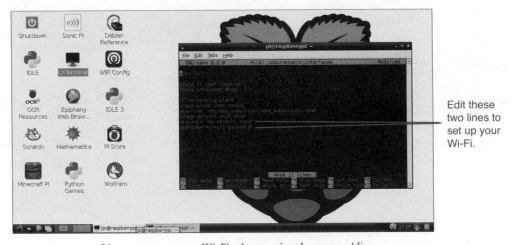

Edit these two lines to set up your Wi-Fi.

It's easy to set up your Wi-Fi adapter using the command line.

5. On your keyboard, tap **Ctrl+X** to save and exit.

6. When prompted, press **Y** to save the file.

Reboot your Raspberry Pi by typing in `Reboot` at the command line. When it's finished booting, your Wi-Fi adapter should now work.

Testing Your Connectivity

Now that your Wi-Fi adapter is up and running, it's time to check that it's working properly. You can do this in one of two ways—via the Midori web browser or the command line.

Here's how to test your connection using Midori:

1. If you're in Raspbian's graphical interface, open Midori by double-clicking its icon on your desktop.

2. Type in a URL—any URL. If it loads, you're connected to the internet and you know your Wi-Fi adapter is up and running.

Here's how to test your connection using the command line:

1. At the command line, type `ping`, followed by a website address. For example, try

   `ping google.com`.

2. If it's working, the command line will output a bunch of numbers.

Now your Raspberry Pi's Wi-Fi should be working correctly.

Troubleshooting

With the newest versions of Raspbian, setting up Wi-Fi is a pretty smooth experience. However, things can go wrong. An adapter might not be included with the Raspbian drivers, or you might run into a problem where the Wi-Fi drops off periodically. Likewise, other Raspberry Pi operating systems don't always come with the drivers needed to use a Wi-Fi adapter out of the box.

In this section, I show you how to manually find and install drivers for your adapter as well as give you a fix for one of the Raspberry Pi's most common Wi-Fi problems.

 PI POINTER

Troubleshooting on the Raspberry Pi can be very difficult because there's often not a lot of support from manufacturers. Thankfully, there *is* a lot of community support for the Raspberry Pi, so if you search online for an answer, you'll likely find responses in forums and on blogs. These are usually just as useful as an official response, so if you're having trouble, be sure to give them a try.

Manually Finding and Installing Drivers

If your Wi-Fi adapter isn't supported out of the box—that is, if your Raspberry Pi doesn't immediately recognize or work well with your adapter—you'll need to do a little bit of digging to find the necessary *drivers* for your adapter to start the setup process. This is most likely only going to happen if you buy a brand-new Wi-Fi adapter that uses a different technology from the older ones your Raspberry Pi already knows, or if you're not running Raspbian.

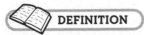 **DEFINITION**

A **driver** is a small bit of software that tells your computer how to interact with hardware. Without a driver, the computer doesn't understand that a new piece of hardware is connected and can't use it.

You'll work from the command line. And you'll need your Raspberry Pi connected to the internet through the Ethernet cable. (If you're using the Model A+, you'll need to use your USB Wi-Fi adapter.) You can run these commands from either LXTerminal or the regular command line:

1. First, check to see if Raspbian recognized your USB Wi-Fi adapter. At the command line, type in ifconfig and look for your wireless adapter listed in the wlan0 section. If it's there, your device is recognized, so go back to the setup section and run through the process again. If it's not listed, proceed to step 2.

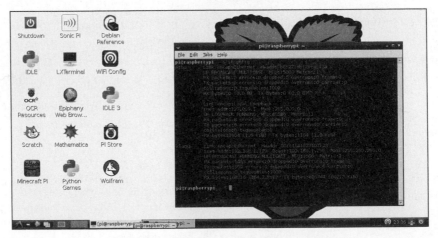

Use the ifconfig screen to check for your adapter.

2. Type in sudo apt-get update to update your package list.

3. Type in sudo apt-get install to install the new package list.

4. Now, you'll search for your Wi-Fi adapter driver. This part's a little tricky because it's different for each adapter. Type in `sudo apt-cache search` *your wi-fi adapter name*, replacing "your wi-fi adapter name" with the manufacturer name. You should see a list that includes your Wi-Fi adapter. You might need to try a few different variations of the name to find it. Make a note of the name listed in the search results.

5. Install the drivers by typing in `sudo apt-get -install` *name from previous step*, replacing "name from previous step" with the name you wrote down in step 4. It should look something like `sudo apt-get -install firmware-ralink`.

6. When the firmware is finished downloading, reboot your Raspberry Pi and run the setup process again.

This should get your Raspberry Pi's Wi-Fi up and running. If not, head to the website of your adapter's manufacturer and look for specific setup instructions.

Fixing Common Drop-Out Issues

One common problem that plagues the Raspberry Pi is random drop-outs, or when your wireless connection loses the connection to the router. This is a pain when you're trying to do just about anything.

Thankfully, the fix is pretty simple. You're going to turn to the command line again and edit a file.

At the command line, type in the following:

```
sudo nano /etc/modprobe.d/8192cu.conf
```

This edits the configuration file. Then, type this:

```
#Disable power saving
options8192cu rtw_power_mgnt=0 rtw_enusbss=1
rtw_ips_mode=1
```

Tap **Ctrl+X** to save and exit the editor. Then reboot your Raspberry Pi. Your connectivity problems should now be resolved.

The Least You Need to Know

- Wi-Fi adapters are an inexpensive way to make your Raspberry Pi a little more portable.

- If you're using Raspbian, your Wi-Fi adapter is probably "plug and play," so all you need to do is plug it in and connect it to your router.

- If you're not using Raspbian, you might need to manually install the drivers for your Wi-Fi adapter. You can do this by searching for drivers from the command line.

- Almost every Wi-Fi adapter available today works with the Raspberry Pi.

Making a Media Center

One of the most popular, and useful, projects you can do with your Raspberry Pi is turn it into a media center. Then, with it, you'll be able to stream movies, store movies on an external hard drive to watch, or stream movies from your home computer to your Raspberry Pi.

If you're not familiar with media centers, they're pretty handy. If you've used a device like a Roku or Apple TV, that's essentially what you'll get here, but you can customize it a lot more than you can with those devices. For example, you can install custom themes to change the look and install apps for online services like YouTube.

To make a media center, you'll create a SD card much like you did with Raspbian in Chapter 8, but instead of using Raspbian, you'll use one of three different media center images. When you're finished, you'll have a small, low-power media center you can hook up to your TV to watch movies and other video any time you want.

In This Chapter

- Media center options for the Raspberry Pi

- Setting up and installing Raspbmc

- Extending your media center's functionality with plug-ins

- Remote control options

In this chapter, I cover the various options for media centers, show you how to set one up, and guide you through the various customization options you have to make your media center your own.

Raspberry Pi–Powered Media Center Capabilities

A Raspberry Pi makes a surprisingly powerful little media center. Typically speaking, building your own media center could cost you around $500, but with the Raspberry Pi, you can build one for around $35.

With your Raspberry Pi–powered media center, you can stream movies and television shows from the internet, your computer, or an external hard drive. Obviously, adding an external hard drive to your media center increases the cost of the project a bit, but it'll be considerably less than $500.

Streaming Content from the Web

The big appeal of a media center is its capability to stream video from online resources. That means you no longer have to hover over a small laptop screen to watch streaming videos.

With a Raspberry Pi media center, you can play just about any online video on your TV. You can stream content from YouTube (youtube.com), Funny or Die (funnyordie.com), College Humor (collegehumor.com), FOX (fox.com), CBS (cbs.com), NBC (nbc.com), and more. Countless websites offer streaming video you can access and play through your media center.

Playing Movies and Music from Your Home Network

In addition to streaming from websites, you can stream movies, television shows, and music from your home computer to your Raspberry Pi.

If you've ripped (copied) your DVD or CD collection to your home computer, you can stream that content from your computer's hard drive to your Raspberry Pi. Then, you have the capability to watch any video you want on your big-screen TV—without having to move your desktop computer over to your TV.

 HARDWARE HELPER

The Raspberry Pi doesn't have a built-in hard drive, so it might seem like an odd choice for a media player. However, with an external hard drive, you can store as many movies and TV shows as will fit, and the Raspberry Pi can stream right from the external drive. Plus, the external drive is portable, so you can use it on any other computer you have.

If your computer has a lot of empty storage space, that's another easy way to keep costs down on this project.

Attaching External Storage to Your Pi

To make it even easier, you don't have to deal with your home computer at all. If you'd prefer, you can attach an external hard drive to your Raspberry Pi and store your movies and music there so your Raspberry Pi can easily access them.

All you need for this is an external hard drive with a USB port so you can connect it to your Raspberry Pi. Then you can transfer movies or music to your hard drive any way you like.

Raspberry Pi Media Center Limitations

The Raspberry Pi makes an excellent media center, but it's important to keep in mind that, at a fraction of the cost, it's not nearly as powerful as other options. It doesn't have the power to stream full 1080p HD videos smoothly, for example, and it's a little slower than most big PC builds.

Likewise, the Raspberry Pi doesn't have the power to do a lot of *encoding*. That means you'll need to get your videos in the proper format before you play them through your Raspberry Pi. It's an easy enough problem to work around though, so don't let that deter you from getting your Raspberry Pi media center set up.

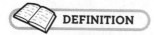 **DEFINITION**

> **Encoding** refers to the video *codec*, the software that enables compression and decompression of a digital video, with which a file is saved. Different types of software save using different codecs, and codecs can change the quality of a video. Codecs that retain HD quality and sound tend to struggle a bit on the Raspberry Pi because there's so much data in them.

Raspberry Pi Media Center Options

You have a lot of options when it comes to operating systems for your Raspberry Pi media center. Three of the most popular are Raspbmc (raspbmc.com), OpenELEC (openelec.tv), and XBian (xbian.org).

Each has its own strengths and weaknesses. They all look pretty much the same, but they work very differently from one another. In addition, some are better suited for different types of use.

Let's break down what they're all best for.

Raspbmc

Like Raspbian, Raspbmc is the default media center on the Raspberry Pi. It's the most widely supported, full-featured media center operating system available.

At a glance, Raspbmc looks just like XBMC on Windows, a Mac, or Linux.

Raspbmc is based on the popular media center *XBMC,* so XBMC users will feel right at home with Raspbmc, right out of the box. Raspbmc runs a full version of Linux, so it's a big file that takes a bit of time to boot up. That said, part of the appeal of Raspbmc is similar to Raspbian: you don't really need to do a lot of work to get it set up and working.

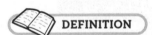 **DEFINITION**

> **XBMC** is media center software initially made for the Xbox. Since its launch, it has come to many different operating systems—the Raspberry Pi included. It's basically a media player and streaming software so you can turn a computer into a media device. It's meant to play videos and music and display photos. Originally, XBMC stood for Xbox Media Center, but in 2014, the team announced the software would change names to Kodi.

Like Raspbian, Raspbmc is based on the Linux distribution Debian. Developer Sam Nazarko, a computer science student from London, created it with the goal of making an XBMC media center on the Raspberry Pi as simple as possible.

Raspbmc is a solid starting point with media centers because it's packed with features that work without any effort on your part. Out of the box, you can stream music, use *AirPlay,* use a *PVR* (personal video recorder), and more. Likewise, pretty much all the add-ons work right away, so you don't need to dig into a bunch of settings or download additional software.

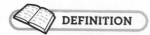 **DEFINITION**

AirPlay is an Apple software that enables your Raspberry Pi to receive a music signal from your home computer. With it, you can stream music from software like iTunes right to your Raspberry Pi—no cables necessary. It's handy when your computer isn't connected to your living room's speakers. **PVR** stands for *personal video recorder*. It's often the device you get with a cable package to record live video from your TV, but it's also used in camcorders. With Raspbmc, you can access the video saved on your PVR so you don't have to go through your cable box.

Raspbmc also comes with a bunch of other features that makes it great for beginners. Wi-Fi works out of the box, installation is easy on any platform, it automatically downloads new updates, and it can even be installed on a hard drive instead of an SD card if you want more storage.

Raspbmc is available from raspbmc.com.

OpenELEC

Whereas Raspbmc is packed full of features, OpenELEC strips them away. The goal of OpenELEC is speed, so it's kept as simple as possible.

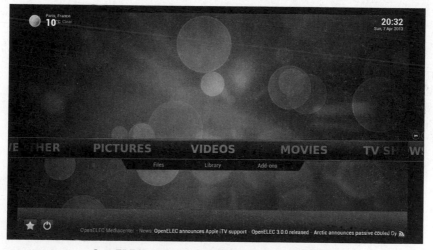

OpenELEC's main screen is nearly identical to Raspbmc.

Unlike Raspbmc, OpenELEC isn't built on top of a previously made Linux distribution. It's just a media center, and it can't do anything else. It's still built around XBMC, but it doesn't bother with the operating system beneath it.

OpenELEC was created to do one thing—be a blazing-fast media center. This means you'll only be able to use your Raspberry Pi as a media center when your OpenELEC SD card is in. It also means installation and support is a little harder for beginner users because it's not packed with every single driver for every single accessory. In many cases, you'll have to go find drivers and plug-ins to get OpenELEC working how you want it to.

OpenELEC doesn't do nearly as much hand-holding as Raspbmc. For the most part, you're left to your own devices to get it installed and running. Once it is, you have to get all your accessories working, download the necessary plug-ins, and set up repositories on your own. It's by no means an unachievable task, but it takes a lot more effort than if you were using Raspbmc.

OpenELEC is available from openelec.tv.

XBian

Raspbmc concentrates on ease-of-use, OpenELEC prioritizes simplicity, but XBian focuses on cutting-edge features.

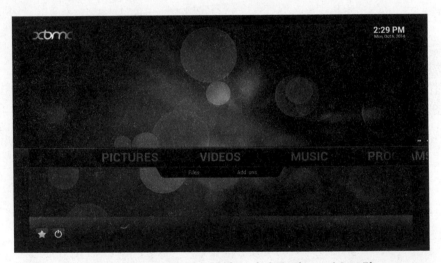

The XBian's main title screen is similar to both Raspbmc and OpenElec.

Like Raspbmc, XBian is built on Raspbian and comes with most of the same packages and add-ons as Raspbmc. This makes it easy to set up and get running without a lot of technical skill. Also like Raspbmc, XBian does just about everything you need right from the start, including supporting Wi-Fi adapters, AirPlay, and more.

However, unlike Raspbmc, XBian still manages to be fast because it's built on a more lightweight version of Debian than Raspbian. (Raspbian is based on Debian.) That makes XBian a little speedier than Raspbmc.

The key difference between Raspbmc and XBian is the media center software itself. XBian is all about the latest features. It's essentially a testing ground for new features, updates, and software, and many times, you get new software and features with XBian before anyone else. It also means XBian is constantly being updated with new builds, so you often need to download software when you start it.

PI POINTER

Remember, all it takes to swap between different operating systems on the Raspberry Pi is a new SD card. So if you're not really certain which media center software is right for you, give them all a try. It only takes a few minutes to format and load an SD card, and you can swap among several different ones quickly to find the one that's right for you.

Sounds great, right? There's a catch, though. With the up-to-the-minute features, you sometimes also get some bugs. Software sometimes won't load properly, videos won't stream cleanly, or in the worst case, you won't be able to turn on your media center at all.

XBian is available from xbian.org.

Media Center Operating System Pros and Cons

Now that you've got a good overview of what each media center operating system does, let's break it all down. The following table offers a pros and cons list to help you make the right choice.

Operating System	Pros	Cons
Raspbmc	Good for beginners; includes all the software you need out of the box; easy to install; has lots of room to customize it however you like	Is slow; has a large installation size; has infrequent updates
OpenELEC	Incredibly fast; has a simple interface that's easy to use; fully customizable	Is harder to set up; requires more work to download extra software; doesn't include as much support for tweaking as Raspbmc does
XBian	Is fast; is very customizable; is easy to set up; cutting-edge new features are added all the time	Potentially has lots of bugs; is slightly more difficult to use than Raspbmc; Fixing bugs usually requires an expert

In the end, the operating system you choose comes down to what you want from a media center. But for this book, let's install Raspbmc. It's the easiest to install, the best suited for new users, and gives a good overview of exactly what a media center can do.

> **SOFTWARE SOLUTION**
>
> If you have some extra time, it's worth installing each of these operating systems and testing them out. You might be surprised by which one you end up preferring. Once you commit to one, it takes up a lot of time to set up a new one, so be sure you're happy with your choice.

Installing Raspbmc

If you already installed Raspbian in Chapter 8, a lot of this section, in which you learn to install Raspbmc, will look familiar to you, as the process is almost identical.

However, the installation process for Windows is significantly easier than if you're on a Mac.

Downloading and Installing Raspbmc

The process for downloading and installing Raspbmc is a bit different depending on what type of personal computer you're using.

Windows:

Windows users get a very easy download and installation process with Raspbmc. You simply download a small installation program, and it downloads the latest release of Raspbmc and installs it onto your SD card. Here's what you need to do:

1. From your Windows computer, head to raspbmc.com/wiki/user/windows-installation and click the link at the top of the page to download the installer.

2. When the installer is finished downloading, double-click the **raspbmc-win32.zip** file to unzip the setup file.

3. Double-click the **setup.exe** file to open the Raspbmc setup utility.

4. Insert your SD card into your computer, and click **Refresh**.

5. Select your SD card in the **Raspbmc Installer**.

6. Check the box marked **I accept the license agreement**.

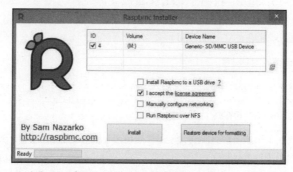

The Raspbmc installer for Windows makes setup easy.

7. Click **Install**, and wait for Raspbmc to do its thing.

When it's finished, eject your SD card and you're ready to go.

Mac:

Raspbmc's installation process is a little more difficult on the Mac, but it's still pretty straightforward. Remember in Chapter 9 when we talked about how OS X uses a similar command line to Linux? You'll be using that here as well.

1. On your Mac, open Terminal by clicking **Applications > Utilities > Terminal**. You're greeted with a command line interface much like the Raspberry Pi's.

The Raspbmc installer on a Mac requires a few more steps.

2. In Terminal, type in the following:

```
curl -O http://svn.stmlabs.com/svn/raspbmc/release/installers/python/install.py
```

3. When this finishes downloading, type in this:

   ```
   chmod +x install.py
   ```

4. Insert your SD card.

5. Type in this:

   ```
   sudo python install.py
   ```

6. Enter your Mac's password.

7. You'll now see a prompt asking you to select your SD card. If you have just an SD card inserted, you'll likely see two options. One of them is your hard drive, and the other is your SD card. Your hard drive is likely much larger and listed as disk0. The SD card should display the same size as what's listed on the SD card and likely is identified as disk2. Type in your SD card as your choice.

> **PI POINTER**
>
> Be very, very careful not to type in your hard drive in step 7. If you select the wrong drive, you'll erase everything on your Mac's hard drive.

8. Type in Y, and press **Enter** when prompted.

9. Wait for the download to complete.

10. When prompted **Would you like to set up your post-installation settings**, type N, and press **Enter**.

When the process is complete, eject your SD card.

The First Run

Now, insert your SD card into your Raspberry Pi, plug in your keyboard and TV, and connect the power cord. Now it's time to run through Raspbmc's first run process.

When you first start up Raspbmc, it'll run some processes in the background and reboot a couple times. This is normal, so let it do what it needs to do. Eventually, you'll be greeted with the Raspbmc main screen.

> **PI POINTER**
>
> When you first start Raspbmc, it'll take a little while because it needs to download extra software, unpack some files, and do some general maintenance. It shouldn't take longer than 5 to 10 minutes, but give yourself some time and walk away while it does its thing.

When it launches, use your keyboard's arrow keys to select the language you prefer.

Now it's time to get your network set up:

1. Use your keyboard's arrow keys to navigate to **Programs > Raspbmc Settings**, and tap the **Enter** key.

2. Use the arrow keys to navigate to the **Network Mode** section. If you're wired, leave it how it is. If you're wireless, tap **Enter** until **Wireless (WIFI) Network** is selected. If you're wired, you're done with the process. If you're on wireless, continue to the next step.

On the first run, you'll set and change some settings in Raspbmc.

3. Scroll down to **Scan Networks**, and tap **Enter**. Select your wireless router's name from the list that comes up, and press **Enter**.

4. Scroll down to the **WIFI Key**, and tap **Enter**. Enter your router's password, and tap **Enter** again.

That's it. Your Raspbmc media center should now be connected to the internet.

Configuring Raspbmc

Raspbmc works out of the box, but you'll need to do a few little things to get everything working properly on your network. You'll also need to configure a few basic settings so Raspbmc looks and operates properly.

Adjusting Resolution

There's a good chance that your first boot of Raspbmc has some display problems. If you can't see the whole screen or the resolution seems wrong, you can adjust both very easily.

1. Scroll over to **System**.

2. Select **Settings**.

3. Scroll down to **System**.

4. Select **Video output**, and press the right arrow key.

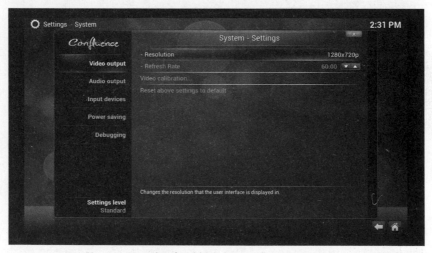

You can customize the video output, audio output, and more.

5. Select **Resolution**, and press **Enter**.

6. Then choose your monitor's resolution. If you're not sure, **1280×720p** is the best resolution for HD monitors and TVs. Tap **Enter** when you've made your choice.

7. Scroll down to **Video calibration…**, and press **Enter**.

8. Use the arrow keys to adjust your screen so the square in the top-left corner is visible. Then press **Enter**.

9. Use the arrow keys to adjust your screen so the square in the bottom-right corner of the screen is visible. Press **Enter**.

10. Move the arrow keys so the blue line on the bottom of the screen is visible. Press **Enter**.

11. Use your arrow keys to adjust the rectangle until it's square. Press **Enter**.

12. Press **Esc** to get back to the main settings screen.

Now you should be able to see the whole screen much better in Raspbmc.

Setting Up Local Network Playback Options

Now you need to be sure your Raspberry Pi can access any servers you're running in your home—your local network.

1. Head to the **Systems** tab, and press **Enter**.

2. Head to **Settings,** and press **Enter**.

3. Scroll down to **Services,** and press **Enter**.

4. Scroll down to **AirPlay,** and press the right arrow key.

5. Navigate to **Allow XBMC to receive AirPlay content,** and press the space bar.

6. Press the left arrow key.

7. Navigate to **UPnP,** and press the right arrow key.

8. Highlight **Allow control of XBMC via UpnP**.

Now you'll be able to access videos and music streamed from other devices on your local network.

If you prefer to play videos directly on your Raspberry Pi, you can plug in an external hard drive or USB flash drive with your favorite videos on it. Raspbmc will recognize the videos right away. Just select the **Videos** tab and then **Files**.

The Risks and Rewards of Overclocking

The Raspberry Pi supports *overclocking,* which is a fancy way of saying it can go a little faster than the 700MHz speed the processor is made to run. Essentially, overclocking means you're pushing your Raspberry Pi's processor a little harder than usual so programs can run faster.

The good news is that overclocking is officially supported, so you don't need to worry about voiding your warranty.

That said, doing so does come with some caveats.

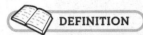 **DEFINITION**

> **Overclocking** refers to making your CPU work harder than it's supposed to. The Raspberry Pi has a 700MHz processor, but you can overclock it up to 900MHz for speed increases. You can overclock your Raspberry Pi with any operating system, including Raspbian. It's not as useful there as it is with Raspbmc, but you might see some benefits with it enabled. Just head to the raspi-config screen and select **Overclocking**, and you should notice some speed increases.

When you overclock your Raspberry Pi, you force the processor to work overtime. This makes the device hotter, which can cause problems if you're running it for too long. Generally, the Raspberry Pi will crash if you're running it overclocked too high, but it could potentially burn the board as well. So it's best to only overclock when you really need it.

You'll see some benefits with overclocking in Raspbmc. The Raspberry Pi isn't that fast, so overclocking can make it a bit more useable and quick to open videos.

There's a nice in-between so you can just overclock it a little. Here's how to do it:

1. Head to the **Programs** tab.

2. Select **Raspbmc Settings**.

3. Select **System Configuration** from the top menu.

4. Scroll down until you get to **System Performance Profile**.

5. Press **Enter** until it reads **Fast**.

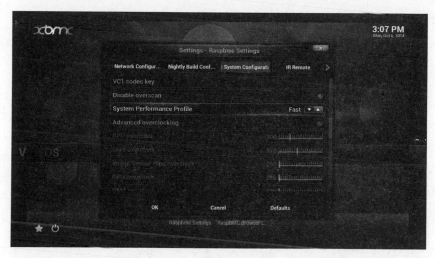

Overclocking is a nice option, but be sure not to overdo it.

6. Scroll down to the **OK** button, and press **Enter**.

7. When it asks you to restart, select **Yes**.

This overclocks your Raspberry Pi just a little bit, but it's a noticeable difference. It's safe, too, so you shouldn't have to worry about your Raspberry Pi overheating at all.

When you're finished with overclock mode, follow these steps to turn it off again.

XBMC Add-Ons and Repositories

You've likely already noticed that Raspbmc is pretty empty when you first load it up. Don't worry. What makes Raspbmc (or any XBMC) special is the add-ons. With add-ons, you can access video content from all over the web.

Browsing the Add-On Repositories

Add-ons are installed from repositories, just like other Linux software. By default, by downloading and installing Raspbmc, you have access to the main add-on directory from XBMC. This should be plenty to get you started with.

Here's how to browse the available add-ons:

1. Head to the **Videos** tab.

2. Select **Add-ons**, and press **Enter**.

3. Scroll down to **Get more…**, and press **Enter**.

Now, you'll find a massive list of all the available add-ons for your Raspbmc.

Raspbmc links to a large selection of add-ons.

Installing Add-Ons

When you've found an add-on you want to install, you need to take a few steps to get it loaded into Raspbmc.

Here's how:

1. Highlight the add-on you want to install, and press **Enter**.

2. When the next screen comes up, highlight **Install**, and press **Enter**.

Raspbmc makes installing add-ons easy.

3. Wait for it to download.

4. To open an add-on, navigate to **Videos** and select **Add-ons**.

5. You're shown a list of the add-ons you have installed. Select the one you want to launch, and press **Enter**.

That's it. Now you've installed an add-on and you're able to check any video you want inside of it. The same works for both image and audio add-ons, so feel free to find some cool media to entertain yourself with.

 SOFTWARE SOLUTION

Similar to Linux, XBMC has a lot of different repositories in addition to the default one built into Raspbmc. Unfortunately, these repositories don't always contain add-ons that are guaranteed to work with the Raspberry Pi. If you don't find an add-on you like, search online to see if someone's made one in a private repository. You can then add that repository to Raspbmc and give the add-on a try.

Popular Plug-Ins

The number of add-ons available for Raspbmc is a bit overwhelming. To help you wade through them all and find some useful ones, here are a few of the most popular:

TV channels: Many TV channels upload videos to their websites, and lots of those are available in Raspbmc. Popular options include CBS News, Discovery Channel, ESPN, FOX News, Food Network, and PBS. You'll also find video streams of specific shows like *South Park, The Daily Show,* and *The Colbert Report.*

YouTube: YouTube gets a special nod here because it's the biggest repository of free videos online. Once you install the YouTube add-on, you have access to every single YouTube video available, right from your Raspberry Pi.

Web series: It's not just about broadcast shows from big name producers; your Raspbmc also is a great place to watch shows from your favorite web series. Popular options include College Humor, Funny or Die, G4, Geek and Sundry, Giant Bomb, How Stuff Works, TED Talks, The Onion, and more.

Play around with different channels, look through the available lists, and find some stuff you like. You might be surprised at how much video content is available online for free.

Remote Controls

If you don't want to deal with using your keyboard and mouse with Raspbmc, you can set up a remote to use instead.

Even better, you can use your smartphone as a remote so you don't need to buy anything new.

Raspbmc-Supported Remotes

Raspbmc supports a handful of remotes out of the box:

- Xbox DVD playback remote
- ATI/X10 remote
- CyberLink 0766:02404 remote
- MCE remote
- Hama remote

Most of these remotes come with a small USB receiver. Just plug the receiver into the Raspberry Pi's USB port, and the remote should work right away.

Smartphone as Remote

If you don't want to purchase a remote control, you can use your smartphone as a remote control very easily. Let's look at how to do it.

First, you'll need to download the remote control app for your smartphone:

1. On an iPhone, open the App Store. On an Android phone, open the Play Store.

2. Search for Official XBMC Remote.

3. Download and install the free application.

With the application downloaded to your smartphone, it's time to get Raspbmc in order.

1. In Raspbmc, navigate to the **System** tab and select **Summary information**.

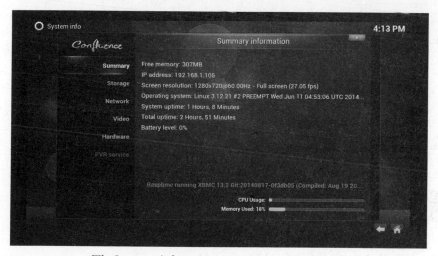

The Summary information screen gives you lots of details.

2. Under **Summary**, you'll see **IP address**. Make a note of that number. It should start with **192.168.1.xxx**.

3. Press **Esc** to head back to the main menu.

4. Select **Settings** under the **System** tab.

5. Navigate to **Services**, and press **Enter**.

6. Select **Webserver**, and press the right arrow key.

7. Be sure **Allow control of XBMC via HTTP** is checked. If not, press **Enter**.

8. Make a note of the Port.

9. On your smartphone, open the XBMC Remote application you downloaded.

10. Tap the **Add Host** option.

11. In the description field, type `Raspberry Pi`.

12. In the host section, type in the number you wrote down in step 2.

13. In the next text field, type in the port number you recorded in step 8.

14. Tap **Save**.

15. Your Raspberry Pi should now be listed on your phone's home screen or a subsequent screen. Tap it to connect your smartphone to your Raspberry Pi.

 PI POINTER

If you don't have a smartphone, you can use your personal computer as a remote. In your computer's web browser, type your Raspberry Pi's URL, a colon, and the port number to access the remote screen. It should read something like 192.168.1.105:80.

Now you can control Raspbmc right from your smartphone or tablet—no keyboard required. You can use the navigation buttons on your phone to move around Raspbmc and pull up movies and TV shows you already have loaded on the Raspberry Pi using the menu button in the top-left corner.

The Least You Need to Know

- Raspbmc is an operating system based on Debian, the same Linux distribution upon which Raspbian is based.

- Once you've set up Raspbmc, you can stream movies from online resources or store movies locally on your Raspberry Pi to play.

- The Raspberry Pi isn't super powerful, but it can handle most video formats.

- You can overclock your Raspberry Pi to get a little more speed out of it.

- You can use your smartphone or tablet as a remote control so you don't have to buy extra equipment (unless you want it!).

Setting Up a Personal VPN

Unless you're really involved in the tech industry, you probably don't know what a *VPN,* or *virtual private network,* is or what it does—nor why you'd want to make one with your Raspberry Pi. VPNs are an easy way to protect yourself and your data online, so it's worth looking into. When you connect to a VPN, it secures your internet connection so nobody can spy on what you're doing. With hacks on bank accounts and public cloud storage becoming more common, a VPN is a simple solution to the problem.

VPNs can help you secure your data no matter where you are. You can connect to it from your phone or computer from inside your house or when you're away from it. This is great when you're not home and using public Wi-Fi somewhere like a coffee shop. Connecting to a VPN means no one else can spy on what you're doing.

A VPN also adds *encryption* to your data so even if someone somehow does get a hold of your information, they can't do anything with it. It's essentially a beefed-up security measure that makes all your online dealings a lot more secure without much effort on your part.

In This Chapter

- Why a VPN is worth having
- Making your local network VPN friendly
- Transforming your Raspberry Pi into a VPN
- Remote VPN control

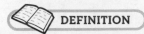

DEFINITION

A **virtual private network (VPN)** acts as a security measure between your computer and the internet. It ensures all data sent through it is encrypted so nobody can steal it. As the name suggests, it's not a physical network; rather, it's created using software on a computer. In this case, that's the Raspberry Pi. **Encryption** is a means of encoding data so only authorized parties can understand it.

The installation process for OpenVPN—the software you use to create a VPN—takes a bit of effort because it's not just about setting up your Raspberry Pi. You also need to configure the VPN itself.

This might all sound overwhelming at first, but let's break down the steps you'll take to make it a little less intimidating:

1. **Configure your home network for VPN:** You need to set up your home network so it can easily find your Raspberry Pi.

2. **Configure your Raspberry Pi for internet access:** The whole point of a VPN is accessibility anywhere, so you need to give your Raspberry Pi an address where you can access it via the internet.

3. **Install OpenVPN:** The installation process is just a few lines you'll type into the command line and then you'll get some special security keys.

4. **Set up your Windows or Mac computer:** You'll install some software on your personal computer and then set up those security keys.

Really, that's all there is to it. The process takes a good amount of time, but it's not necessarily difficult. You should be pretty familiar with your Raspberry Pi at this point, but be sure you're comfortable with the command line before you start this project. When you've got everything set up, you'll be able to use your VPN safely and securely from anywhere in the world.

In this chapter, I walk you through the specifics of what a VPN is, why you'd use it, and how it helps your security.

PI POINTER

You need Raspbian installed on your Raspberry Pi before you can start this process. If you need to, check back to Chapter 8 for instructions on getting Raspbian up and running.

What Is a VPN?

A VPN is a group of computers linked together via the internet. Typically, a business uses a VPN to connect data centers, and individuals can then use those VPNs to access that network, even if they're not physically on-site. VPNs are essentially virtual tunnels that connect remote computers. VPNs also encrypt any communication that passes over them, so they're often used when a company wants to keep its data private. Everyday internet users can benefit from this encryption, too.

Typically, you launch a VPN client such as OpenVPN on your computer, log in, and wait while your computer exchanges some information with the server. After both computers verify each other, all the communication that goes through the VPN is encrypted and secured so no one can eavesdrop.

Physically, a VPN can be any computer as long as it's running special software. This is exactly why the Raspberry Pi is perfect as a VPN. You can keep it connected all the time so you can access it from anywhere; it's tiny so it doesn't get in the way; and because it's not on your primary computer, you don't have to worry about hogging resources. In addition, it's optional. You can use it when you need security, like when you're looking at your bank statements via the coffee shop Wi-Fi, but skip it when you don't need it.

Because VPNs secure and encrypt your data, they tend to slow down your internet connection speed. For most web browsing, it's usually not very noticeable, but you'll likely notice a slowdown enough to make it annoying when you're just trying to watch Netflix, for example. In such cases, it's usually best to ignore the VPN and only use it when you're sending private data.

Security and Encryption

Generally, when you connect to the internet, your computer links directly to a website and the data transferred between the two is sent in an easily readable plain text format. With a VPN, your computer goes through the VPN, where your information is encrypted and made anonymous before your computer connects to a website. The same process works in reverse, so all data you request from a site is encrypted before it reaches your computer.

 PI POINTER

As more and more online retailers are hacked, security is becoming increasing important for all of us. A VPN gives you the peace of mind to browse whatever you want, wherever you are because it makes your connection secure. If you often use coffee shop Wi-Fi or you're an international traveler, this is very helpful.

A VPN can do this through a variety of different security protocols, but here are the most popular methods:

Point-to-Point Tunneling Protocol (PPTP): PPTP creates a tunnel between computers so they can easily connect to each other. This data is private, but it's not encrypted. PPTP has been around for a long time, but due to its lack of encryption, it's not used much anymore.

Layer 2 Tunneling Protocol (L2TP) and **Internet Protocol Security (IPsec):** Alone, L2TP works similar to PPTP, but combined with IPsec, it benefits from encryption. IPsec encrypts data, secures a data channel, and checks the data to ensure it's never compromised.

Secure Sockets Layer (SSL): This is the same type of security you get when you log on to your bank's website or any other site that starts with *https*. SSL essentially creates a secure connection between two computers so the data sent between them is encrypted instead of being sent as plain text.

Secure Shell (SSH): SSH creates both the VPN tunnel between two computers and the encryption that protects that data. The data itself is never encrypted, but the tunnel through which it travels is.

Basically, a VPN modifies the data that goes through it so your internet service provider, hackers, or even the government can't tell what it is.

Why Use a VPN?

You might be thinking that this type of security is overkill for you. But VPNs are important for every internet user.

VPNs are useful for students and remote workers who need to access their school or employer network remotely. (In such cases, the school or business probably already has a VPN set up, but it's still good to know how they work.) If you work on public Wi-Fi a lot, VPNs are an easy way to secure everything you do on those networks. It's surprisingly easy for a hacker to grab your data when you're somewhere like a coffee shop, so using the extra layer of security is essential.

If you're in a country that has a lot of government-enforced restrictions on internet access, a VPN enables you to get around those restrictions. Not only can VPNs encrypt and secure your data, they also can spoof your location so it looks like you're accessing the internet from another place.

VPNs are important for securing your private data—everything from your passwords to your bank account info—when you're online. There's really no harm in setting one up, especially if you're trying to find a good use for your Raspberry Pi.

An Introduction to OpenVPN

OpenVPN, the VPN client you'll use for this project, is free and open source. It's also compatible with a lot of different operating systems.

OpenVPN uses the SSL security protocol. This makes it highly secure but still pretty easy to use. The encryption is handled by OpenSSL, another bit of open-source software. The end result is a free, easy-to-use, DIY security solution.

I call for OpenVPN on your Raspberry Pi for a number of reasons. First, it's very secure. Second, it's easy to set up. Third, it's likely always going to be free. Other Raspberry Pi VPNs have gone to a pay model that includes subscriptions. OpenVPN will likely always be free as long as you're the one doing the installation. You learn exactly how to do that in this chapter.

OpenVPN is also widely supported across several operating systems. You won't have any trouble bringing up OpenVPN on your Windows computer, Mac machine, or even your smartphone.

 SOFTWARE SOLUTION

> You might be noticing an open-source software theme. The Raspberry Pi itself is open source, as is its operating system and much of the software it runs is open source. This is ideal for the Raspberry Pi enthusiast, because it means you can load your device with all the software you need for free.

James Yonan conceived OpenVPN while he was traveling internationally and noticed that logging in to computers remotely was difficult in countries where there were security concerns. So he decided to create a VPN solution that was both secure and easy to use. As a result, OpenVPN was born in 2001.

The name *OpenVPN* is also a nod to OpenSSL and meant as a clear indication that this is free and open-source software. It might seem that making the software open source is a bad idea with security, but it's actually helped strengthen it and make the security stronger. With more eyes on the OpenVPN source code, more people understand how it works, and subsequently more people can find potential bugs and security flaws.

OpenVPN was initially made for Linux, and without the support of the Linux community, it would have had a much harder time gaining ground. Now, OpenVPN is one of the most popular VPN solutions around and has an active group of people talking about it.

Setting Up Your At-Home VPN

Before you can install and set up OpenVPN, you need to get your home network and Raspberry Pi ready for it. To do that, you need to log in to your home router and adjust some settings.

If you've never logged into your home router before, this might seem intimidating. But it's not as difficult as you might think, and you only need to poke around in a few settings to get everything working.

Changing Your Home Network for a VPN

To access your Raspberry Pi remotely, you need to be able to access your home network from anywhere. This means connecting your Raspberry Pi to the internet at large, making your Raspberry Pi a server that's accessible just like any other website you might visit.

To do this, you need to set up your Raspberry Pi with a *static IP address*. This gives your Raspberry Pi a set place on your home network. You also need to assign your Raspberry Pi a *DNS address* so it's accessible over the internet. Essentially, you're going to open your Raspberry Pi to the internet at large, but you'll do so in a way that only you have access to it.

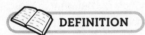 **DEFINITION**

A **static IP address** is a set spot where your Raspberry Pi is always located, no matter how many times you reboot. Your router assigns each device on your network a number when it logs into it. This is usually done automatically based on when you turn on each device. So if you power on your computer first in the morning, it's number 2 (the router's 1), your phone is 3, and so on. This can be a bit random, so it's best to give your Raspberry Pi a set, or static, address so you can always find it without looking up the number. A **DNS (domain name server) address** is basically the internet's phone book. To get to a website, you type in a name, but behind that name is a series of numbers, much like your IP address.

Logging in to Your Home Router

First, you need to log in to your home router. This process is a little different on every router, but I'll try to provide a general-enough outline on how to do this so you'll be able to make it work with your particular router.

To log in to your router, you'll need to determine your router's IP address. This is usually something like 192.168.X.X or 10.0.X.X. When you've figured out your router's IP address, you can access it from your computer's web browser.

But first you need to figure out the address. Here's how:

Windows:

It takes a bit of effort to track down your router's IP address in Windows. You'll be using the command line:

1. Open the Windows Command Window. Click **Start > Run**, and type cmd. Press **Enter**.

2. Type ipconfig into the command line, and press **Enter**.

3. Look for **Default Gateway** in the displayed results. This is your router's IP address.

4. Type that address into your computer's web browser to load your router's login page.

When you get to the login page, type the username and password for your router.

 PI POINTER

If you've never logged in to your router before (on either a Windows PC or a Mac), consult the manual that came with your router for your username and password.

Mac:

Determining your IP address on a Mac is very easy. You'll just make a single click of the mouse:

1. When you're connected to your router's Wi-Fi, tap the **Option** key on your keyboard and right-click the Wi-Fi symbol in your Mac's top menu bar.

2. Look for the **IP Address:** address. Type that number into your computer's web browser to get to the login page.

When you get to the login page, type your username and password for your router.

Assigning Your Raspberry Pi a Static Internal IP Address

Now that you're logged in to your router, let's give your Raspberry Pi a static internal IP address where it will be accessible anytime you need it. Typically, when your Raspberry Pi logs into your router, it takes whatever number is available. Assigning it a static IP address means it's always at the same address, login after login.

You'll do this from the command line on your Raspberry Pi. Be sure your Raspberry Pi is connected to the internet, and open the command line in LXTerminal or Raspbian:

1. Type `ifconfig`, and press **Enter**.

2. Look for the section titled **eth0** if you're connected to Ethernet or **wlan0** if you're connected to Wi-Fi.

The `ifconfig` menu shows you a ton of information about your Wi-Fi network.

3. Write down the numbers listed after **inet addr** (you'll use this for the "address" section in step 8), **Bcast** (for the "broadcast" section in step 8), and **Mask** (for the "netmask" section in step 8).

4. Type in `netstat -nr`, and press **Enter**.

5. Write down the numbers listed under **Gateway Address** (for the "gateway" section in step 8) and **Destination Address** (for the "network" section in step 8).

6. Type in `sudo nano /etc/network/interfaces`, and press **Enter**.

7. Look for the line that reads **iface eth0 inet dhcp**, and edit it to **iface eth0 inet static**.

8. Right below that line, type in the following, substituting the numbers you wrote down in steps 3 and 5 for the X's:

```
address xxx.xxx.x.xx
netmask xxx.xxx.xxx.x
network xxx.xxx.x.xx
broadcast xxx.xxx.x.xx
gateway xxx.xxx.x.xx
```

9. Press **Ctrl+X** to exit and save your changes.

Now, your Raspberry Pi has a static IP address and will always be accessible at the same place.

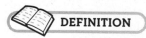

> **PI POINTER**
>
> Be very careful when writing down all the information in this exercise. Even one wrong number can make the whole system not work. Type data into the command line carefully, too. Take your time and double-check your work throughout so you don't have to troubleshoot later. For longer sections of information you need to type in (5 lines or more), such as that in step 8, you can log on to idiotsguides.com/raspberrypi and copy and paste.

Assigning Your Raspberry Pi a Static External IP Address via Dynamic DNS

After your Raspberry Pi has a static *internal* IP address, you need to set it up with a static *external* IP address as well. You'll do this through a service called *dynamic DNS*.

> **DEFINITION**
>
> **Dynamic DNS** simply means a DNS name is automatically updated even when the number behind it changes. This is helpful for your server because your ISP will change your address from time to time. Dynamic DNS ensures you can still find it, even when it changes.

Giving your Raspberry Pi an external IP address through dynamic DNS makes it accessible from the internet. This enables you to access your Raspberry Pi from anywhere in the world you have an internet connection.

You have a lot of options for getting a dynamic DNS address, but for this lesson, let's use DNSdynamic (dnsdynamic.org).

Here's what to do:

1. Head to dnsdynamic.org.

2. Check for a domain availability by typing a domain name you'd like to assign to your Raspberry Pi in the **check availability** box. You can use whatever you want here. Follow the instructions, and you'll get a host service that reads something like *myraspberrypi*.dnsdynamic.com. You'll also get some more configuration settings. Hold on to these for step 7.

3. Head back to your Raspberry Pi, and open the command line.

4. Type in `sudo apt-get install ddclient`, and press **Enter**. This installs the dynamic DNS client. Wait for it to download and install.

5. When it's finished, it will run automatically. Select the DNS server you picked, or select **Other** if you're using DNSdynamic.

6. Enter the address of the DNS server you registered in step 2.

7. Now you need to edit the file to include your information. Type in `sudo nano /etc/ddclient/ddclient.conf`, and press **Enter**. Write in all the information you gathered in step 2.

8. Finally, add one more line to the top of the file that reads `daemon=600`. This tells your internet service provider to check the address every 600 seconds, or 10 minutes.

9. Press **Ctrl+X** to save and exit the project.

10. Now type in `ddclient`. This launches the dynamic DNS client so your Raspberry Pi is accessible online.

Before you can get to it, you'll need to configure your router to allow access from the internet. Assuming you're still logged into your router, here's what you need to do:

1. Look for a tab or setting that reads **NAT /QoS**, and click it.

2. Find the **Port Forwarding** tab, and click it.

3. Typically, you'll need to click an **Add** button to add a new port forwarding address.

4. In the boxes, enter your Raspberry Pi's static IP address under address and **1194** under port. Save it, and exit your router.

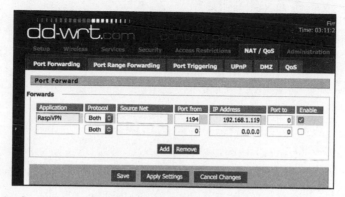

Configuring your router to allow external internet access takes just a few steps.

Your Raspberry Pi is now accessible via the internet.

 PI POINTER

Remember, all routers are a little different, so if you can't find your router's port forwarding section, refer to your owner's manual.

Other Dynamic DNS Options

DNSdynamic isn't your only choice for getting a dynamic DNS address. Here are a few other suggestions if you'd like to try something different:

- Duck DNS (duckdns.org)

- DtDNS (dtdns.com)

- No-IP (noip.com)

- YDNS (ydns.eu)

- FreeDNS (freedns.afraid.org)

All these options are free and will do the job, so you can choose any one you like. Remember to make a note of the address you get from the dynamic DNS server though. You'll need it later.

Preparing Your Raspberry Pi for OpenVPN

Before you can set up OpenVPN, you need to make a few changes on your Raspberry Pi. In this section, I show you how to install Raspbian, secure your Raspberry Pi with a better password, enable SSH so you can access your Raspberry Pi from your home computer, and set up a remote connection on your computer.

Installing Raspbian

OpenVPN can work on any version of Linux, but Raspbian's your best option. If you haven't done so already, refer to Chapter 8 for the full guide to installing Raspbian.

You can use an existing SD card upon which you have Raspbian installed.

Changing Your Default Password

If you didn't change your password when you set up Raspbian, you need to do it now. By the end of this project, your Raspberry Pi will be accessible from the internet and will be used for sending encrypting data. The last thing you want to do is keep the default password.

Here's what to do:

1. From the command line in Raspbian or LXTerminal, type `raspi-config`, and press **Enter**.

2. Scroll down to **Change password for 'pi' user**, and press **Enter**. Then type in a new password.

Don't exit out of raspi-config just yet. You've got one more setting to change.

Installing SSH for Remote Connectivity

Now you need to set up *SSH* on your Raspberry Pi. This enables you to remotely connect to your Raspberry Pi from your home computer.

Here's how:

1. In raspi-config, scroll down to **Enable or Disable SSH Server**, and press **Enter**.

2. Turn the setting to **On**.

3. Exit raspi-config.

Now, SSH is on and you have a solid new password. It's time to connect to your Raspberry Pi remotely from your home computer.

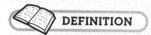

DEFINITION

SSH stands for *Secure Shell*. It's a network protocol made for secure data communication over the command line. In this case, it's a way for you to log in to your Raspberry Pi's command line from your home computer.

Connecting to Your Raspberry Pi Remotely

Your next step is to remotely connect to your Raspberry Pi from your Windows or Mac computer. This is one of the coolest things you can do with SSH.

When you're connected, you can easily transfer files between your computer and your Raspberry Pi, and you even can access the command line from your home computer. You don't even have to connect your Raspberry Pi to a monitor if you don't want to.

The remote SSH screen looks just like your Raspberry Pi's command line.

Earlier in this chapter, you gave your Raspberry Pi a static IP address. With it, you can SSH into your Raspberry Pi at the same address every time. You'll do this differently on a Windows PC than you will on a Mac.

Windows:

On Windows, you'll need to download some software before you can SSH into your Raspberry Pi.

Here's what to do:

1. Head to www.chiark.greenend.org.uk/~sgtatham/putty/download.html and download PuTTY.

2. When the file has downloaded, open **putty.exe**.

3. Enter your Raspberry Pi's IP address under **Host Name**.

4. Tap **Enter** to open a command line.

5. Enter your Raspberry Pi's username and password and press **Enter**.

Now, you're connected to your Raspberry Pi on your Windows PC. You can control your Raspberry Pi just like you would if you were in front of the device itself.

Mac:

If you own a Mac, you already have SSH built in to your computer, and you can access your Raspberry Pi using the Terminal app. Here's how:

1. Launch Terminal on your Mac from **Applications > Utilities > Terminal**.

2. Type in `ssh pi@`*`yourIPaddress`*. Replace *yourIPaddress* with the static IP address you assigned your Raspberry Pi earlier. For example, ssh pi@192.168.1.105.

3. When prompted for the password on your Raspberry Pi, type it in and press **Enter**.

That's it. You can now control your Raspberry Pi from Terminal on your Mac just like you would from the command line on the Raspberry Pi. You should also see your Raspberry Pi in Finder, so you can drag and drop files onto it if you need to.

PI POINTER

Once you have SSH enabled, you can do all sorts of things with your Raspberry Pi without ever needing to touch it. You can control it from your personal computer's command line, set up file transfers, and even poke around in the file system. You'll do all that and more throughout this chapter.

Installing OpenVPN on Your Raspberry Pi

Okay, now that all the preliminary stuff is out of the way, it's time to actually install OpenVPN. This process is super easy and works just like downloading other software onto your Raspberry Pi.

Downloading OpenVPN

To download and install OpenVPN, you use the command line. In the previous section, you set up a connection between your Raspberry Pi and your computer. That means you can run these commands from your personal computer, or you can stick to your running them from your Raspberry Pi.

Either way, here's what to do:

1. At the command line, type in `sudo apt-get update`, and press **Enter**.

2. Next, type in `sudo apt-get upgrade`, and press **Enter**.

3. Finally, type in `sudo apt-get install openvpn`, and press **Enter**.

OpenVPN should now download and install. When it's done, you can move on to generate your security keys and certificates.

Generating Your Security Keys

Just like a real key, security keys give you access to your Raspberry Pi while blocking out anyone else. It's essentially the same as locking the door to your house.

Here's how to set up your security keys:

1. First you need to give yourself superuser access for everything you do. To do this, at the command line, type in `sudo -s`. This opens a new window where you're always logged in as the superuser.

2. Now, you're going to copy a directory. Type in the following to copy the directory and everything underneath it:

   `cp -r /usr/share/doc/openvpn/examples/easy-rsa/2.0 /etc/openvpn/easy-rsa`

3. Type in `cd /etc/openvpn/easy-rsa`. This moves you over to your new directory.

4. Now it's time to edit the file you just moved. Type in `nano vars`. This opens your text editor.

5. Next you need to edit a single line in the text file. Look for the line that starts **export EASY_RSA**, and change it to `export EASY_RSA="/etc/openvpn/easy-rsa"`. This simply tells your Raspberry Pi where to store your encryption keys.

6. Press **Ctrl+X** to save and exit the editor.

That's the first part of getting the security keys ready to go. Next you'll build the certificates.

Generating Your Security Certificates

With your key generator set up, next you need to get your *security certificates* in order. Certificates verify the ownership of a key and ensure that only a person with the key can access your Raspberry Pi. This type of key is the same thing you'd see in your browser's URL when you log into your bank's website.

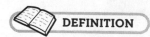 **DEFINITION**

> A **security certificate** is the information that allows another computer to decrypt an encrypted message you send. Without the certificate, the two computers can't understand each other.

This is one of the more complicated parts, so be sure you type everything in this section exactly.

Here's what to do:

1. At the command line, type in `cd /etc/openvpn/easy-rsa`, and press **Enter**.

2. Type in `source ./vars`, and press **Enter**. This loads the document you were editing earlier.

3. Type in `./build-ca`, and press **Enter**. This builds your certificate.

When you finish the command, you'll get an output with your security certificates.

Your Raspberry Pi will now ask you a bunch of questions about location, names, and more. These are optional. Fill them out if you want, or just press **Enter** to skip through them.

Building certificates takes a bit of time, but you'll see the encryption process in action as it does its job.

One area you need to address is setting a name for your server. Type in the following, replacing *SERVERNAME* with the name you want:

```
./build-key-server SERVERNAME
```

It can be anything you want, so be creative. For the purposes of this lesson, I'm calling it raspberrypiVPN.

 PI POINTER

> Be sure to write down your server name somewhere you'll remember it. You'll need it in some of the upcoming steps. It's good practice to do this with any information you manually enter.

In addition, fill in these prompts:

- **Common Name:** Enter the name you gave your server here.

- **A challenge password?** Leave this blank.

- **Sign the certificate?** Type Y.

- **1 out of 1 certificate requests certified, commit?** Press Y.

With your server set up, it's time to build your keys. You'll make a key for each of the devices you want to connect to the VPN. You can get by with just creating one, but then only one device can access the VPN at once. It's best to create a few for each of your devices.

Here's what to do:

1. At the command line, type in `./build-key-pass` *name*, replacing *name* with the device you want to make the key for. For example, you could do `./build-key-pass client1`. Do this for every device you want a key for. You can name them however you like. Just be sure you remember or jot down the names.

2. When you build a key pass, you get three prompts:
   Enter PEM pass phrase: Make a password. Be sure it's something you'll remember.
   A challenge password? Leave this blank.
   Sign the certificate? Enter in Y here, and press **Enter**.

3. After the key is generated, type in `cd keys`, and press **Enter**.

4. Finally, type in `openssl rsa -in DEVICENAME.key -des3 -out DEVICENAME.3des.key`, replacing *DEVICENAME* with the name you used in step 1, and press **Enter**. For example, using the device name *client1*, you'd type `openssl rsa -in client1.key -des3 -out client1.3des.key`.

That's it for the certificates and keys.

Building the Key Exchange

Next up, you need to build the key exchange. Think of this like handing the keys over to a friend so they can get into your house.

Here are the steps to take:

1. Type in cd /etc/openvpn/easy-rsa, and press **Enter** to return to the key directory.

2. Type in ./build-dh, and press **Enter**. This builds the key exchange. It might take a little while.

3. When it's finished, you're going to add one more layer of protection. Type in openvpn -genkey -secret keys/ta.key, and press **Enter**.

Your keys and your certificates are now established. Your Raspberry Pi has a static IP address, and it's accessible online. You're almost there. Now you need to edit the OpenVPN configuration file.

Writing the OpenVPN Configuration File

Unfortunately, the OpenVPN software isn't smart enough to take everything you worked through already in this chapter and integrate it into its own configuration file. That means you'll have to make your own. This will require a lot of typing—or copying and pasting from idiotsguides.com/raspberrypi—so get comfortable.

Here's how to write the OpenVPN configuration file:

1. Type in nano /etc/openvpn/server.conf. This will create a new blank file.

2. Now you're going to need to type in a lot of information. Type all of this into the text file you just created, substituting your own information from the previous steps when noted.

```
local 192.168.1.0 #Enter the IP address of your Raspberry Pi that you
    got up above here.
dev tun
proto udp
port 1194
ca /etc/openvpn/easy-rsa/keys/ca.crt
cert /etc/openvpn/easy-rsa/keys/Server.crt #Enter in your server
    certificate you generated above here. In our example it's
    raspberrypiVPN.crt
key /etc/openvpn/easy-rsa/keys/Server.key #Enter the server key you
    made above here, in our example, it's raspberrypiVPN.key
dh /etc/openvpn/easy-rsa/keys/dh1024.pem
server 10.8.0.0 255.255.255.0
ifconfig 10.8.0.1 10.8.0.2
push "route 10.8.0.1 255.255.255.255"
push "route 10.8.0.0 255.255.255.0"
push "route 192.168.2.0 255.255.255.0" #Enter your Raspberry Pi's IP
    address here after "route
"dhcp-option DNS yourdynamicaddress.server.com" #Enter your Dynamic DNS
    address here
push "redirect-gateway def1"
client-to-client
duplicate-cn
keepalive 10 120
cipher AES-128-CBC
comp-lzo
user nobody
group nogroup
persist-key
persist-tun
status /var/log/openvpn-status.log 20
log /var/log/openvpn.log
verb 1
```

The OpenVPN configuration file has a lot of stuff to set up. Take your time getting it right.

3. Tap **Ctrl+X** to save the file and exit the editor.

PI POINTER

Remember, in programming, the # symbol is used to "comment out" a line. This tells the program not to read anything after the symbol. It's often used to add comments to code so other people can understand it or to just leave notes for yourself. In this case, it's helpful to note where you need to add your own information.

Be sure you remove the # from this line; otherwise, your VPN won't work.

I know that was a lot of typing, but you're not quite finished yet. You need to edit a couple more files. These next two are really easy though:

1. Back at the command line, type in `nano /etc/sysctl.conf`.

2. Find the line that reads **Uncomment the next line to enable packet forwarding for IPv4**. Delete the # sign on the line below that. This allows the Raspberry Pi to relay information between your computer and the internet.

3. Tap **Ctrl+X** to save and exit the editor.

4. Finally, type in `sysctl -p`, and press **Enter**. This reloads the file you just edited with the changes you just made.

The configuration file is all set up. One last edit on your Raspberry Pi, and you're good to go.

Setting Up Your Raspberry Pi's Firewall

By default, the Raspberry Pi has a *firewall* set up that ensures nobody can access your Raspberry Pi from the internet. This is great for security, but you need to access your Raspberry Pi from anywhere.

The solution is to create a hole in the firewall for the VPN. You also need to be sure your Raspberry Pi loads all the details at launch.

 **DEFINITION**

A **firewall** is a network security system that controls the traffic on a device. It creates a barrier between a trusted network like your router and another untrusted network, like the internet. This denies access from any unapproved network connections.

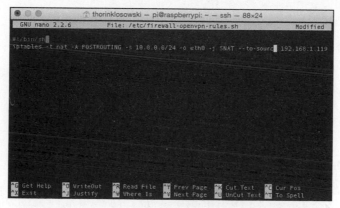

These are the rules of your firewall. You can alter them as you see fit.

1. At the command line, type in `nano /etc/firewall-openvpn-rules.sh`, and press **Enter**.

2. This creates a blank document in which you're going to write a script that'll load at launch to open the firewall a little. Type this into the file:

```
#!/bin/sh
iptables -t nat -A POSTROUTING -s 10.8.0.0/24 -o eth0 -j SNAT -to-source
   192.168.X.X
```

   Replace *192.168.X.X* with the IP address of your Raspberry Pi. If your device is wireless and not connected to your router with an Ethernet cable, replace **eth0** with `wlan0`.

3. When you're done, press **Ctrl+X** to save and exit the document.

4. Back at the command line, you'll change the permissions for the files you created. This makes them accessible where they need to be and ensures others can't edit them. Type in `chmod 700 /etc/firewall-openvpn-rules.sh`, and press **Enter**.

5. Type in `chown root /etc/firewall-openvpn-rules.sh`, and press **Enter**.

That changes your permissions.

Finally, you need to edit your network configuration file so it loads all your stuff at startup. Here's how:

1. Type in `nano /etc/network/interfaces`, and press **Enter**.

2. Find the line reads **iface eth0 inet static**. Add a new line below that by pressing **Enter**.

3. Press **Tab** to create an indent.

4. Type in `pre-up /etc/firewall-openvpn-rules.sh`, and tap **Ctrl+X** to exit and save the document.

Your Raspberry Pi is now set up as a VPN server. Reboot to be sure all the settings are loaded. Type in `sudo reboot`, and wait for the system to reboot.

> **PI POINTER**
>
> If you're connected to the Raspberry Pi over SSH, you need to reconnect after the system reboots. Just give it a few minutes to do its thing, and type in the SSH command again. Remember, it's probably something like `ssh pi@192.168.1.2`.

Configuring Keys for Each Client

Your Raspberry Pi is a fully functional VPN server now, but unfortunately, you still can't do much with it. You need to create a configuration file for each of the clients you want to connect to your Raspberry Pi.

Remember earlier in the chapter where you created a bunch of different keys for each of your devices? In this section, you're going to configure your Raspberry Pi so it works with those devices. You're going to create a program that runs and does this for you automatically. The program comes from Eric Jodoin of the SANS Institute.

First, you'll need to create text file to store some information:

1. At the command line, type in `sudo nano /etc/openvpn/easy-rsa/keys/Default.txt`, and press **Enter**. This creates a blank text file.

2. Type the following into the text file (or copy and paste from idiotsguides.com/
    raspberrypi), replacing *YOUR PUBLIC IP ADDRESS* with the dynamic DNS address you
    got earlier in this chapter:

```
client
dev tun
proto udp
remote YOUR PUBLIC IP ADDRESS 1194
resolv-retry infinite
nobind
persist-key
persist-tun
mute-replay-warnings
ns-cert-type server
key-direction 1
cipher AES-128-CBC
comp-lzo
verb 1
mute 20
```

3. Press **Ctrl+X** to exit and save the document.

Next, you create the program that will compile information for all your keys.

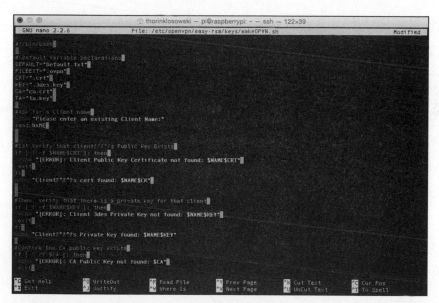

*This is your key generation program. It's a little complex, but mostly it uses commands
you've seen before.*

1. Type in `sudo nano /etc/openvpn/easy-rsa/keys/MakeOPVN.sh`, and press **Enter**.

2. Type the following into the file (or copy and paste from idiotsguides.com/raspberrypi), being sure to avoid typos:

```bash
#!/bin/bash
# Default Variable Declarations
DEFAULT="Default.txt"
FILEEXT=".ovpn"
CRT=".crt"
KEY=".3des.key"
CA="ca.crt"
TA="ta.key"
#Ask for a Client name
echo "Please enter an existing Client Name:"
read NAME
#1st Verify that client's Public Key Exists
if [ ! -f $NAME$CRT ]; then
echo "[ERROR]: Client Public Key Certificate not found: $NAME$CRT"
exit
fi
echo "Client's cert found: $NAME$CR"
#Then, verify that there is a private key for that client
if [ ! -f $NAME$KEY ]; then
echo "[ERROR]: Client 3des Private Key not found: $NAME$KEY"
exit
fi
echo "Client's Private Key found: $NAME$KEY"
#Confirm the CA public key exists
if [ ! -f $CA ]; then
echo "[ERROR]: CA Public Key not found: $CA"
exit
fi
echo "CA public Key found: $CA"
#Confirm the tls-auth ta key file exists
if [ ! -f $TA ]; then
echo "[ERROR]: tls-auth Key not found: $TA"
exit
fi
echo "tls-auth Private Key found: $TA"
#Ready to make a new .opvn file--Start by populating with the
default file
cat $DEFAULT > $NAME$FILEEXT
#Now, append the CA Public Cert
echo "<ca>" >> $NAME$FILEEXT
cat $CA >> $NAME$FILEEXT
echo "</ca>" >> $NAME$FILEEXT
#Next append the client Public Cert
echo "<cert>" >> $NAME$FILEEXT
cat $NAME$CRT | sed -ne '/-BEGIN CERTIFICATE-/,/-END CERTIFICATE-/p' >>
    $NAME$FILEEXT
echo "</cert>" >> $NAME$FILEEXT
#Then, append the client Private Key
```

```
echo "<key>" >> $NAME$FILEEXT
cat $NAME$KEY >> $NAME$FILFEXT
echo "</key>" >> $NAME$FILEEXT
#Finally, append the TA Private Key
echo "<tls-auth>" >> $NAME$FILEEXT
cat $TA >> $NAME$FILEEXT
echo "</tls-auth>" >> $NAME$FILEEXT
echo "Done! $NAME$FILEEXT Successfully Created."
#Script written by Eric Jodoin
\ No newlineat end of file
```

3. When you're finished, press **Ctrl+X** to exit and save.

4. Type in cd /etc/openvpn/easy-rsa/keys/, and press **Enter**.

5. Next you need to change the permissions so you can run the program. Type in chmod 700 MakeOPVN.sh, and press **Enter**.

6. Now, it's time to run your program. Type in ./MakeOPVN.sh, and press **Enter**.

7. As the script runs, it will ask you for the names of your clients. You generated keys for each of your devices and named them earlier. Type those names in here (our example was *client1*). Repeat the process for each client.

With that, your VPN is fully up and running and accessible from all your computers. You're going to grab these configuration files you just created a little later when you're setting up your clients. Let's get to actually using it.

Terminal Commands to Start and Stop the VPN

You already set up your VPN to run on startup, but if you need to manually start or stop it, you'll need to know a couple terminal commands:

- To start OpenVPN, type in sudo openvpn *servername*.conf (replace *servername* with your server's name), and press **Enter**.

- To stop it, type in sudo killall openvpn, and press **Enter**.

You shouldn't have to deal with this much, but it's good to know how to do it, just in case.

Installing OpenVPN on Your Computer

Finally, it's time to get OpenVPN onto your personal computer. Your VPN is up and running on your Raspberry Pi, but you need to tell your personal computer how to route its traffic through it so everything is secured—it doesn't do this automatically.

To install the OpenVPN client you'll need to download some software.

Windows:

To access your Raspberry Pi's VPN, you need special software on Windows. You'll do this through software called OpenVPN:

1. Download the newest version of OpenVPN for your operating system from openvpn.net/index.php/open-source/downloads.html.

2. When the file is finished downloading, double-click it to launch the installer.

3. Launch the software by double-clicking the OpenVPN file that was just installed.

After you launch the software, you'll get some prompts to set it up. Move on to the "Setting Up Security Keys and Config Files" section to get the files you need here.

Mac:

On your Mac, you'll use software called Tunnelblick to access your VPN:

1. Download Tunnelblick from code.google.com/p/tunnelblick.

2. Double-click the DMG file you downloaded to open it.

3. Double-click the Tunnelblick.app icon to launch the installer.

4. When it's finished installing, navigate to **Applications > Tunnelblick**, and click it to launch the app.

When you first launch Tunnelblick, it'll ask you for some configuration files. You need to grab those from the Raspberry Pi.

 PI POINTER

You also can set up VPN on your smartphone or tablet. Look for OpenVPN clients in your smartphone's store to find the app to help you set it all up.

Setting Up Security Keys and Config Files

To use your VPN, you need to install the configuration files on your computer. These are the files you created earlier when you ran the program you made. These OpenVPN files are your keys. Think of this step as handing over keys to all your friends you want to let in.

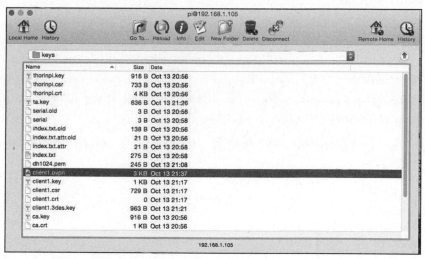

You'll need to copy your security keys for each computer that uses the VPN.

Windows:

On Windows, you need to connect to your Raspberry Pi with the WinSCP software:

1. Download WinSCP from winscp.net/eng/index.php.

2. Launch WinSCP. In the **Connect to:** box, type in your Raspberry Pi's internal IP address. You probably have this memorized by now.

3. Type in pi for the username.

4. Click the **Connect** button. When prompted, enter your password.

5. You're now connected to your Raspberry Pi. Navigate to the **/etc/openvpn/easy-rsa/keys/** folder, and find the OpenVPN file for the client. It should be called something like *client1.opvn*. Drag it to your desktop.

6. Double-click the **client1.opvn** file. This opens it in Tunnelblick and automatically sets it up for you.

Mac:

On a Mac, you need to connect to your Raspberry pi with Fugu SSH:

1. Download Fugu SSH from sourceforge.net/projects/fugussh.

2. Open the software. In the **Connect to:** box, type in your Raspberry Pi's internal IP address.

3. Type in pi for the username.

4. Click the **Connect** button. When prompted, enter your password.

5. You're now connected to your Raspberry Pi. Navigate to the **/etc/openvpn/easy-rsa/ keys/** folder, and find the OpenVPN file for the client. It should be called something like *client1.opvn*. Drag it to your desktop.

6. Double-click the **client1.opvn** file. This opens it in Tunnelblick and automatically sets it up for you.

Your personal computer now has the key to your VPN so it can access it.

 SOFTWARE SOLUTION

The nice thing about using this SSH software is it gives you access to your Raspberry Pi's file system. If you need to copy files from your primary computer over to your Raspberry Pi, or if you want to copy files from your Raspberry Pi to your computer, you can do so easily with this software.

Connecting to Your Pi VPN Remotely

Are you ready to use your VPN? You now can securely browse the web and also access files on your Raspberry Pi or home computer remotely over a secure connection. All your hard work is about to pay off because now that you're set up, this process is very easy—and will continue to be in the future.

Establishing a Connection

From here on out, connecting to your Raspberry Pi and using the VPN is just a couple clicks away. Whether you're at a coffee shop in Budapest or an airport Wi-Fi network in Buffalo, you'll always have a secure connection as long as your Raspberry Pi is powered up.

Windows:

1. Launch the OpenVPN Connect software, and click the **connect** *yourclientname* button.

2. Enter your password. You're now browsing on a secure connection.

Mac:

1. Launch Tunnelclick, and click the **Connect** *yourclientname* button.

2. Enter your password, and all your browsing will be secure.

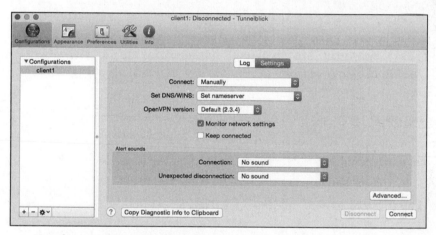

Now that everything is set up, connecting to your VPN remotely is just a click away.

Accessing Files and Folders Remotely

In addition to getting a secure connection for browsing the web, you can access all your files on your Raspberry Pi—and any other computer connected to your VPN—from anywhere. This means that even if you're away from home, you can access your home computer's files from your laptop.

As long as your VPN on your Raspberry Pi is on and you leave your home computer connected to it, you'll see the option to connect to your home computer remotely from your laptop in either Explorer on Windows or Finder on a Mac. Just click on your computer, and you're connected.

The Least You Need to Know

- Setting up a VPN gives you a secure connection to the internet from anywhere in the world.

- Your VPN client runs right on top of Raspbian, so you don't need to create a separate SD card for this project.

- VPNs encrypt all the data you transfer through them, so they're great when you need to connect to public Wi-Fi.

- The process of setting up your VPN is time-consuming and might seem a little difficult, but once you have it up, it's very easy to use.

Creating a Streaming Internet Radio

It seems like just about all of our electronic devices can play music these days, but it can be annoying to have to leave your phone plugged in to your stereo or a speaker just to play music around the house. With a Raspberry Pi, you can build an entire music streaming system that connects right to your stereo so you can use it as part of your home audio setup without dealing with any extra cables and wires, or lack of portability with your phone.

When you have your Raspberry Pi streaming radio set up, you can control your device from your smartphone or computer—no wires required. You'll do this using two pieces of software: Pianobar, a command line music player that uses Pandora, and Pi MusicBox, a bit of software that enables you to stream from services like Spotify, SoundCloud, and Google Music. You'll even be able to stream music from your phone to your Raspberry Pi if you want.

Once you get your software up and running, you'll also be able to connect a USB sound card for improved audio. The Raspberry Pi's audio output isn't that great, so adding in a sound card can really improve the quality. And when everything is working, nobody will be able to tell you're running such high-quality sound out of an inexpensive little computer you built yourself.

In This Chapter

- Handy music apps to use with your Raspberry Pi

- Streaming Pandora, Google Music, and more

- Making a remote control

- Selecting and setting up a USB sound card

In this chapter, you learn the setup process for both music players, connect everything to your home audio setup, and start playing music right away.

What Can a Pi-Powered Internet Radio Do?

Your Raspberry Pi–powered internet radio system can stream audio from many different online audio sources. You'll also be able to stream music from your other devices to your Raspberry Pi. You can control it from your computer, smartphone, or tablet.

The best part is that this is actually one of the easier-to-use Raspberry Pi projects. Just about anyone will be able to use it, regardless of their technical skill (except for navigating Pandora, which requires the command line).

Internet Radio in Home Theater Setups

The big appeal here is the ease with which you can connect your home theater to internet streaming services. Typically, you'd need to buy expensive accessories or plug your device directly into your stereo to do this. With the Raspberry Pi, however, you can control everything wirelessly, so you don't need to worry about buying a bunch of cables.

All you need to connect your Raspberry Pi to your home stereo is a single cable and a good set of speakers. From there, you'll be playing music wirelessly right away.

Support for Pandora, Spotify, Google Music, and Others

In this chapter, you're going to build a Raspberry Pi internet radio that supports many different services and features. Here's a breakdown of what you get:

- Spotify support
- Google Music support
- SoundCloud support
- Pandora support
- Subsonic support

- AirTunes/AirPlay support for playing music from your phone or tablet
- Last.fm scrobbling
- Podcast player
- MP3/OGG/FLAC/AAC player

 PI POINTER

If you haven't already, now's a good time to sign up for any or all of the preceding services. Most are free and only require an email address to sign up.

For this project, you'll need to have accounts set up for Pandora, Spotify, Google Music, SoundCloud, and Last.fm. With Spotify, you'll need a premium account ($9.99/month) before it will work on your Raspberry Pi, but free accounts on all the other services are just fine. Just be sure you have your usernames and passwords ready because, you'll need those during the setup process.

Installing Pi MusicBox

To build your Raspberry Pi music streaming device, you need two bits of software—Pi MusicBox and Pianobar. First, you'll set up Pi MusicBox.

Pi MusicBox is a Raspberry Pi operating system based on Raspbian. Like Raspbian, it works right out of the box so you shouldn't need to do much setup for your Wi-Fi adapter, USB sound card, or anything else. You'll just burn the image and start using it.

Pi MusicBox turns your Raspberry Pi into a server you can access from your phone, computer, or tablet. In fact, you don't even need to plug Pi MusicBox into a monitor or TV at any point. All you need to do is connect it to a set of speakers and start playing music.

Preparing Your SD Card for a Pi MusicBox Image

You'll install Pi MusicBox on your SD card, the same way you installed Raspbian and Raspbmc. Here's how:

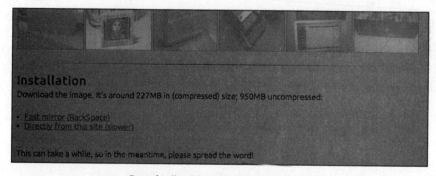

Downloading Pi MusicBox from this link.

1. Download the Pi MusicBox image from woutervanwijk.nl/pimusicbox/index.html.

2. Burn the image onto an SD card using the same method you used to burn Raspbian in Chapter 8. Just substitute the Pi MusicBox image in for the Raspbian one.

Now you have the image on your SD card, but you're not quite done yet. Keep the SD card in your computer because you're going to edit some settings.

PI POINTER

If you haven't noticed already, the installation process for most of these operating systems is the same. Once you've figured it out, it's a pretty simple procedure. In fact, it can be fun to experiment with different operating systems, if you have a few spare SD cards around.

Changing Your Pi MusicBox Settings

Pi MusicBox works a bit differently from Raspbian in how you change the settings. Instead of working with the command line to get everything set up, you use a text editor on your computer to add some login information so you can use Pi MusicBox easily. This actually makes things a lot easier to get set up.

Here's what to do:

1. When Pi MusicBox is on your SD card, double-click your card (it's now called Pi MusicBox) to open it in Explorer on your Windows PC or in Finder on your Mac.

2. Double-click the **Config** folder.

3. Find the **settings.ini** file, and double-click it to open it in your text editor. This is the settings file for Pi MusicBox, and you'll edit this text file to connect to your Wi-Fi network, enter passwords, and more.

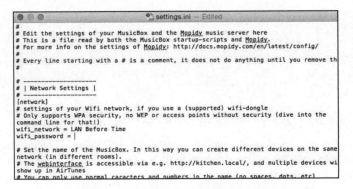

You can configure Pi MusicBox's settings in the settings.ini file.

4. The line that reads [network] is where you add your Wi-Fi network name and password. After **wifi_network =**, type in your network name, surrounded by apostrophes, and after **wifi_password =**, type in your network password, also surrounded by apostrophes. For example, **wifi_network = 'My Network'** and **wifi_password = 'Password'**. You'll need to use the apostrophes any time you enter a password. Also, this section is case sensitive, so be sure your network name and password are correct.

5. Find the line that reads `name =`, and type whatever name you want your Pi MusicBox to be called.

6. Find the line that reads `enable_ssh = false`. You want SSH on so you can install Pianobar later, so change this to read `# enable_ssh = true`.

7. Now enter in your username and password for any of the services you want to use. Find the **Spotify, Last.fm, SoundCloud, Google Music, Dirble, Subsonic, TuneIn Radio, Internet Archive**, and **SomaFM** sections, and add your username and password for the appropriate services. For example, in the Spotify section, put your username after `username =` and your password after `password =`. Be sure you put your responses between apostrophes like you did in step 4. And change the `enabled = false` section under each service to `enabled = true`.

8. Podcasts are set up a bit differently. You need to manually enter any podcast feeds you want to subscribe to. You can find these feeds on a podcast's website under the RSS or Subscribe section. They usually look something like this: *http://www.npr.org/rss/podcast.php?id=510019.* Just put each URL followed by a comma after the `feeds =` line in the **Podcast** section. For example, `http://www.npr.org/rss/podcast.php?id=510019,` `http://www.npr.org/rss/podcast.php?id=510253.` You can enter as many podcast feeds as you want.

9. Find the line that reads `resize_once = false`, and change it to `resize_once = true`. This resizes your SD card so the file system takes up the entire card.

10. When you're finished, save the document and exit. Then eject your SD card.

With that, Pi MusicBox is all set up. Now it's time to plug it in to your Raspberry Pi and begin listening to some tunes.

 PI POINTER

Don't worry if you don't have all this stuff set up right now. Pi MusicBox has a Settings panel you can come back to and make changes. I show you how to find it a little later in this chapter.

Connecting to External Audio

The one thing that's a little different with Pi MusicBox is that because it's all about music, you need to connect it to a set of speakers. You can do this with a 3.5mm to RCA cable. Just plug the 3.5mm jack into your Raspberry Pi and the RCA cables into your stereo. If your stereo system is more high tech, you can use an HDMI cable as an audio output.

When you're all set up for audio, plug your SD card into your Raspberry Pi and power it up.

Booting Pi MusicBox

Pi MusicBox doesn't actually require you to plug your Raspberry Pi into a monitor or TV to work, but it's helpful on the first boot just so you can see what's happening.

The first time you start Pi MusicBox can take a little while. It needs to set itself up, connect to your network, and expand the file system. So grab a cup of coffee, settle in, and watch it do its thing, addressing any problems that might come up. (Such as if you entered the wrong password for your Wi-Fi network. If this happened, you'll see that Pi MusicBox can't connect.)

Eventually, you'll see a login screen. You don't need to log in here.

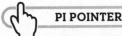

> **PI POINTER**
>
> You can run Pi MusicBox as a *headless machine,* which just means it's not connected to a monitor. Everything you need to do in Pi MusicBox is controlled through the web interface or SSH, so once it's set up, you can just plug in your Raspberry Pi and it'll be ready to use.

Using Pi MusicBox

When Pi MusicBox finishes its installation process, you can start using it right away. From here on out, you won't actually touch your Raspberry Pi. Rather, you'll do everything from your computer or smartphone's browser.

To log in to Pi MusicBox, you need to be on the same network as your Raspberry Pi. Then, point your computer or smartphone browser to musicbox.local. When you're greeted by the Pi MusicBox window, you're up and running.

The Pi MusicBox page is pretty self-explanatory, but let's go through the left-side sidebar so you know what everything means:

Setting up Pi MusicBox from the web interface is simple.

Now Playing: This takes you to the song or podcast that's currently playing.

Playlists: This leads you to any playlists you've created on any of the services you signed in with.

Browse: Here you can look through your music library by the services you've set up. Just click the service name, and you're taken to a page for that service, where you can get any songs you want.

Queue: This is your song queue. You can always play full albums, but if you want to queue up certain songs, click the three dots to the right of the track to get a menu where you can add it to your queue.

Search: You can search for any songs in your library here.

Radio: This is the radio function. You can load any radio stations you want by tracking down a URL of the station's stream and adding it here.

Fullscreen: This loads Pi MusicBox in full-screen mode.

Settings: This is your Settings panel. You can add new services here, change login information, and more. You also can toggle services on and off, change network information, or configure anything else you didn't do in the original settings.ini file. You also can add new URLs for podcasts here instead of editing the INI file. This makes things a lot easier when you want to extend your new Pi MusicBox a little.

System: You can shut down or reboot the system here.

Now it's time to start playing music. Find the track you want to play, click it, and you should hear it playing from your home audio's stereo.

Playing Music Remotely from Your Smartphone or Computer

In addition to being able to play music from a wide variety of online outlets, your Raspberry Pi can receive music from your smartphone or computer. This means you can select your Raspberry Pi as a speaker and play whatever music you have stored on your smartphone or computer as long as that device supports AirPlay.

This process varies depending on what music-playing software you're using, but as long as your device and your Raspberry Pi are on the same Wi-Fi network, you'll see an option for Pi MusicBox under the AirPlay icon. (The AirPlay icon is a square with a small triangle in the middle.) In iTunes, you'll find AirPlay next to the volume bar. On iOS, you can access it by pulling up the Control Center and selecting **Pi MusicBox** from the AirPlay area.

Once you're connected to your Raspberry Pi, all you need to do is select a song on your device and it'll start playing on your Raspberry Pi. You can change tracks, pick new songs, and even control the volume, all from your device.

Access AirPlay on your iPhone via the Control Center.

> **SOFTWARE SOLUTION**
>
> You can install AirPlay separately on any Raspberry Pi operating system with software called Shairport (lightweightdream.com). The nice thing about Pi MusicBox is that it's all set up from the start, so you don't have to do anything special to get it to work.

Installing Pianobar for Pandora

Pi MusicBox doesn't natively support the music-streaming service Pandora, but you can add it using software called Pianobar. Pianobar (6xq.net/projects/pianobar) is a command line–based music player. With it you don't get the fancy web interface Pi MusicBox has, but it works just as well.

You actually don't need Pi MusicBox to install Pianobar. If you only care about Pandora, you can install Pianobar on your Raspbian SD card if you want. In these instructions, however, I use Pi MusicBox.

The installation process can be tricky because Pianobar often has a bit of initial trouble on Raspbian for some reason. So you're going to download it directly from the source, compile the program on your own, and establish your own configuration settings. Don't be intimidated at the thought of this. I walk you through it, and you only need to run through this process once.

Downloading Pianobar to Your Pi

Because of Pianobar's initial hang-ups on the Raspberry Pi, you need to manually install it, alongside a few other bits of software, to get it working correctly. This is a little time-consuming, but it doesn't take that much actual effort.

Installing Pianobar to your Raspberry Pi takes a bit of command line work.

Here's what to do:

1. From the Terminal, log in to Pi Musicbox. The username is `root`, and the password is `musicbox` (unless you changed these).

2. In Terminal, type in `sudo apt-get update`, and press **Enter**.

3. Type in the following, and press **Enter**:

   ```
   sudo apt-get install git libao-dev libgcrypt11-dev libgnutls-dev
      libfaad-dev libmad0-dev libjson0-dev make pkg-config
   ```

   Type `Y` when prompted.

4. When that's finished, type in the following and press **Enter**:

   ```
   git clone https://github.com/FFmpeg/FFmpeg.git
   ```

   Then wait for FFmpeg to download. (FFmpeg is streaming software for your Raspberry Pi.)

5. Type in `apt-get install build-essential`, and press **Enter**. Again, wait for all this stuff to download.

6. Type in `cd FFmpeg`, and press **Enter**.

7. Type in `./configure`, and press **Enter**. This builds a configuration file for FFmpeg.

8. Type in `make clean`, and press **Enter**.

9. Type in make, and press **Enter**. This builds the FFmpeg file. It might take an upward of a couple hours to complete this, so feel free to walk away from your Raspberry Pi for a while.

10. When that's finished, type in sudo make install, and press **Enter**.

11. Follow that with cd .. to go back to the original root directory.

12. Now to download the newest version of Pianobar from GitHub, type in git clone https://github.com/PromyLOPh/pianobar.git, and press **Enter**.

13. When that's finished, type in cd pianobar, and press **Enter**.

14. Type in make clean, and press **Enter**.

15. Type in make, and press **Enter**. This compiles Pianobar into actual software you can use. It'll take a little while to complete.

16. Finally, type in sudo make install, and press **Enter**.

That's it for getting Pianobar downloaded and installed, but it's not quite the end of the process. You still need to make a few adjustments to get Pianobar set up and working properly.

> **PI POINTER**
>
> Pianobar isn't required, but it's certainly nice to have if you're a fan of Pandora. The installation process takes a chunk of time, so be sure you set aside a whole afternoon for it. It's not complicated at all, just time-consuming.

Setting Up Pianobar and Logging in to Pandora

As mentioned earlier, Pianobar takes a little effort to get working properly on the Raspberry Pi, and you need to make a few more adjustments in the configuration settings.

From the command line, here's what to do:

1. Type in pianobar, and press **Enter**.

2. Enter your Pandora username and password. If you don't have an account, point your computer's browser to pandora.com and create one.

3. Select the radio station you want to play from the list, and press **Enter**.

Pandora should start playing from your Raspberry Pi.

Remote Control via SSH or the Command Line

To control Pianobar remotely, you need to SSH into it from your computer. Remember setting up SSH on your home computer in Chapter 13? It works pretty much the same here, but changing Pi MusicBox's SSH setting is a little different:

1. When you're on the same network as your Raspberry Pi, point your computer's browser to musicbox.local.

2. Select the **Settings** option.

3. Scroll down to **Network**, and click it.

4. Toggle the **Enable SSH** box to **On**.

5. Click **Update Settings**.

This reboots your Raspberry Pi with SSH turned on. When it restarts, you'll be able to log in to your Raspberry Pi from a local computer. Now to set up SSH on your computer.

 ## Setting Up a Static IP Address and SSH

To effectively use SSH to log in to your Raspberry Pi, you need a static, or fixed, IP address so you can access your Raspberry Pi at the same address every time you turn it on. If you don't set up a static address, you'll have to hunt for its new IP address every single time.

Navigate to the Pi MusicBox command line on your Raspberry Pi, and be sure your Raspberry Pi is connected to the internet. Here's what to do:

1. Type `ifconfig`, and press **Enter**.

2. Look for the section titled **eth0** if you're connected to Ethernet or **wlan0** if you're connected to Wi-Fi.

3. Write down the numbers listed after **inet addr** (you'll use this for the "address" section in step 8), **Bcast** (for the broadcast section in step 8), and **Mask** (for the netmask section in step 8).

4. Type in `netstat -nr`, and press **Enter**.

5. Write down the numbers listed under **Gateway Address** (for the gateway section in step 8) and **Destination Address** (for the network section in step 8).

6. Type in `sudo nano /etc/network/interfaces`, and press **Enter**.

7. Look for the line that reads **iface eth0 inet dhcp**, and edit it to `iface eth0 inet static`.

8. Right below that line, type in the following, substituting the numbers you wrote down in steps 3 and 5 for the x's:

```
address xxx.xxx.x.xx
netmask xxx.xxx.xxx.x
network xxx.xxx.x.xx
broadcast xxx.xxx.x.xx
gateway xxx.xxx.x.xx
```

9. Press **Ctrl+X** to exit and save your changes.

10. Reboot your network settings. Type in `sudo /etc/init.d/networking restart`, and press **Enter**.

Now your Raspberry Pi has a static IP address and will always be accessible at the same place.

PI POINTER

The set-up process for a static IP address is the same across all operating systems, so once you get the hang of it, you'll be able to do it for others easily. It's handy when you need to access your Raspberry Pi remotely.

Setting Up SSH

Your next step is to set up SSH on your computer. (Or you can use an SSH program on your smartphone or tablet.)

Windows:

On a Windows PC, you need to download some software before you can SSH into your Raspberry Pi. Here's how:

1. Head to www.chiark.greenend.org.uk/~sgtatham/putty/download.html and download **PuTTY**.

2. When it's downloaded, open **putty.exe**.

3. Enter your Raspberry Pi's IP address under **Host Name**.

4. Tap **Enter** to open a command line.

5. Enter your Raspberry Pi's username and password.

Now, you're connected to your Raspberry Pi on Windows, and you can control your Raspberry Pi just like you would if you were in front of it. This also means you can wirelessly control Pianobar.

Mac:

If you own a Mac, you already have SSH built in to your computer and you can access your Raspberry Pi using the Terminal app. Here's how:

1. Launch Terminal on your Mac from **Applications > Utilities > Terminal**.

2. Type in ssh pi@*yourIPaddress*, replacing *yourIPaddress* with the static address you established earlier. For example, ssh pi@192.168.1.105.

3. When prompted for your Raspberry Pi's password, type in your password and press **Enter**.

That's it. You can now control your Raspberry Pi from Terminal on your Mac just like you would from the command line on the Raspberry Pi itself and navigate Pianobar wirelessly.

Keyboard Controls for Pianobar

Using Pianobar to play Pandora radio isn't the most intuitive thing in the world, but you have lots of keyboard shortcuts to work with. With Pianobar running, you can do whatever you need by pressing these keys:

> **+:** Thumbs up the current song.
>
> **−:** Thumbs down the current song.
>
> **n:** Skips to the next song.
>
> **e:** Explains why the current song is playing.
>
> **g:** Adds a genre station.
>
> **c:** Creates a new station.
>
> **r:** Renames the current station.
>
> **p:** Pauses the radio.
>
> **d:** Deletes the current station.
>
> **q:** Quits Pianobar.

Controlling Pianobar from the command line is easier than it sounds.

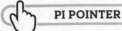

PI POINTER

If you forget the keyboard controls at any point, remember that you can ask Linux for a manual. Type in man pianobar at the command line to get the full list of shortcuts.

Adding Better-Quality Sound with a USB Sound Card

The Raspberry Pi's sound output is okay, but you can improve it significantly with a USB sound card. A USB sound card works just like a USB Wi-Fi adapter, but instead of connecting your Raspberry Pi to a wireless network, it processes audio and sends out a high-quality signal to your speaker.

A USB sound card improves the quality of your Raspberry Pi's sound output.

It's best to go through the preceding tutorials, listen to your music, and then decide if you're happy with it or not. Music quality is a little different for everyone, so it's totally possible that you'll be fine with the quality of music you hear from your Raspberry Pi.

If you want something better to listen to, get a USB sound card.

Choosing the Right USB Sound Card

Nearly any USB sound card should work with Pi MusicBox. Remember, it's based on Raspbian so it also comes with Raspbian's accessory support and already contains the software needed to use the USB sound card.

Sound cards range in price from about $10 to $50, but even the inexpensive models will improve the audio quality quite a bit.

For an up-to-date list of compatible sound cards, head to elinux.org/RPi_VerifiedPeripherals#USB_Sound_Cards.

Setting Up and Installing a USB Sound Card

This will be easy. All you need to do to install your USB sound card is plug it into your Raspberry Pi's USB port. Then plug in a 3.5mm audio cable to the sound card and into your home stereo. When that's hooked up, turn on your Raspberry Pi. The USB sound card automatically does the rest, and you should notice a pleasant increase in the sound quality.

The Least You Need to Know

- Turning your Raspberry Pi into a specialized music streaming device requires an operating system called Pi Musicbox.

- You can stream music from a variety of online services, including Pandora, Spotify, Google Music, and more.

- Pandora setup requires an extra bit of work, but after that, you'll be able to play any Pandora station you want.

- Transforming your Raspberry Pi into a streaming radio enables you to wirelessly control your Raspberry Pi from your computer, smartphone, or tablet.

Building a Private Minecraft Server

Minecraft is one of the most popular games of the last several years. It's available on PC and Mac, Android and iOS, Xbox, PlayStation, and countless other devices. Your Raspberry Pi makes an excellent Minecraft server you and your friends can access to build your own world. And with your Raspberry Pi, you can leave your server running all day without incurring a lot of electricity costs.

If you've already installed Raspbian on your Raspberry Pi, you've probably noticed that Minecraft is usually included with it, but this is a little different. Instead of just playing Minecraft on your Raspberry Pi, in this chapter, you turn your Raspberry Pi into a *server*. This means anyone on your network can access and play in your Minecraft world, which could lead to some great collaboration.

The version of Minecraft included with Raspbian is just a single-player game. You can't connect and play online. So instead, you need to purchase a copy of Minecraft for your computer to use this server. If you don't already have it, you can buy it from minecraft.net.

In This Chapter

- Creating a Minecraft server on your Raspberry Pi

- Working with Java

- Configuring your Minecraft server settings

- Accessing your server remotely

In this chapter, you take a look at Minecraft as a game, learn a little about servers, and set up your own private Minecraft server. In addition, you discover how to customize your Minecraft world.

What You Get with a Minecraft Server

A Minecraft server is a little different from a regular game of Minecraft. You can customize the settings in a number of ways to make it work however you want, and you can play with a select group of friends, which makes world-building a much more collaborative effort.

First off though, let's talk about what Minecraft really is.

 PI POINTER

Your Raspberry Pi isn't the only device that can run a Minecraft server. Any computer with Minecraft installed can do it. What makes the Raspberry Pi nice is the fact that you can just plug it in and leave it running all the time and it won't consume a lot of power. Likewise, if you have another personal computer, it doesn't take up memory running in the background.

Getting to Know Minecraft

Minecraft is an open-world sandbox game originally created by developer Markus "Notch" Persson. More recently, it's been developed and published by the company he founded, Mojang.

Minecraft is a world you can explore and make your own.

The original version of Minecraft was released as a public alpha version in 2009. Originally, the game was simply a playground where players could build and craft items. Over time, the game was updated with new features, including a survival mode where players are tasked with staying alive by building houses and gathering resources.

Minecraft was moved out of alpha and into beta in 2011. By that time, 1 million copies had sold. As of April 29, 2014, Minecraft had sold 54 million copies across all its platforms with more than 100 million registered users. It's still in development today and is available on Windows, Mac, Linux, Raspberry Pi, Xbox 360, PS3, Vita, PS4, Xbox One, Android, and iOS.

Minecraft is now best known as an open-world game that allows players to do whatever they want. There are no specific goals or game elements. Instead, the core gameplay revolves around breaking blocks and placing them to build structures. The game looks decidedly old, with a blocky, 1980s look.

The Minecraft world itself is *procedurally generated;* it's created on the fly, at random, each time you launch a new game. So the world is a little different every time you play. Amazingly, the world itself is also nearly infinite because it's generated by the computer as you reach the edge of the map.

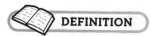 **DEFINITION**

> **Procedurally generated** means the world map is randomly generated with an algorithm each time you start a new world. Essentially, there's no game designer who creates the world; rather, it's created by the computer. Nearly infinite world maps can be created. Every world is a little different, and no two games are the same.

The Minecraft world consists of all types of terrains, including plains, forests, caves, mountains, and bodies of water. You also can come across everything from jungles to snowfields.

As you explore, you encounter all kinds of animals, villagers, and enemies, such as zombies, skeletons, and spiders. One of the most popular of the enemies is the Creeper, which sneaks up on you and tries to explode.

Minecraft has four basic game modes: Survival, Creative, Adventure, and Multiplayer. In Survival mode, you're tasked with staying alive as long as possible as enemies attempt to kill you. You can do this by building a shelter to keep you safe as well as seeking out resources to craft weapons, better shelters, and more.

Creative mode is more about building a world. Unlike Survival mode, you instantly have access to everything you need in Creative mode to build whatever you want. You can even fly around the map to anywhere you want without worrying about enemies.

Adventure mode works more like a traditional game where you're trying to achieve a goal. The goals are defined by other users just like you.

Multiplayer mode is what you'll be using with your Raspberry Pi. As the name implies, it's all about playing with other people. With multiplayer mode, people can access your server with your predefined rules and play Minecraft together in any mode.

The appeal of Minecraft is hard to pin down because so much depends on the player. Some people love Survival mode, while plenty of others just enjoy building their worlds. The beauty of running your own server means you'll be able to customize your game however you like.

Minecraft Versus a Server

Running your own Minecraft server comes with some caveats. The main difference between your own server and running Minecraft on your computer is that you'll be able to play with anyone you want. You and the other players can run around the world together, fight monsters in tandem, or just build up the world as a team.

With your own server, everything you and your friends do is recorded and saved on the server. As long as your Raspberry Pi is powered on, you and your friends can access the server.

The best part about running your own server is the customization options. You can restrict the size of the world, get rid of enemies, or change the game in countless other ways. You can determine what gains experience points, change the weather, or instantly create any blocks you need in a particular moment.

Otherwise, Minecraft on your server is pretty much the same as Minecraft on your own.

Installing Raspbian

For this lesson, you're going to install Minecraft on your Raspbian SD card. If you haven't made one, refer to Chapter 8 for instructions.

Technically, you can use pretty much any Linux distribution for this, but Raspbian makes things a little easier. You do need to change some of Raspbian's main settings though. You're going to overclock your Raspberry Pi to make it a bit faster, change the memory configuration so the device can use more of its CPU power, and enable SSH so you can remotely log in to your Raspberry Pi from your home computer. Because this is a server, there's no real reason to have your Raspberry Pi connected to a TV or monitor.

Configuring Raspbian with Optimal Minecraft Settings

Minecraft is a bit of a resource hog, so you'll want to give your Raspberry Pi all the power you can for it to work well. It's not recommended that you try this on Models A+, B, or B+. The extra RAM in the Model 2 (1GB versus the Model A+'s 256MB and Models B and B+'s 512MB) make it a much better option for Minecraft.

Here's what you need to do to get your Raspberry Pi ready:

1. Load the Raspbian configuration file by pulling up the command line. Type in `sudo raspi-config`, and press **Enter**.

2. In raspi-config, select **Overclock**. Choose the last option, **Warp5 1000MHz ARM, 500MHz core, 600MHz SDRAM, 6 overvolt**, and press **Enter**. This overclocks your Raspberry Pi to take full advantage of the processor and make it fast enough to run your server. You'll get some warnings about this when you enable it, but don't worry. Your device will be safe.

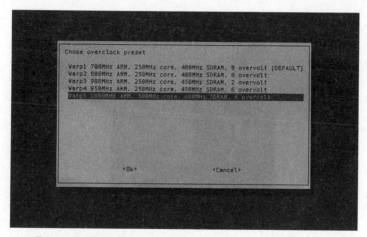

For your Minecraft server, you need to overclock your Raspberry Pi.

3. Back at the main raspi-config menu, select the **Enable Boot to Desktop/Scratch** option, select **Console Text console**, and press **Enter**.

4. At the main raspi-config menu again, select **Advanced Options** and press **Enter**.

5. Select **SSH**, and enable it. This gives you remote access to your Raspberry Pi.

6. Load **Advanced Options** again, and select **Memory Split**. Change the memory on the GPU to **16MB**. You do this because your Minecraft server runs without a graphical user interface, and you don't need the GPU to have that much memory.

7. Back in **Advanced Options**, select **Hostname** and press **Enter**.

8. Change the hostname to whatever you want. If you want people to be able to find it easily, *Minecraft* is a good name.

9. Scroll down to the bottom of the screen, select **Finish**, and press **Enter**.

With that, your Raspberry Pi will reboot and you can move on to getting Minecraft set up and working.

 PI POINTER

Overclocking your Raspberry Pi this much can cause some instability. If you have troubles with your Raspberry Pi, drop down the overclocking a bit. Overclocking is officially supported by the Raspberry Pi Foundation, so it won't void your warranty. And the worst-case scenario is that your SD card won't work anymore. If that happens, you'll just need to remake the Raspbian image.

Setting Up SSH

You're going to run your Raspberry Pi in headless mode, or without a monitor. Therefore, it's best to set up and use SSH so you can control your Raspberry Pi from your personal computer. This step is totally optional, if you want to use your keyboard, mouse, and monitor on your Pi that's fine, but this makes things a little easier.

Windows:

On Windows, you need to download some software before you can SSH into your Raspberry Pi:

1. Head to www.chiark.greenend.org.uk/~sgtatham/putty/download.html and download PuTTY.

2. Once it's downloaded, open **putty.exe**.

3. Enter your Raspberry Pi's IP address under **Host Name**.

4. Tap **Enter** to open a command line.

5. Enter your Raspberry Pi's username and password, and press **Enter**.

Now, your Windows computer is connected to your Raspberry Pi. You can control your Raspberry Pi from the command line just as if you were sitting in front of it.

Mac:

If you own a Mac, you already have SSH built into your computer and you can access your Raspberry Pi using the Terminal app. Here's what to do:

1. Launch Terminal on your Mac from **Applications > Utilities > Terminal**.

2. Type in `ssh pi@yourIPaddress`, replacing *yourIPaddress* with the IP address of your Raspberry Pi. For example, `ssh pi@192.168.1.105`.

3. When prompted for your Raspberry Pi password, type it in and press **Enter**.

That's it. You can now control your Raspberry Pi from Terminal on your Mac just like you would from the command line on the Raspberry Pi itself.

Installing Java

In order for Minecraft to work, you need the newest version of *Java* installed on your Raspberry Pi. As is the case with most things on the Raspberry Pi, Java is free and open source.

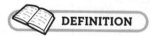

DEFINITION

Java is the programming language Minecraft was written in, and it's universal across a variety of platforms. Java was originally released in 1995 by Sun Microsystems. Because Java is made to run on every platform imaginable, its original promise was to allow programmers to "Write once, run anywhere."

Why You Need Java

Java isn't always installed on computers out of the box. Typically, most operating systems avoid installing Java because it's often a security risk. Java wasn't optimized to work on the Raspberry Pi at first either, but now a version of Java is built specifically for ARM computers and works terrifically on the Raspberry Pi.

The reason you need it is simple: Minecraft was coded in Java and requires Java to run. Java is a programming language that's compatible on a ton of different systems, so it's a good way to develop for different platforms without learning an entirely new type of coding.

In this case, Java was used simply because that's the language Markus Persson knew best. Because of this, Minecraft has been built on Java since the alpha was first launched. When you play Minecraft on your computer or game console, you probably don't even realize this, but when you're running your own server you'll have to launch it using a specific Java command, so you'll become familiar with it pretty quickly.

Downloading and Installing Java

Installing Java is a pretty straightforward process. Many distributions of Linux already have it, but it's a good practice to check and be sure you have the most recent version before you proceed.

Here's what to do:

1. At the command line, type in `sudo apt-get install oracle-java7-jdk`. This downloads and installs the most recent version of Java for the Raspberry Pi.

The Java install will take a bit of time, so be prepared to wait.

2. Type in `java -version`, and press **Enter** to ensure the newest version of Java was installed.

With that, Java is now installed on your Raspberry Pi.

Installing and Setting Up the Minecraft Server

Let's download and set up your Minecraft server. First, you're going to download the server files directly from the Minecraft site.

Installing the Minecraft Server Files

If you're not already there, head back to the command line:

1. Type in `cd /MCServer`, and press **Enter**.

2. Type in `sudo wget https://s3.amazonaws.com/Minecraft.Download/versions/1.8/minecraft_server.1.8.jar`, and press **Enter**.

3. Wait for the file to download.

4. You'll need to agree to the terms of service. Type in `sudo nano eula.txt`, and press **Enter**.

5. Scroll down to **eula=false**, and change it to `eula=true`.

6. Press **Ctrl+X** to save the file and exit.

Minecraft is updated fairly often, so if the link in step 2 doesn't work, head to minecraft.net/ download and look for the link in the Multiplayer Server section.

That's it for the installation of the server. It's time to launch it.

PI POINTER

As of this writing, the official Minecraft server files are the only ones available. However, until recently, another version called Spigot was available specifically for the Raspberry Pi. Spigot was taken offline due to some copyright violations, but if those are worked out and it's re-released, it's a good alternative to the official Minecraft files. Check at spigotmc.org to see if it's available. If you want to use Spigot, the instructions throughout this chapter are the same with the exception of from where you download the file.

Starting and Stopping Your Server

Because your server is open to the world, you don't want to leave it on all the time. When you and your friends aren't using it, it's best you turn it off.

You'll start and stop your Minecraft server from the command line. The process is pretty straightforward:

1. To start the server, type in `sudo java -Xms256M -Xmx496M -jar minecraft_server.1.8.jar nogui`.

2. Press **Enter**.

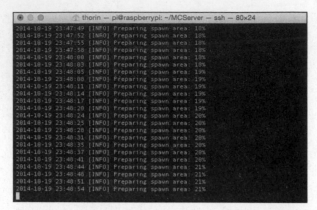

Starting the server works just like starting any other program,
but the screen is packed with information about the server itself.

It'll take a long time to get started, so sit back and let it do its work. This is telling Java to open the Minecraft server file with no graphical user interface, keeping it nice and lightweight. The Xms and Xmx commands are for your memory distribution. You're assigning RAM and CPU speed to your Minecraft server so it can run fast enough.

Here's how to stop the server:

1. At the command line, type `stop`.

2. Press **Enter**.

With that, you server is running. You've also learned how to launch any other Java program you might come across in your Raspberry Pi adventures.

Accessing Your Minecraft Server from Your Computer

Now you need to load your server on your copy of Minecraft. Here's how:

1. Open Minecraft on your computer, and be sure you're connected to the same Wi-Fi network as your Raspberry Pi.

2. Click **Multiplayer**.

3. Look for your server name in the list, click it, and click **Join Server**.

Find your Minecraft server on the list of available servers. It should be the only one on your network.

You're now ready to play around in your private Minecraft world. It might be a little clunky right now, so it's worth adjusting some of the settings to get it running smoothly.

 PI POINTER

As long as people are on your home network, they'll be able to connect to your Minecraft server as easily as this. If they have trouble, they can click the **Direct Connect** button and type in your Raspberry Pi's IP address to access the server directly.

 ## Changing Your Server's Settings

The best part of running your own Minecraft server is that you can customize the settings. You can change when it gets dark, if animals are on the map, and so much more. You do this by editing the Properties file.

Here's what to do:

1. At the command line, type in `sudo nano server.properties` and press **Enter**.

2. Here, you'll find all the various server settings. I've changed a few settings to help it run better on the Pi, so make yours match the following:

```
#Minecraft server properties #(File modification datestamp)
op-permission-level=4
allow-nether=false
level-name=world
enable-query=false
allow-flight=false
announce-player-achievements=true
server-port=25565
level-type=DEFAULT
enable-rcon=false
force-gamemode=false
max-build-height=256
spawn-npcs=true
white-list=true
spawn-animals=true
hardcore=false
snooper-enabled=true
online-mode=true
pvp=true
difficulty=1
enable-command-block=false
player-idle-timeout=0
gamemode=0
max-players=10
spawn-monsters=true
generate-structures=true
view-distance=5
spawn-protection=16
motd=Pi server
```

3. When you're finished editing the file, tap **Ctrl+X** to save and exit the file.

You can play with the settings as you like, and once you get into running your own Minecraft server, you'll likely want to alter a few settings. Most are pretty self-explanatory, but you can find a specific explanation for each line on the Minecraft Wiki page at minecraft.gamepedia.com/Server.properties.

Setting Your Server to Start on Boot

If you're not using your Raspberry Pi for anything other than a Minecraft server, you might want to have it launch automatically each time you boot up. This is optional, of course, so only work through this step if you're interested in running only your Minecraft server on your Raspberry Pi. You can set this up in many different ways, but you're going to use a service called Crontab.

Here's what to do:

1. At the command line, type in `sudo crontab -e`, and press **Enter**.

2. Add the line `@reboot sudo java -Xms256M -Xmx496M -jar minecraft_server.1.8.jar nogui`.

3. Press **Ctrl+X** to exit and save the file.

Now your Minecraft server will automatically start when you boot your Raspberry Pi. If you want to stop this behavior, just follow these steps and remove the `@reboot sudo java -Xms256M -Xmx496M -jar minecraft_server.1.8.jar nogui` command.

PI POINTER

> If you're using your Raspberry Pi for anything other than a server, you probably don't want to launch it automatically on boot. Your Minecraft server takes a ton of resources to work, so you likely won't be able to do much else on it.

Moderating Your Server

Running your own server isn't just about playing Minecraft; it's also about playing with your friends. To get the best experience, assign yourself *operator status*. Operator status gives you moderation capabilities so you can ban players, access server commands, and move around the map quickly.

Here's what to do:

1. At the command line, type in `cd MCServer`, and press **Enter**.

2. Type in `sudo nano ops.txt`, and press **Enter**.

3. Add your Minecraft username to the TXT file, and press **Ctrl+X** to exit and save the file.

You can do your moderator tasks by launching the Minecraft chat window. To launch the window, press /. Here, you can enter commands to trigger actions in Minecraft, much like you do from the command line.

As a moderator on your Minecraft server, you can do all kinds of cool things.

There are a ton of commands available, but here are some of the most useful:

Giving achievements: You can give players achievements with the `achievement` command. For example, you can type in `achievement give achievement.overkill` *username* to give someone named *username* the overkill achievement. Replace `give` with `take` to remove an achievement.

Rewarding players: Want to reward someone for their hard work? You can grant them experience points. Type in `xp amount` *username* to reward them. For example, `xp 5000` *username* gives the player *username* 5,000 points.

Giving items: To give a user an item, use the `give` command in place of `clear`. If you're busy building a world and need to give a player a specific item, type in `give` *username itemname* `amount`. For example, you could type in `give` *username* `minecraft:planks 40`.

Removing inventory: Removing items from a player's inventory is also possible. You just need to use the `clear` command. For example, if you want to remove everything from someone's inventory, type in `clear` *username*. If you'd prefer to remove a single item, type in `clear` *username* `minecraft:`*itemname*.

Banning players: You can completely ban players from being allowed on your server if they're not behaving. Type in `ban` *username* to ban someone with the name *username*. If you need a refresher on who you've banned, type in `banlist players` at any point.

Kick players off your server: If someone's causing you grief, you can easily kick them off of your server with the `kick` command. Just type in `kick` *username* to remove them. Unlike banning, this is a temporary suspension.

Changing game mode: You can change the default game mode for your server very easily. Type in `defaultgamemode` followed by the game mode name—`survival`, `creative`, `adventure`, or `spectator`. For example, to set the game mode to survival, type in `defaultgamemode survival`.

Adjusting difficulty levels: You can change the difficulty of Minecraft on your server very easily with the `difficult` command. Just type in `difficult` followed by the level you want—`peaceful`, `easy`, `normal`, or `hard`.

Changing the weather: Not a fan of the current weather on your server? Type in `toggledownfall` to change it. If it's raining or snowing, it'll stop. If it's a clear day, it'll start to rain or snow. Likewise, you can set the weather directly with the `weather` command. Type in `weather` followed by either `clear`, `rain`, or `thunder`, and follow that with the duration you want it to last in seconds. For example, `weather thunder 60` would make it thunder for 1 minute.

Debugging your server: If you're having issues on the server, you can start a debug mode to get more information. Type in `debug start` to load the debug menu. You can stop the debugging with `debug stop`.

Removing status effects: If someone on your server has some nasty status effects and needs your help, you can assist with the `effect` command. Type in `effect _username_ clear` to remove status effects from any player. Likewise, you can give an effect by typing in `effect _username_ effectname`.

Checking who's playing: If you need to quickly see who is on the server at any point, type in `list` to see everyone who's connected.

Saving: By default, your server is saving its state every few minutes, but you can manually save them as well. Type in `save-all` to save the server files to the disk manually.

That's just a few of the more useful tools you'll use, but there are tons more. At any point, type in `help` to get a list of every command available to you.

 PI POINTER

> Moderating your server might seem like a lot of work, but it's actually the best part about running your own server. You control who has access, what they get, and how they play. Think of it like being your own game designer.

Accessing Your Server Remotely

As it stands now, your Minecraft server is only accessible by people on your Wi-Fi network. That's great, but if you want to play with friends who live out of town, you'll need to do a little more work. Specifically, you'll need to set up port forwarding on your home router.

Every router works a little differently, so I can't give you an exact guide on how to set up your specific router, but you can usually find your router's manual online if you don't have one.

The process usually goes something like this:

1. Connect to your home router and log in. (Remember, your router's address is usually something like 192.168.1.1.)

2. Find the port forwarding section. It's usually listed under a tab titled **NAT/QoS** or **Services**.

3. Click the **Add** button to create a new port forward.

4. Type the name Minecraft into the **Application**, **Label**, or **Name** section.

5. Select **TCP/UDP** under **Protocol.**

6. Under **External Port** (sometimes also called **Redirect Port**), type in 25565.

7. Under **Internal IP Address**, type in your Raspberry Pi's IP address. If you don't know it, head back to your device, type in ifconfig, and look for the number listed after **inet address**.

8. To access your server remotely, you'll need to figure out your computer's public IP address. Head to yougetsignal.com/tools/open-ports and you'll see your IP address. It should be a number that reads something like **24.56.65.205**. For players to access your server, they'll need to add this number followed by the port to their Minecraft game. For example, 24.56.65.205:25565.

You'll now be able to access your server from anywhere, provided it's turned on. As always, be careful with this. You're giving people access to your home network this way, and although they should only be able to use it to play Minecraft with you, be cautious about who you give it to.

The Least You Need to Know

- You can create a private Minecraft server for you and your friends fairly easily.

- Setting up your own Minecraft server gives you full control over how it works and who plays.

- You can get your server set up and working on any copy of Raspbian you already have on an SD card.

- You can access your server from any computer with an internet connection.

Setting Up a Home Surveillance System

Even at the low end, a home surveillance camera typically runs around $1,000—and that's just for a simple camera you can access remotely via the internet. With the Raspberry Pi, however, you can build a similar system for a little over $100.

In this chapter, you learn how to turn your Raspberry Pi into a camera system you can monitor locally, on your home computer, or remotely, online. You'll also set it up so you get an email notification anytime the camera senses movement, which makes it possible to use a DIY security system to protect your home.

For this project, you need to pick up a few extra parts. You need a camera (about $29) and a housing for the camera (about $10). You also need a set of standard gear for your Raspberry Pi, like a power supply, a SD card, and a Wi-Fi adapter.

In This Chapter

- Creating a Raspberry Pi-powered home surveillance system

- Choosing the best camera housing

- Setting up a motion detector

- Accessing your system remotely

Using the official Raspberry Pi Camera Module, which hooks right into your Raspberry Pi without any special equipment or skill, is quick and easy. Even the housing is simple enough that you don't need to worry too much about any extra skills required to put it all together. For the overall setup, you'll be using a lot of skills you've already learned in previous chapters, including installing Raspbian, hooking up a Wi-Fi adapter, and downloading other software.

By the end of this chapter, you'll have a pretty nice little home security camera you built yourself from scratch.

What a Raspberry Pi Surveillance System Can Do

At a glance, the Raspberry Pi doesn't look like much of a security system, but you'll be surprised at what you can do with it and a few extra parts. When you finish this project, you'll have a camera you can mount outside your home or office, within range of your Wi-Fi network, that records video when it senses movement. You'll also be able to access a live stream remotely or retrieve any saved video later. And you're going to tuck the Raspberry Pi and the camera inside a fake camera housing, so the whole thing will look legit to anyone who comes across it.

If you're using a Raspberry Pi Model B, B+, or 2, you'll get HD video. If you're on the Model A+, you'll have SD video, but it's still perfectly capable for this project.

 HARDWARE HELPER

The Raspberry Pi Foundation released the Raspberry Pi Camera Module in 2013. It's a 5-megapixel camera that's pretty simple, but it gets the job done. You won't be able to add filters, zoom in or out, or change lenses, but as a point-and-shoot camera, it works well.

This isn't a full-blown security system by any means, but it can give you peace of mind that your house is being monitored when you're away—at a fraction of the cost. Plus, you have full control of the setup process, so you can alter any settings you want.

What You Need

As mentioned, to complete this project, you need a few more components beyond the usual stuff necessary to operate your Raspberry Pi.

Be sure you have an extra SD card, a power supply, and a Wi-Fi adapter. And because you'll be storing HD video on the SD card, consider getting a card that's at least 32GB in size.

You'll need to get a few other parts. Let's take a closer look at exactly what you'll want to pick up before you start this project:

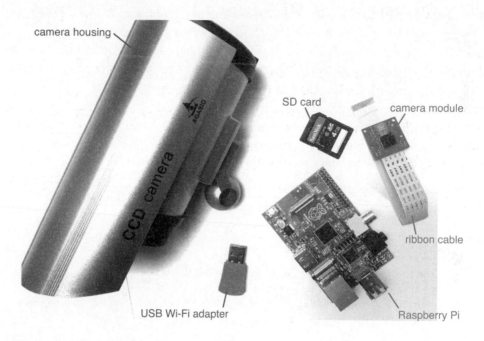

Raspberry Pi: Model B, B+, or 2 is recommended if you want to record HD video, but the Model A+ works if you don't mind SD. Also pick up a power supply if you don't already have one.

Camera module: The Raspberry Pi Camera Module is a custom camera made specifically for the Raspberry Pi by the Raspberry Pi Foundation. It attaches to the Raspberry Pi via a ribbon cable that connects to the top of the Raspberry Pi. The board itself is actually pretty tiny. It's about 25 by 20 millimeters and weighs only 3 grams. The camera is a 5-megapixel camera that's capable of taking still images at 2592×1944, 1080p video, 720p video, and 640×480 video. The ribbon cable only transmits pixel data, so it's surprisingly fast. It costs $29.95 as of this writing.

HARDWARE HELPER

The camera module comes in two variations—the normal version that shoots regular video, and the Pi NoIR, which can record in low light using infrared. The setup process for both cameras is the same, so go with whichever one you think is best for your needs.

Camera housing: You'll also need to purchase a housing for your camera system. Perhaps surprisingly, there's a large market of dummy security cameras, and many are less than $10. These camera housings are made to look like a real security camera, but they're hollow inside with no camera or other electronics inside—ideal for housing your Raspberry Pi and camera module. Find one that can fit your specific model of Raspberry Pi inside. You should be able to purchase a camera housing at a department store near you or online. For this project, I used one from UniquExceptional I purchased from Amazon for $8 (amazon.com/gp/product/B004D8NZ52).

SD card: Your SD card is not only going to store Raspbian for this project; it's also going to store the video you record on your camera, so the bigger the better. Get at least a class 10 32GB SD card for this project; you can go up to 128GB if you want. (If you're not sure an SD card is compatible, you can check it at elinux.org/RPi_SD_cards.)

That's it for the extra stuff you'll need. Depending on the size of your housing, you might also want to mount your Raspberry Pi inside the camera housing more securely, so be sure you have hook-and-loop tape or a similar adhesive to do that.

Camera Module Sources

Like the Raspberry Pi, it's best to purchase your Raspberry Pi Camera Module from a reputable seller. Its list price is $29.95 as of this writing, so don't spend more than that.

If you can, it's best to buy a housing from a store local to you. That way, you can bring your Raspberry Pi into the store and eyeball it to be sure it'll fit inside the housing. This isn't required, of course, but it does help ensure you don't waste $10 on housing that's too small.

If you're having trouble tracking down a housing locally, here are a few online stores you can try:

Adafruit: Adafruit (adafruit.com) typically has the camera module in stock and is a great resource for all things Raspberry Pi–related, including the camera. You can order it from adafruit.com/product/1367.

SparkFun: SparkFun (sparkfun.com) is an electronics and hardware distributor that sells all kinds of fun stuff, including several Raspberry Pi accessories. You can order the camera module from sparkfun.com/products/11868.

MCM Electronics: MCM Electronics (mcmelectronics.com) is one of the official distributors of the Raspberry Pi so it should come as no surprise it also carries the camera. Find it at mcmelectronics.com/product/28-17733.

With those options, you should have no problem tracking down a Raspberry Pi Camera Module.

 PI POINTER

> Be sure the housing you purchase is capable of being mounted to a wall or the side of a building. If you're planning on using it outdoors, it's good to check that it's listed for outdoor use. That might not mean it's waterproof, but because it's plastic, it should be fine. That said, many cases are cheap plastic, so don't expect them to hold up under extreme weather conditions.

Storage Considerations

The Raspberry Pi's hard drive is just an SD card, so you're limited to the space supported on a card for video storage. Fortunately, you have a few different options for dealing with this.

As one option, you can select a smaller video size during the setup process. If you shoot in SD, your videos will take up less space on your SD card and so you have room for more videos. You also can get a bigger SD card, but even that will fill up fast if you're not deleting the camera's footage daily or transferring it to another drive.

Provided you have another computer that's connected to the same Wi-Fi network as your Raspberry Pi, you can set up a system to automatically dump the security video onto your personal computer. I explain how in this chapter.

Video Limitations

It's also worth noting that the HD video itself isn't perfect. At 1080p, you only get a maximum of 30 frames per second, which is pretty slow for a security camera but should be fine for catching any intruders in your house. You can bump that up to 60 frames per second if you drop the video quality down to 720p. Which you use is really up to you. If you want a truly high-quality HD stream, use the 1080p video.

Recording at this higher quality, however, takes up a lot of space. A 1-hour video recorded at 1080p at 60 fps takes up about 11GB of space—far too much for just an SD card. In this chapter, I show you how to set up your video recording system so you're not wasting too much space with high-quality video you might not need. You can drop down your frames per second and the quality so you can store more video at the sacrifice of a little quality.

Note you won't be recording live video with this project. Instead, you'll set up your camera so it shoots at a very low frame rate. This makes the video choppy, but it also means you can save a lot more information on the SD card. Unless you're using your camera to capture Batman, this shouldn't be a problem.

PI POINTER

It's important to note that this security system doesn't have many of the conveniences of a commercial system. No security guard will come by your house if something goes wrong, and it's probably not as reliable as those $1,000 systems. So although it's probably just fine for your personal needs, don't try to secure a bank with it.

Camera Limitations

Unfortunately, there is a downside to this system: you can only use one camera at a time. You can certainly set up multiple cameras with multiple Raspberry Pis, but they won't be linked together like a modern security system.

To create a multiple-camera system, you'll need to purchase multiple Raspberry Pis and multiple camera modules. This is still a lot less expensive than a commercial security system.

Setting Up and Configuring Raspbian

Before you assemble the camera module, housing, and other hardware, you need to get Raspbian up and running properly.

Installing Raspbian

This project uses Raspbian as the basis because it's preloaded with the bulk of the software you'll need. Refer to Chapter 8 to install it if it's not already on your SD card.

Then, come back here because you need to adjust a few settings.

Setting Up SSH

Your camera's likely going to need to be wireless and not connected to a television of any kind, so you'll want to set up SSH so you can log in to your Raspberry Pi remotely.

Here's what to do:

1. At the command line, type in `sudo raspi-config`, and press **Enter** to get to the Raspberry Pi configuration menu.

2. Scroll down to **Advanced Options**, and press **Enter**.

3. Select **Enable SSH**, and press **Enter**.

4. Select the **Enable** option.

5. Press **Esc** to get back to the command line.

When you have SSH enabled, you'll need to set up your Wi-Fi card.

Enabling Wi-Fi

I covered establishing your Wi-Fi connection in Chapter 11, but here's the short version if you need a refresher:

1. From the command line, type in `sudo nano /etc/network/interface`, and press **Enter**.

2. Edit the file so it matches the following, replacing *YOUR ROUTER NAME* and *WIFI PASSWORD* with your network information:

```
allow-hotplug wlan0
iface wlan0 inet dhcp
wpa-ssid "YOUR ROUTER NAME"
wpa-psk "WIFI PASSWORD"
```

3. When you're done, press **Ctrl+X** to exit and save.

4. Restart your Wi-Fi interface to be sure everything takes effect. Type in `sudo /etc/init.d/networking restart`, and press **Enter**.

Your Wi-Fi card is set up, and SSH is enabled. You have one more thing to do before you start assembling hardware.

Assigning Your Raspberry Pi a Static IP Address

Because you're going to be accessing your Raspberry Pi remotely all the time, it's smart to give it a static IP address so you can easily find it on your network each time you boot your Raspberry Pi. The process is really easy to do from the command line:

1. Type `ifconfig`, and press **Enter**.

2. Look for the section titled **wlan0**.

3. Write down the numbers listed after **inet addr** (you'll use this for the "address" section in step 8), **Bcast** (for the "broadcast" section in step 8), and **Mask** (for the "netmask" section in step 8).

4. Type in `netstat -nr`, and press **Enter**.

5. Write down the numbers listed under **Gateway Address** (for the "gateway" section in step 8) and **Destination Address** (for the "network" section in step 8).

6. Type in `sudo nano /etc/network/interfaces`, and press **Enter**.

7. Look for the line that reads **iface wlan0 inet dhcp**, and edit it to `iface wlan0 inet static`.

8. Right below that line, type in the following, substituting the numbers you wrote down in steps 3 and 5 for the X's:

   ```
   address xxx.xxx.x.xx
   netmask xxx.xxx.xxx.x
   network xxx.xxx.x.xx
   broadcast xxx.xxx.x.xx
   gateway xxx.xxx.x.xx
   ```

9. Press **Ctrl+X** to exit and save the changes.

10. Restart your Wi-Fi interface one more time. Type in `sudo /etc/init.d/networking restart`, and press **Enter**.

You just set a static IP address for your Raspberry Pi so it's always accessible at the same place on your network.

PI POINTER

Every time your Raspberry Pi logs on to your home network, it needs to find an IP address. This can change every time you power on your Raspberry Pi, so picking a static IP address ensures it's in the same place every time, which makes it easy to find.

Updating Raspbian

Because you're using a lot of external components, you'll want to ensure your Raspberry Pi and your camera module are both up to date. You can do this from the command line.

Here's how:

1. Type in `sudo apt-get install rpi-update`, and press **Enter**.

2. Type in `sudo rpi-update`, and press **Enter**. This updates Raspbian if there's anything to update.

3. Type in `sudo apt-get update`, and press **Enter**.

4. Type in `sudo apt-get upgrade`, and press **Enter**. This ensures all your software is up to date, including drivers for the camera.

Now everything's ready to go. You just need to check that SSH works properly.

Connecting to Your Pi Remotely

With SSH on and Wi-Fi enabled, you can now log in to your Raspberry Pi remotely from your computer. You'll do this through SSH with some additional software.

Windows:

On Windows, you need to download some software before you can SSH into your Raspberry Pi.

Here's what to do:

1. Head to www.chiark.greenend.org.uk/~sgtatham/putty/download.html and download PuTTY.

2. When the file is downloaded, open **putty.exe**.

3. Enter your Raspberry Pi's IP address you assigned earlier under **Host Name**.

4. Tap **Enter** to open the command line.

5. Enter your Raspberry Pi's username and password.

Your Raspberry Pi and Windows computer are now connected. You can control your Raspberry Pi via your Windows PC as if you were in front of your Raspberry Pi itself. Test this out before you assemble your hardware so you don't have to disassemble it to troubleshoot later.

Mac:

If you own a Mac, you already have SSH built into your computer and you can access your Raspberry Pi using the Terminal app. Here's what to do:

1. Launch Terminal on your Mac from **Applications > Utilities > Terminal**.

2. Type in `ssh pi@`*yourIPaddress*, and replace *yourIPaddress* with the IP address you gave your Raspberry Pi. For example, `ssh pi@192.168.1.119`.

3. When you're prompted for your Raspberry Pi password, type it in and press **Enter**.

That's it. You can control your Raspberry Pi from Terminal on your Mac just like you would from the command line on your Raspberry Pi. You should also see your Raspberry Pi in Finder, so you can drag and drop files onto it. Before you assemble your hardware, test this connection so you don't have to disassemble it to troubleshoot if problems arise later.

 PI POINTER

When you use SSH, you control your Raspberry Pi from the command line just like you would if you were sitting in front of your Raspberry Pi. All the same commands work here. Just remember, if you reboot the Pi, you'll have to reconnect.

Assembling the Hardware

When you have everything connected and the preliminary setup finished, you can assemble your camera. As with any construction-type project, pay close attention to what you're doing, and always keep an eye on your small parts so they don't disappear.

Connecting the Camera Module

First, let's get that nifty camera module installed. Here's what to do:

1. Look at your Raspberry Pi Camera Module. You should see a blue strip at the end of the ribbon cable. On the opposite side of that is a bit of metal. You're going to connect that metal part to your Raspberry Pi.

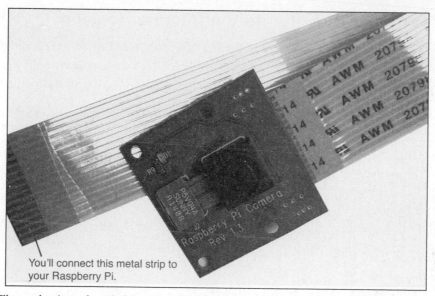

You'll connect this metal strip to your Raspberry Pi.

The metal strip on the end of the camera module is how you attach the camera to your Raspberry Pi.

2. Connect the ribbon cable to your Raspberry Pi's Camera Module insert. It's located right next to the Ethernet. Insert it so the metal on the ribbon cable touches the metal on the board. (The blue bit should be facing the Ethernet connector.) You might need to use a little bit of force to insert it.

Ethernet connector

camera module ribbon cable connection

Connect the camera module's ribbon cable to your Raspberry Pi.

Fitting Your Raspberry Pi into the Camera Housing

Next, you'll fit your Raspberry Pi, with the camera module attached, into the empty camera housing. This process will be a bit different depending on which camera housing you purchased, but you should still be able to follow along with these instructions and your specific housing.

The nice thing about these dummy cases is that they look like cameras, but they're basically empty inside. So taking them apart and putting them back together again is incredibly simple.

If you purchased the same case from Amazon I shared earlier in this chapter, you just need to unscrew the four screws in the front and the four in the back to gain access to the inside of the housing. You can remove the wires inside because there's no reason to have a light on. Then, place your Raspberry Pi inside the housing and push the camera module into the housing's front plate. You can secure it with adhesive tape or hook-and-loop tape now if you want. Then close the case, ensuring your power cable is connected and hanging out of the case.

Fit your Raspberry Pi into the empty camera housing.

Every housing is going to be a bit different, so you might have to play around with your model here to see what works best. Just be sure you keep track of the screws as you take apart the housing because you'll have to put it back together again if you want it to actually look like a camera.

Setting Up Your Software

Now that everything's put together, it's time to tackle the software portion and get your camera working properly. This means installing a bunch of drivers, changing some configuration files, and taking a look at a few different ways to view your video stream.

Enabling the Camera

Getting the camera up and running isn't difficult. You'll do this in the raspi-config menu. Here's what to do:

1. Open the command line.

2. Type in `sudo raspi-config`, and press **Enter**.

3. Scroll down to the **Enable Camera** option, and press **Enter**.

4. Select **Enable**.

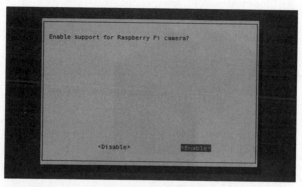

Enable support for Raspberry Pi camera?

<Disable>   <Enable>

Enabling the camera on your Raspberry Pi is pretty simple.

Exit out of the raspi-config menu. Your camera is now set up.

 PI POINTER

This is always how you enable the camera, so if you decide to tackle a different camera project, the camera setup will be the same for that project as it is here. You can do lots of fun stuff with the camera. I share several more projects in Chapter 18.

Installing Motion-Detection Software

The camera is pretty cool, but right now, it's still completely useless. To fix that, you need some additional software—in this case, motion-detection software so the camera knows when to record.

You're going to use Motion. Motion is open-source software that works as a motion detector. When it's installed, it triggers your camera to record only when it sees movement.

Here's what to do:

1. Open the command line.

2. Type in `sudo apt-get install motion`, and press **Enter**. This downloads the Motion software.

3. Motion isn't currently set up to work with the Raspberry Pi Camera Module, so you'll need some additional files. This part's a little tricky to type in, so be careful. Start by typing in `cd /tmp`, and press **Enter**.

4. Type in the following and press **Enter**:

   ```
   sudo apt-get install -y libjpeg62 libjpeg62-dev libavformat53
       libavformat-dev libavcodec53 libavcodec-dev libavutil51 libavutil-dev
       libc6-dev zlib1g-dev libmysqlclient18 libmysqlclient-dev libpq5
       libpq-dev
   ```

5. Now you need to get the most current link for the Raspberry Pi version of the Motion software. Head to github.com/dozencrows/motion/tree/mmal-test in your computer's browser, and scan the page to find a download link. It should look something like **https://www.dropbox.com/s/jw5r1wss32tdibb/motion-mmal-opt.tar.gz**. Make a note of that link.

6. Type in the following, replacing the link with the one you got in step 5, and press **Enter**:

   ```
   wget https://www.dropbox.com/s/jw5r1wss32tdibb/motion-mmal.tar.gz
   ```

7. To unzip the file you just downloaded, type `tar zxvf motion-mmal.tar.gz` and press **Enter**.

8. Now, you need to modify the version of Motion you downloaded in step 1 so it integrates this new software. Type in `sudo mv motion /usr/bin/motion`, and press **Enter**.

9. Type in `sudo mv motion-mmalcam.conf /etc/motion.conf`, and press **Enter**.

10. Type in `sudo nano /etc/default/motion`, and press **Enter** to open the text editor.

11. When you're in the text editor, change **start_motion_daemon=no** to `start_motion_daemon=yes`. Then press **Ctrl+X** to exit the editor.

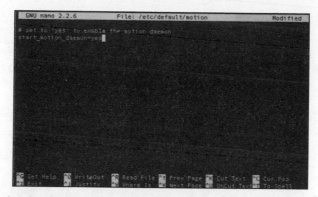

Starting the motion detection takes a few steps but isn't overly difficult.

That's it for installing the motion detection software. Customizing it for your use is next.

Adjusting Your Motion-Detection Software

Now to fine-tune the motion detection software. I show you how to set it up so it works well on a Raspberry Pi operating in a pretty low-key neighborhood, but you might need to alter some of these settings for your specific use.

First, you need to get your permissions in order. Because you're using a modified build of Motion, you need to give it proper permissions before you can proceed.

Here's how:

1. At the command line, type in sudo chmod 664 /etc/motion.conf, and press **Enter**.

2. Type in sudo chmod 755 /usr/bin/motion, and press **Enter**.

3. Type in sudo touch /tmp/motion.log, and press **Enter**.

4. Type in sudo chmod 775 /tmp/motion.log, and press **Enter**.

This should set all your permissions.

PI POINTER

Remember, when you're editing configuration files, be careful to type everything exactly as you see it here. One small typo, and the whole system won't work. Fortunately, if something is wrong when you try to launch Motion, you'll get a list of errors. You can usually troubleshoot where you made a mistake by comparing the lines you'll find here and there.

Now to actually edit that configuration file:

1. To open the file, type in `sudo nano /etc/motion.conf`, and press **Enter**.

2. Now you're in the configuration file. You have a ton of options to edit here, so let's go through each of the important ones:

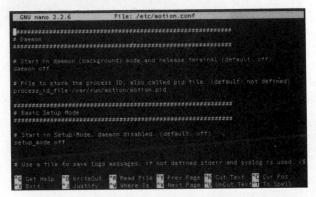

The motion configuration file has plenty of options to configure.

Daemon off: Change this to `daemon on`. This ensures the motion detector is always running.

Logfile /home/pi/motion.log: Change this to `logfile /tmp/motion.log`. This ensures you don't have to actually log in to your Raspberry Pi for it to record.

Width 640: If you want to record HD video, change this to `width 1280`. This will record in HD width.

Height 576: Because you changed the width, you also need to change the height. Change this to `height 720` for HD video.

Pre_capture 0: With motion-sensor software, it's useful to record a little before the motion and also a little after. Change this to `pre_capture 2` to record 2 seconds before the motion.

Post_capture 0: This is what's captured after movement. Change this to `post_capture 2` to record 2 seconds after the motion.

Max_movie_time 0: This is the maximum amount of time the camera can record. Because you don't need to record forever, you're going to change it to read `max_movie_time 600`. This makes the maximum record time 600 seconds, or 10 minutes.

Ffmpeg_video_code mpeg 4: This is the format the camera records in. You're going to adjust this so it's a little more compatible with other software. Change it to `ffmpeg_video_code msmpeg4`.

Locate_motion_mode off: Your camera can find and draw a box around any motion it sees. If you want that box, change this to `locate_motion_mode on`.

stream_localhost on: This tells your Raspberry Pi to not send the video outside your network. If you want to access it remotely from anywhere, change this to `stream_localhost off`.

Stream_auth_method 0: If you want to access your video stream remotely, you'll want a password. Change this to `stream_auth_method 2` so it requires authentication.

Stream_authentication username:password: This is your username and password for your live video stream. Type in whatever username you want in place of *username* and whatever password you want in place of *password*.

PI POINTER

The configuration file here is pretty large, but it's easy to navigate. Remember, anything that's proceeded with a # is a comment, so don't worry about editing those lines. Instead, you're looking for the lines without that symbol.

3. When you're done editing, press **Ctrl+X** to exit and save.

4. Reboot the system by typing in `sudo reboot`.

Those are the core settings, but as you're going through the configuration file, you'll probably notice some other things you want to tweak. The description for each configuration change is in the file itself, so take your time going through it and change whatever you like to match your needs.

You should now be able to access the live stream of your video by pointing your web browser to *YOURRASPBERRYPIIPADDRESS*`:8081`. For example, you might use something like `192.168.1.119:8081`.

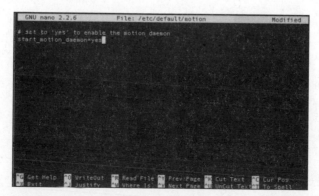

Your Raspberry Pi–powered camera can detect and record anything that moves within its view, such as in a tree outside your window.

PI POINTER

I had trouble getting the video stream to work in both Google Chrome and Internet Explorer. If you're having trouble, try another web browser like Safari or Firefox. You should also be able to access this video on your smartphone, provided it's on the same Wi-Fi network as your Raspberry Pi.

Storing Videos on Your Computer

Your stream is up and running, and the camera is recording video whenever it senses movement. But your Raspberry Pi doesn't have a ton of storage, even if you purchased a large SD card. You might want to set it up so all the recorded video is automatically sent over to your home computer, where you have more storage capacity.

Windows:

Here's how to put that video transfer in place in Windows:

1. Create a folder to share with your Raspberry Pi. Call it something like *Surveillance* so it's easy to remember.

2. Right-click the folder, and select the **Share** option.

3. Select the **Everyone** option, and change the **Permission Level** to **Contributor**.

4. Click the **Share** button, and make a note of the network path. It should read something like *yourcomputer*\users\documents\surveillance.

5. Head back to your Raspberry Pi's command line. Type in `sudo nano /etc/fstab`, and press **Enter**. This loads a startup configuration.

6. Add this line to the configuration file, substituting in the information you wrote down in step 4:

   ```
   //PATHFROMSTEP4 /mnt/surveillance cifs
      username=YOURFOLDERUSERNAME,password=YOURFOLDERPASSWORD,iocharset=ut
         f8,file_mode=0777,dir_mode=0777 0 0
   ```

7. Your Raspberry Pi now has access to that shared folder on your Windows computer. You just need to change your camera's settings so it knows to save videos there. Type in `sudo nano /etc/default/motion.conf`, and press **Enter**.

8. Find the line that says **target_dir**, and change it to `target_dir /mnt/surveillance`.

9. When you're done, press **Ctrl+X** to save and exit.

Your Raspberry Pi will now save all the videos and images it records right on your Windows computer for easy access.

Mac:

Storing videos on a Mac is pretty simple to do as well. You'll just need to share a folder with the Raspberry Pi. Here's how:

1. Create a folder to share with your Raspberry Pi. Call it something like *Surveillance* so it's easy to remember.

2. Open System Preferences by clicking the Apple logo in the top menu bar and selecting **System Preferences**.

3. Navigate to the **Sharing** option, and click it.

4. Click the **+** button next under **Shared Folders**, and select the folder you want to share.

5. Now head back to the main System Preferences panel, and select **Network**. Look for your IP address here. You'll need it in step 8.

6. Head over to your Raspberry Pi, and pop into the command line. Type in `sudo apt-get install afpfs-ng`, and press **Enter**. This installs the file-sharing protocol your Raspberry Pi needs to access your Mac.

7. Type in `sudo nano /etc/fstab`, and press **Enter**.

8. Add these lines to the configuration file, substituting your own information for *YOURMACUSERNAME, MACPASSWORD, YOURMACIPADDRESS, FOLDERFROMSTEP3,* and *YOURUSERNAME:*

    ```
    afpfs#afp://YOURMACUSERNAME:MACPASSWORD@YOURMACIPADDRESS/FOLDERFROMSTEP3/
        mnt/surveillance fuse
          user=YOURUSERNAME,group=fuse 0 0
    ```

9. Save and exit the file by tapping **Ctrl+X**.

10. Next, type in `sudo nano /sbin/afps`, and press **Enter**.

11. Type the following into the blank text file:
    ```
    #!/bin/bash
    mount_afp $3 $4 $1 $2
    ```

    Tap **Ctrl+X** to save and exit the file when you're done.

12. Now to make the file you just created an executable program, type in `chmod +x /sbin/afpfs` and press **Enter**.

13. Your Raspberry Pi has access to that shared folder on your Mac computer; you need to change your camera's settings so it knows to save it there. Type in `sudo nano /etc/default/motion.conf`, and press **Enter**.

14. Find the line that says **target_dir**, and change it to `target_dir /mnt/surveillance`.

15. When you're done, press **Ctrl+X** to save and exit.

Your Raspberry Pi should automatically connect to your Mac so it can store information there.

> **PI POINTER**
>
> The Mac configuration is a little trickier because Macs use a different type of file sharing than Windows or Linux. Pay careful attention to what you're doing here to get it right. There's always a chance this won't work if any of the sharing preferences get changed, so if you're struggling, additional resources are available online.

Accessing Saved Videos

If you set up your Raspberry Pi to automatically save videos to your personal computer, you can access all your saved footage there. If not, you'll need to pull it off the Raspberry Pi directly. You can do that remotely, too.

Windows:

On a Windows computer, you can access your saved videos through SSH software called WinSCP. Here's how:

1. Download WinSCP from winscp.net/eng/index.php.

2. Launch WinSCP. In the **Connect to:** box, type in your Raspberry Pi's IP address.

3. Type in `pi` for the username.

4. Click the **Connect** button.

5. When prompted, enter your password.

6. Now that you're connected to your Raspberry Pi, navigate to the **/tmp/** folder. Your videos are saved here. You can drag them to your desktop or play them remotely.

If you need to clear up space, you can delete old videos from this folder.

Mac:

To access files on your Raspberry Pi from your Mac, you'll need additional software called Fugu SSH. Here's what to do:

1. Download Fugu SSH from sourceforge.net/projects/fugussh.

2. Open the software. In the **Connect to:** box, type in your Raspberry Pi's internal IP address.

3. Type in pi for the username.

4. Click the **Connect** button.

5. When prompted, enter your password.

6. Now that you're connected to your Raspberry Pi, navigate to the **/tmp/** folder, where your videos are saved. Drag them to your desktop, or play them remotely from here.

If you need to make room on your SD card, you can remove old videos from the /tmp/ folder.

Remotely Reviewing Footage

If viewing and accessing your surveillance video from your home computer isn't enough for you, you also can remotely access it online. To do this, you'll need to register a DNS address for your Raspberry Pi and set up some port forwarding on your router.

Setting Up a DNS Address for Your Raspberry Pi

You have many options for getting a DNS address. In this project, we'll use DNSdynamic (dnsdynamic.org). In Chapter 13, I share a few alternative options.

1. Head to dnsdynamic.org.

2. Check for a domain availability by typing in a domain name in the **check availability** box. You can use whatever you want here. Follow the instructions, and you'll get a host service that reads something like myraspberrypicamera.dnsdynamic.com. You'll also get some more configuration settings. Hold on to these for use in step 7.

3. Head back to your Raspberry Pi, and open the command line.

4. Type in sudo apt-get install ddclient, and press **Enter**. This installs the dynamic DNS client. Wait for it to download and install.

5. When it's finished, it'll run automatically. Select **Other** if you're using DNSdynamic.

6. Enter the address of the DNS server you registered in step 2.

7. Now you need to edit the file to include your information. Type in sudo nano /etc/ddclient/ddclient.conf, and press **Enter**.

8. Then type in all the information you gathered in step 2.

9. Finally, add one more line to the top of the file that reads daemon=600. This tells your internet service provider to check the address every 600 seconds, or every 10 minutes.

10. Press **Ctrl+X** to save and exit the file.

11. Type in `ddclient`. This launches the dynamic DNS client so your Raspberry Pi is accessible online.

12. To be sure ddclient is always running when you reboot your Raspberry Pi, type in `sudo /etc/init.d/ddclient start` and press **Enter**. This adds ddclient to your boot process.

Your Raspberry Pi now has a permanent address on the internet. You're almost done. You just need to tell your router it's okay to broadcast that signal.

> **PI POINTER**
>
> Dynamic DNS is a great way to give your Raspberry Pi a permanent address online. Your internet service provider constantly changes your IP address, so a dynamic DNS ensures you can always find your Raspberry Pi at the same address every time. Plus, it's a lot easier to remember a phrase you come up with yourself than it is to remember a string of seemingly random numbers.

Enabling Port Forwarding on Your Router

Before you can access your Pi's camera remotely, you need to set up port forwarding on your router. Every router is a little different, so consider this a loose guide to get you started:

1. Access your router from your computer's web browser. It's typically **192.168.1.1** or **10.0.0.1**.

2. When prompted, type in your router's username and password.

3. Look for a tab or setting that reads **NAT/QoS**, and click it.

4. Find the **Port Forwarding** tab, and click it.

5. Typically, you'll need to click an **Add** button to add a new port forwarding address.

6. In the boxes, enter your Raspberry Pi's IP address under **Address** and 8081 under **Port**.

7. Save it, and exit your router.

As mentioned earlier, all routers are a little different, so if you can't find your router's port forwarding section, refer to your owner's manual.

With that, your Raspberry Pi is accessible over the internet. You should be able to access your camera feed by going to *nameyoupickedabove*.com:8081.

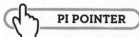

PI POINTER

Every internet service provider varies in the settings they allow. If port 8081 doesn't work for you, try another like 80, 20, or 8080.

Setting Up Email Alerts

A motion-sensing camera is only so good without some kind of alert system. Fortunately, you can set up your Raspberry Pi to send you an email every time the camera detects motion. This way, when you get an alert, you know to boot up your remote camera and see what's going on.

Here's what to do:

1. From the command line on your Raspberry Pi, type in `sudo nano /etc/motion.conf`, and press **Enter**.

2. Edit the line **on_picture_save value** so it reads `on_picture_save mpack -s Alert %f` *youremail@youremail.com*, replacing *youremail@youremail.com* with your personal email address. This ensures you'll get an email alert any time the camera detects motion and snaps a picture or video.

3. Press **Ctrl+X** to save and exit the document.

Get ready to check your email because now you'll get alerts when your Raspberry Pi camera senses motion.

Mounting Your Camera

Now that everything is set up and working on the software side, you can get the hardware in place.

When you're deciding where to mount your camera system, look for the most trafficked area. This is probably your front door, but it really depends on what you're trying to capture on film. Be sure it's located within Wi-Fi range of your router and that your power cord reaches an electric outlet. It's also best to keep it someplace out of the weather. It's in a case, sure, but that doesn't mean you want to leave it out during a hailstorm. Finally, point the camera's eye at what you want to film. You might need to test it and adjust it a bit before you're finished.

With your camera in place where you want it, plug in your Raspberry Pi and boot up your browser to check the feed.

The Least You Need to Know

- Using a camera module and some motion-detecting software, you can turn your Raspberry Pi into a simple security system.

- You can set up your surveillance system for access locally or remotely via the internet.

- For ease of use, you can access your saved video from your home computer.

- Like many projects, this one uses Raspbian as its backbone, so you should have no problem getting started.

Making a Wireless Router

If you've been following along with the projects in this book so far, you've already used your Raspberry Pi for a host of projects, including turning it into a server you can access from anywhere. But you might not realize your Raspberry Pi can be used as an actual wireless network router, too.

It might not look like it from the outside, but your home Wi-Fi router is actually just a small computer. It might even run Linux. So with some work, some downloads, and some tinkering with configuration files, you can turn your Raspberry Pi into a router that works just like one you'd buy at a store.

Building your own router means you can bring it with you anywhere you might need a Wi-Fi connection. For example, it's great for hotels that notoriously have terrible Wi-Fi but decent wired connections. It's also a handy, inexpensive way to share an internet connection wherever you are. The best part about building your own device is that you can customize it however you like. You can set it up and use whatever components you want and change settings to suit your specific needs. You're basically creating your own little Wi-Fi hot spot, so make it yours.

In This Chapter

- Turning your Raspberry Pi into a Wi-Fi spot

- Setting up your Wi-Fi adapter as an access point

- Enabling internet forwarding

In this chapter, you learn to set up Wi-Fi on your Raspberry Pi, configure it to access the internet, and route that internet connection to external devices. All you need is your Raspberry Pi, a power adapter, an SD card, an Ethernet cable, and a Wi-Fi adapter.

This one's going to take a lot of work in the command line, so get your typing fingers ready.

What a Raspberry Pi Router Can Do

A Raspberry Pi router works similarly to a Wi-Fi hot spot. It won't have the same configuration screen or complicated settings an off-the-shelf router has, but it will connect your computers and get them online.

It also will be able to link all your computers so they can communicate with each other. And when your router is all set up, it really won't require you to do anything with it other than leave it plugged in to your modem. You'll even be able to upgrade it easily with the newest wireless tech simply by buying a new Wi-Fi adapter, instead of purchasing a whole new machine.

 HARDWARE HELPER

Not all Wi-Fi cards are created equal. Some are faster than others and broadcast at different rates. The same goes for routers. The nice thing about using your Raspberry Pi as a router is that you can upgrade the speed without buying a whole new unit by just upgrading the Wi-Fi adapter.

Installing Raspbian

As you've likely come to realize over the course of this book, Raspbian is the backbone of most Raspberry Pi projects. The same is true for this project.

But in this case, you need to make a brand-new Raspbian SD card instead of trying to multitask with one you've used for another project. You're going to tinker around with how your Raspberry Pi operates a lot throughout this chapter, and it isn't going to work the same way you'd need it to with other projects. After all, you're setting it up so the internet comes *out* of your Raspberry Pi, not *into* it, so it's fundamentally a different type of machine.

So if you haven't already, turn back to Chapter 8 and follow the directions to install Raspbian on a new SD card. When it's all set up, head back here.

Choosing a Wireless Adapter

You need a USB Wi-Fi adapter for this project. I covered wireless adapters pretty extensively in Chapter 11. As a reminder, check out elinux.org/RPi_USB_Wi-Fi_Adapters for a list of all the Wi-Fi adapters that work on the Raspberry Pi.

The Wi-Fi adapter you choose should support something called *AP mode*. *AP* stands for "access point," and it enables the adapter to receive incoming Wi-Fi connections from multiple sources as a host.

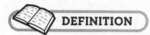

DEFINITION

> **AP mode** stands for *access point mode* and basically just means that the wireless adapter can act as an interface for a router or server.

Countless affordable Wi-Fi adapters support AP mode, so be sure to check before you purchase an adapter. If you're not sure if yours does, I show you how to do a second check in an upcoming step to verify it's working properly.

Setting Up SSH

You're going to run your Raspberry Pi in headless mode, which means you don't need a monitor connected. You'll set up and use SSH so you can control your Raspberry Pi from your personal computer.

Windows:

On Windows, you need to download some software before you can SSH into your Raspberry Pi. Here's what to do:

1. Head to www.chiark.greenend.org.uk/~sgtatham/putty/download.html and download PuTTY.

2. When it's downloaded, open **putty.exe**.

3. Under **Host Name**, enter your Raspberry Pi's IP address. If you don't know your Raspberry Pi's IP address, hook your Raspberry Pi to a screen and type in `ifconfig`. Under **inetaddress:** you'll see your IP address number.

4. Tap **Enter** to open a command line.

5. Enter your Raspberry Pi's username and password.

Now, you're connected to your Raspberry Pi on Windows. You can control your Raspberry Pi from the command line just as if you were sitting in front of it. Because your Raspberry Pi is only operating as a router, this is really all you need to do.

Mac:

If you own a Mac, you already have SSH built into your computer and you can access your Raspberry Pi using the Terminal app. Here's how:

1. Launch Terminal on your Mac from **Applications > Utilities > Terminal**.

2. Type in `ssh pi@yourIPaddress`. For example, `ssh pi@192.168.1.105`. If you don't know your Raspberry Pi's IP address, hook your Raspberry Pi up to a screen and type in `ifconfig`. Under **inetaddress:** you'll see your IP address number.

3. When prompted for your Raspberry Pi password, type it in and press **Enter**.

That's it. You can now control your Raspberry Pi from Terminal on your Mac just like you would from the command line on your Raspberry Pi. Your Raspberry Pi is just acting as a router here, so this is all you need to do.

Installing the Required Components

Now to get the various components installed. You can do this with the `apt-get install` command in the command line, or you can do it in bulk by following the command with as many apps as you need.

First, let's take a look at what you're installing.

 SOFTWARE SOLUTION

Before you start any project, run the update commands for the Raspberry Pi. Start with `sudo apt-get update`, and follow that with `sudo apt-get upgrade`. These two commands check for updates online and ensure all your installed software is the newest version. It's the same basic idea as updating apps on your phone, but you have to manually type in a command instead of tapping an icon.

To set up your router, you need to install a few different bits of software. Some of this stuff is usually included in Raspbian, but it's good to double-check that everything is up to date.

rfkill: This wireless utility allows you to query the state of different interfaces. Some wireless adapters can use this and some can't, but it's good to have it installed for this project.

zd1211-firmware: This is a common firmware for wireless adapters. Chances are that Raspbian has your firmware installed already, but this ensures you're covered.

hostapd: This is an authenticator for wireless adapter. It makes it so your wireless card can properly communicate with your network.

hostap-utils: This is a set of extra tools for hostapd.

iw: This is a wireless configuration utility.

dnsmasq: This is the tool that allows you to use your Raspberry Pi as a router.

bridge-utils: This is used for devices connected over Ethernet and makes it possible for your Pi to connect to your modem.

The installation process for your tools is super easy. Before you start, be sure your Raspberry Pi's Wi-Fi adapter is plugged in and you're plugged in to your modem with the Ethernet cable.

Here are the steps:

1. Open the command line either on your Raspberry Pi or on your computer over SSH.

2. Type in `sudo apt-get install rfkill zd1211-firmware hostapd hostap-utils iw dnsmasq bridge-utils`, and press **Enter**.

The `sudo apt-get install` command lets you install multiple pieces of software at once with one line of text.

3. Wait for all your utilities to download and install.

With everything installed and ready to go, it's time to get to work.

SOFTWARE SOLUTION

Before you set up just about any new piece of hardware, it's a good idea to search for, download, and install any software updates available, even if your hardware seems to work out of the box.

Configuring Your USB Wireless Adapter

You need to do a bit of work before your wireless adapter will operate as a router. Essentially, you need to set it up as a bridge between the computers on your network and your modem.

Testing Your USB Wireless Adapter

Before you do anything, you need to be sure your wireless adapter will work for this project.

Here's what to do next:

1. At the command line, type in `lsusb` and press **Enter**.

2. Look for your USB wireless adapter on the list displayed. If it's included, your Raspberry Pi recognizes it. If not, head back to Chapter 11 to learn how to find and install the proper drivers.

3. Next, you need to verify that your wireless adapter supports AP mode. Type in `iw list`, and press **Enter**.

4. You'll get a list of information about your wireless adapter. Find the line that reads **Supported interface modes:** and be sure **AP** is included in the list.

The results from iw list tell you if your adapter supports AP mode.

Now that you've verified that your wireless adapter works, it's time to configure it.

Configuring a Wireless Interface

Configuring your wireless adapter is a bit complicated. You're also going to create backups of everything you edit so you can roll back to the default settings if anything goes wrong.

Here's what to do:

1. First, you're going to back up your network preferences. At the command line, type in `sudo cp /etc/network/interfaces /etc/network/interfaces.old` and press **Enter**.

2. Now that it's backed up, it's time to edit. Type in `sudo nano /etc/network/interfaces`, and press **Enter**.

3. You're greeted with the text editor and your network preferences. Here, you're going to add a bunch of information and change some stuff around. Delete everything in the text file and replace it with the following:

```
auto lo
auto br0
iface lo inet loopback
iface eth0 inet dhcp
allow-hotplug wlan0
allow-hotplug eth0
iface wlan0 inet manual
iface br0 inet dhcp
   bridge_fd 1
   bridge_hello 3
   bridge_maxage 10
   bridge_stp off
   bridge_ports eth0
```

4. When you're done, tap **Ctrl+X** to save and exit.

5. Next, restart the Wi-Fi interface. Type in `sudo ifdown wlan0`, and press **Enter**.

6. Type in `sudo ifup wlan0`, and press **Enter**.

Now your wireless adapter is ready. Let's configure your router settings.

 PI POINTER

If you don't really need a router, you can use this project as an access point or range extender to make your home network's Wi-Fi go a little farther. This is helpful if you have rooms in a basement or attic that don't have access to the internet because they're too far away from a router.

Configuring hostapd

Now you need to tell your Raspberry Pi how to behave as a router. This requires some more typing and changing of your configuration files.

Here's what to do:

1. First, you need to see which driver your wireless adapter is using. At the command line, type in lsusb -t and press **Enter**.

2. Look for your wireless adapter on the list. Under **Driver=** you should see the driver it's using. Make a note of it; you'll need it in the upcoming steps.

3. You're going to make a backup of your hostapd settings. Type in sudo cp /etc/hostapd/hostapd.conf /etc/hostapd/hostapd.conf.old, and press **Enter**.

4. Now hop into the text editor, type in sudo nano /etc/hostapd/hostapd.conf, and press **Enter**.

5. You're not editing the hostapd.conf file, but you need to modify it so it looks like this, replacing everything in all caps with your information:

```
interface=wlan0
bridge=br0
driver= #TYPE YOUR WI-FI DRIVER NUMBER HERE, IT'S LIKELY NL80211 IF YOU
    PURCHASED A GENERIC ADAPTER
country_code= #TYPE YOUR COUNTRY HERE; THE DEFAULT IS US AND SHOULD
    FOLLOW ISO 3166-1 FOR OTHER COUNTRIES
ctrl_interface=wlan0
ctrl_interface_group=0
ssid="NAME YOUR ROUTER"
hw_mode=g
channel=1 #THIS IS YOUR BROADCAST CHANNEL
wpa=3
wpa_passphrase= #MAKE UP A PASSWORD FOR YOUR ROUTER HERE
wpa_key_mgmt=WPA-PSK
wpa_pairwise=TKIP
rsn_pairwise=CCMP
beacon_int=100
auth_algs=3
macaddr_acl=0
wmm_enabled=1
eap_reauth_period=360000000
```

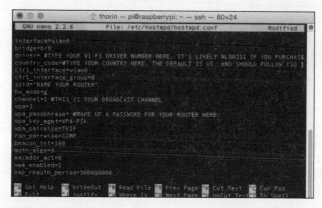

The hostapd.conf screen is where you set up the specifics of your router.

6. When you're done, press **Ctrl+X** to save and exit.

7. Now you need to restart everything. Type in `sudo service networking restart`, and press **Enter**.

8. Type in `sudo service hostapd restart`, and press **Enter**.

Now your Raspberry Pi will show up when you scan for Wi-Fi networks on your computer. But you're not done yet.

PI POINTER

Remember that when you're typing in any command or text into a text editor, it's incredibly important to get it exactly right. Not only do you need to ensure the letters and numbers are correct, you also have to be sure the spacing and even capitalization is the same.

 Configuring DNS Settings

Next, you need to configure the DNS settings so your Raspberry Pi understands that it's supposed to communicate with the internet.

Here's what to do:

1. You're going to copy and backup the configuration file again. Type in `sudo cp /etc/dnsmasq.conf /etc/dnsmasq.conf.old`, and press **Enter**.

2. Type in `sudo nano /etc/dnsmasq.conf`, and press **Enter** to open the text editor.

3. You're looking for three different lines in the text editor to uncomment. Find these three lines, remove the # before each of them, and add wlan0 to the **interface=** line:

```
domain-needed
interface=wlan0
dhcp-range=192.168.2.1,192.168.2.254,12h
```

4. Now, verify you did everything correctly by typing in cat /etc/dnsmasq.conf | grep -v "#" | sed '/^$/d', and press **Enter**. If it's correct, you'll get a reading with the three lines in step 3.

5. Type in sudo service dnsmasq restart, and press **Enter**.

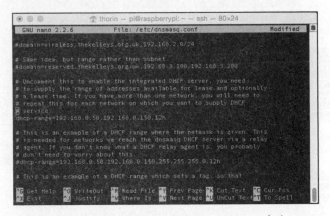

The DNS screen shows that your device can connect to the internet.

This restarts the DNS with the new settings. Although you still need to do one more thing to get access to the internet, at this point, you should see your Raspberry Pi router pop up on your computer like this:

image

If you see this, you know everything's working. Now you just need to bridge the gap between the internet, your Raspberry Pi, and your computer.

Accessing the Internet

To access the internet as a whole, you need to enable port forwarding and network address translation (NAT). This basically allows your Raspberry Pi to take information from the internet and communicate it to your computer.

Enabling Port Forwarding

For your Raspberry Pi to work as a router, you need to enable a feature called *port forwarding*.

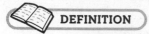 **DEFINITION**

Port forwarding enables your router to communicate with the internet. It translates the address online into a packet of information. A port is a number that makes it possible for your internal IP address to communicate with the outside internet.

To get port forwarding working on your Raspberry Pi, you only need to type in one command:

```
sudo sysctl -w net.ipv4.ip_forward=1
```

Press **Enter**, and port forwarding is now enabled. Just one more step until you're done.

Enabling NAT

NAT is required for just about anything communicating with the internet. It enables multiple computers on your home network to talk with one router.

To enable NAT, type in the following and press **Enter**:

```
sudo iptables -t nat -A POSTROUTING -j MASQUERADE
```

 **DEFINITION**

Network address translation (NAT) makes it possible for your computer to communicate with the internet by setting up your internal IP address and a second group of IP addresses for external traffic.

With that, your Raspberry Pi is acting as a router. On your computer, open the Wi-Fi menu, and select your Raspberry Pi from the list. Open your web browser, and open a test site. If everything's working, you should have full access to the internet.

Setting Everything to Start on Boot

Finally, you want all these processes to start right when you boot up your Raspberry Pi. Here's how to make that happen:

```
● ● ●                     ⌂ thorin — pi@raspberrypi: ~ — ssh — 80×24
Listening on LPF/br0/00:c1:41:23:07:23
Sending on   LPF/br0/00:c1:41:23:07:23
Sending on   Socket/fallback
DHCPDISCOVER on br0 to 255.255.255.255 port 67 interval 6
DHCPDISCOVER on br0 to 255.255.255.255 port 67 interval 17
DHCPREQUEST on br0 to 255.255.255.255 port 67
DHCPOFFER from 192.168.1.1
DHCPACK from 192.168.1.1
bound to 192.168.1.105 -- renewal in 32884 seconds.
Internet Systems Consortium DHCP Client 4.2.2
Copyright 2004-2011 Internet Systems Consortium.
All rights reserved.
For info, please visit https://www.isc.org/software/dhcp/

Listening on LPF/eth0/b8:27:eb:29:ac:3a
Sending on   LPF/eth0/b8:27:eb:29:ac:3a
Sending on   Socket/fallback
DHCPDISCOVER on eth0 to 255.255.255.255 port 67 interval 3
DHCPREQUEST on eth0 to 255.255.255.255 port 67
DHCPOFFER from 192.168.1.1
DHCPACK from 192.168.1.1
bound to 192.168.1.147 -- renewal in 37892 seconds.
done.
pi@raspberrypi ~ $
```

Be sure your router settings start on boot so you don't have to start them manually.

1. First, verify everything is working properly. Type in sudo service hostapd start, and press **Enter**.

2. Type in sudo service dnsmasq start, and press **Enter**.

3. If both of these services start with no errors, you can add them to startup. Type in sudo update-rc.d hostapd enable, and press **Enter**.

4. Type in sudo update-rc.d dnsmasq start enable, and press **Enter**.

5. Finally, you need to remove one thing from the startup process. Type in sudo mv /usr/ share/dbus-1/system/services/fi.epitest.hostap.WPASupplicant.service~/, and press **Enter**.

Now your router processes will load when you boot up your Raspberry Pi, no extra configuration required.

> **PI POINTER**
>
> Be sure your Raspberry Pi has a good, strong password enabled. The Wi-Fi signal is broadcasting just like a home router, so you don't want neighbors or anyone passing by to be able to just log in because your password is *password*.

The Least You Need to Know

- You can easily turn your Raspberry Pi into a wireless router you can use anywhere to network computers together.

- You need a wireless adapter for this project, but otherwise you just need your Raspberry Pi.

- You also need a new copy of Raspbian installed before you can start this process.

- Enable port forwarding and NAT in order for your Raspberry Pi to communicate with the internet.

Creating a Web Server

Running a *web server* can be a complicated task and requires a lot of work, but the act of actually putting together a server is pretty simple. After all, although it seems complex, a server is really nothing more than a computer with special software installed that's accessible from the internet.

Your Raspberry Pi makes an excellent little web server, provided you don't expect to see a large amount of traffic. When you get it set up, it works just like any other web server on the internet. You can type an address into your web browser, and you'll load a website that's housed on your Raspberry Pi. It'll be a little slow, but considering it's basically a free option to host your own website, it has quite a few different uses.

In this chapter, you learn how to turn your Raspberry Pi into a web server that has numerous extra features. In addition to hosting what's needed for a website, you also discover how to install your own cloud storage software, establish a blog, set up various server utilities, and make the whole thing accessible from the internet. Basically, you'll be running your own website from your Raspberry Pi.

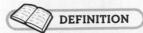 **DEFINITION**

A **web server** is a computer that has software set up to display web pages and store information about a website. It's really nothing more than a computer and hard drive that's accessible online.

Running your own server calls for much of what you've learned in this book so far. You need to install programs, configure databases, edit configuration files, and push your Raspberry Pi to the limits. Server administration is a complicated job that takes years of training to get right, but this chapter gets you started on a hobby that can easily become a career.

You won't learn much about web design in this chapter. That's an entire book in itself. You'll get your server up and running though, and with services like WordPress installed, you'll be able to put together a simple website pretty quickly if you want.

All you need for this project is your Raspberry Pi, an Ethernet cable to attach your Pi to your home router, and a spare SD card. You can technically host everything you need on an 8GB SD card, but if you really want to power a whole website, an external hard drive is recommended. Opt for at least a 100GB drive. Anything larger than that is fine as well.

This project will take an entire day, if not more, to complete, so before you start, be sure you have the time to finish. It's easy to stop at nearly any point if you need to, but still give yourself plenty of time to work on this project.

What a Raspberry Pi Web Server Can Do

At its most basic level, a web server is a computer that serves up files in the form of web pages. If you go to any website online, there's a server behind it that stores those files.

This project teaches you how to turn your Raspberry Pi into a Linux server, and by the end of it, your Raspberry Pi will be the same kind of web server as one you'd expect to find hosting sites anywhere else online. Typically speaking, if you wanted to set up a website for yourself, you'd usually buy server space from an online provider. This negates that process and hosts your website right on your own Raspberry Pi.

In this chapter, you learn how to install everything needed to run your server. This includes all the backend software websites need to work as well as software to create your own blog.

However, it's not just about hosting a website, so if you have no interest in running your own blog or site, that's okay. You also learn to install software called ownCloud in this chapter. ownCloud is cloud storage software that works similar to something like Dropbox. You can easily sync files, music, and media between computers using ownCloud and your Raspberry Pi without having to pay another service to do it for you.

PI POINTER

Running a professional web server can certainly be a full-time job, but don't let that dissuade you from trying this project. From a hobbyist's point of view, it's a great way to learn about how websites work from multiple angles. Setting up the server is just half the process. You eventually need to learn how to actually make a website, too.

What's Included

Because this is such a large project, let's take some time to really dig in to what you'll be doing before you get into it. You spend more time with each of the following elements throughout the chapter, but it's a good idea to know what you're getting into before you take on this project. Here's what will end up on your server:

Webmin administration interface: Webmin (webmin.com) is a server management web interface. After you install it, Webmin is essentially your hub for everything on your server. You can install new stuff, upload files, and more. Think of it like your server's operating system.

Shell in a Box: Instead of running the command line on your Raspberry Pi or through SSH, you'll use Shell in a Box throughout this lesson. Shell in a Box (code.google.com/p/shellinabox) is basically just a web interface for the command line. So instead of downloading special software, you can run command line commands from your browser. It makes things a lot easier.

Apache web server: This is the actual server end of your server. Apache (apache.org) is open source, so it's free and up to date with modern web standards. It's also secure and pretty easy to add new functionality to.

MySQL: MySQL (mysql.com) is open-source database software. Databases are required for just about every website, especially anything that includes login information or complex lists.

PHP 5: PHP (php.net) is a server-side scripting language. It's pretty standard on servers and required for any website that uses dynamic content like a blog or cloud server.

FTP access: If you want to upload files to your server remotely, FTP is the easiest way to do it. In this case, FTP access is useful because you can dial into your server to manage the file system remotely.

Samba: Samba (samba.org) is similar to FTP but only works on a local network. If you're managing your server from the same network, Samba is an easy way to transfer files from a computer to your server.

ownCloud: ownCloud (ownCloud.org) is a cloud storage platform. With it, you can store files, sync contacts, create calendars, and even edit documents—you can basically have your own private cloud storage system you host yourself.

WordPress: WordPress (wordpress.com) is an open-source blogging system. It's one of the most popular blog content management systems because you can customize it in countless ways. Once you get it installed, you'll easily be able to run your own blog on your Raspberry Pi.

That covers the essentials. You'll also download a handful of smaller tools to help get your server up and running.

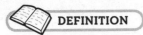 **DEFINITION**

> **MySQL** is a database management system. Working with MySQL can be advanced stuff, but you can still run a server on your Raspberry Pi without really touching it. **PHP** (PHP: Hypertext Preprocessor) is an open-source scripting language that can be embedded into HTML and is often used to run the back end of web servers so small scripts can run on websites. It's a language in itself and difficult to learn, but in this case, you'll mostly just install it on your Raspberry Pi so basic websites can function. **FTP** (file transfer protocol) is a network standard used to transfer files from one computer to another, usually over the internet. If you're away from your server, you'd use FTP to get files onto it.

This is by no means the only way to run a server. You have a ton of options, and you can customize your server in a variety of ways. In fact, what's in this chapter is just one of many ways to set up a server on your Raspberry Pi. This is plenty to get you started if you want to explore other ways of doing it after you work through this lesson.

Limitations of a Raspberry Pi Web Server

Before we get too deep into this, I should remind you that the Raspberry Pi is a pretty slow little computer. It can't handle a ton of things at once, so any web pages you host on it will be a little slow as well. For that reason, it's recommended you stick with simple and small-scale projects here.

Your Raspberry Pi server is perfect for hosting your résumé website, for example, because it probably doesn't get a lot of traffic. You also could use it to host other one-off projects, like your wedding landing page or a graduation announcement. It's not recommended for anything that would get a lot of traffic, like your email or social media pages, because the Raspberry Pi simply can't handle it.

This isn't a bad thing by any means, but it's something to think about before you continue.

Installing Raspbian Turnkey

Before you do anything else, you need to get your basic server set up. You're going to use a variation on Raspbian called Turnkey (turnkeylinux.org). Turnkey is a Linux distribution made specifically for turning a machine into a web server. In this project, you'll use a distribution created by GitHub user ghoulmann that's built specifically for the Raspberry Pi. This makes the process as quick and simple as possible, although you'll still have to do some work to get everything actually going.

Let's get Turnkey onto your SD card and work through the initial setup for your Raspberry Pi. Here's what to do:

1. Download the Turnkey image from github.com/downloads/ghoulmann/ Raspliance-Core/raspliance-core-02.img.tar.gz.

2. Double-click the **tar.gz** file to unzip it.

3. Burn the IMG file to an SD card using the same method you used to burn Raspbian in Chapter 8. With the image on your SD card, plug it in to your Raspberry Pi.

4. Connect your Raspberry Pi to a monitor and a keyboard, and boot it up.

 HARDWARE HELPER

> The monitor and keyboard connections in step 4 are just temporary. You only need to keep your Raspberry Pi attached to a keyboard and monitor for this initial setup.

5. The operating system will take a little while to boot up. When it does, it'll ask you for a password. Create a password, and enter it twice.

6. At this point, you might see the raspi-config screen. If you do, select the first option, **Expand rootfs**, and press **Enter**. When it's done, exit to get back to the Turnkey setup.

7. Next, you'll see your network information in the CORE appliance services menu. Make a note of all these numbers because you'll need them later.

That's it for the initial Turnkey setup. You can power off your monitor and disconnect your keyboard if you want. You won't need them attached to your Raspberry Pi again for this project.

Updating Webmin

Now your Raspberry Pi has the basic software needed to run a server. Technically, you could skip to the end of this chapter and put it online, but it won't do you much good at this point. Your version of Webmin is pretty old and needs to get updated, and you need to set up a few other things before your server is actually useable. However, if you really just wanted a static web page that just displays a block of text, you could do that right now if you wanted. Assuming you want more than that, let's move on.

Webmin (webmin.com) is the interface for your server. Think of it like your operating system. Although you can jump to the command line and do everything you need to, the interface makes it a lot easier to use.

PI POINTER

Webmin is one of many different graphical interfaces for servers. Other similar software include cPanel (cpanel.net), OpenPanel (openpanel.com), Ajenti (ajenti.org), and ZPanel (zpanelcp.com). Many of these are also free, so you can experiment with alternatives once you're set up.

You can access Webmin from any web browser. Once you're in, you'll find all kinds of utilities for managing your own website. You can configure a variety of different apps, including PHP and MySQL through the web interface.

Webmin runs primarily on Linux, so it's perfectly functional on the Raspberry Pi. It's not required by any means—in fact, if you wanted to, you could do everything in this chapter from the command line—but Webmin makes things a lot easier to manage.

Logging in to Webmin

Now to log in to Webmin. Remember those numbers you wrote down in step 7 of the initial setup process earlier? You need those now.

1. Open your main computer web browser, and type in the address you wrote down from Webmin earlier. It should read something like `https://192.168.1.112:12321`. Be sure you use *https* or the page won't load. The initial string of numbers is your Raspberry Pi's IP address. The numbers after the colon are the port.

2. Your browser might give you a warning that the connection isn't private. That's okay for now, so skip through it. (The warning is simply saying the site you're connecting to can't be verified, which is true, because you haven't set anything up yet.)

3. At the Turnkey Linux login page, log in with the username root and the password you created during the initial setup process.

After you log in, you'll see the Webmin main page.

The initial Webmin login page is where you finally start configuring everything.

Upgrading Webmin

Everything looks like it's ready to go, but before you start setting up your server, you need to update Webmin. Click the **Upgrade Webmin Now** button to start the update process.

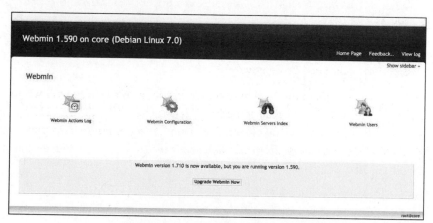

Before you proceed, you need to upgrade Webmin.

You'll then see a bunch of text on the screen about various things downloading and uncompressing. Just let Webmin do its thing. It will take a few minutes to work. At certain points, it will say something like *Download complete* or *Package signature verified successfully*. This doesn't mean the update is finished, so let it go until you see *Webmin has been installed and started successfully*.

When it's complete, click the **Return to Webmin Configuration** button. You'll see a lot of cool-looking stuff to mess around with here, but hold off for a second. You need to do a few other things first.

Logging in over the Shell Interface

Included in your Turnkey distribution is software called Shell in the Box, which enables you to log in and use the command line on your Raspberry Pi server from your web browser. It also makes things a lot easier to manage and allows you to run your Pi without a monitor.

Shell in a Box is a web-based terminal emulator. It gives you access to the command line on your Raspberry Pi server from any web browser. This is helpful with a web server because you often need to get into the command line to do things Webmin can't do. You might need to download a specific set of files, for example, or move things around quickly. With Shell in a Box, you can do everything you can normally do in the command line. The only difference is you're not directly in front of your Raspberry Pi.

Shell in a Box is included with the Turnkey distribution you're using, so you don't need to do anything extra to get it working.

> **SOFTWARE SOLUTION**
>
> You don't have to use Shell in the Box. If you'd prefer to use SSH and your computer's shell program, that's another option. The nice thing about Shell in the Box is that you don't need extra software, so you can access it anywhere.

Logging in Through Your Browser

Because you don't need any special software, you can log in to Shell in the Box from your computer's browser. Here's how:

1. In your web browser, type in the web shell address you wrote down earlier. It'll read something like `https://192.168.1.112:12320`.

2. You'll likely see the unsafe warning again. Skip it, and you're greeted with a shell login that looks just like the command line.

```
core login: root
root@core's password:
Linux core 3.2.27+ #250 PREEMPT Thu Oct 18 19:03:02 BST 2012 armv6l

The programs included with the Debian GNU/Linux system are free software;
the exact distribution terms for each program are described in the
individual files in /usr/share/doc/*/copyright.

Debian GNU/Linux comes with ABSOLUTELY NO WARRANTY, to the extent
permitted by applicable law.
Last login: Mon Nov 10 20:25:43 2014
root@core ~#
```

The shell interface looks just like the command line on your Raspberry Pi, but it's in your browser.

3. Type in root for the username and your password for the password. From here on out, you'll be using this shell just like you would if you set up SSH.

You're now logged in to your Raspberry Pi server and can interact with the command line. Let's change up some settings.

Changing Your Host Name

Chances are, you don't want your server to be called *CORE,* which is the default host name. The good news is, you can change it to whatever you want. Here's what to do:

1. At the command line, type in nano /etc/hostname, and press **Enter**.

2. Replace **CORE** with whatever you want your host name to be.

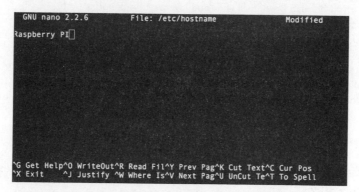

```
GNU nano 2.2.6            File: /etc/hostname            Modified
Raspberry PI




















^G Get Help^O WriteOut^R Read Fil^Y Prev Pag^K Cut Text^C Cur Pos
^X Exit    ^J Justify ^W Where Is^V Next Pag^U UnCut Te^T To Spell
```

You can edit your host name to whatever you'd like it to be.

3. Tap **Ctrl+X** to save and exit.

4. Type in reboot to reboot the system so your change takes effect.

Now, your server has the host name you want.

Mounting an External Hard Drive (Optional)

If you want to store a lot of stuff on your web server, you should attach an external hard drive. This isn't required by any means, but if you plan on hosting anything more than a couple static websites with a lot of text, you'll want an external drive.

External hard drives are inexpensive, and just about any of them will work for this project. Get something big so you don't need to upgrade in the future. Any hard drive larger than 100GB should be plenty for what you need.

Downloading NTFS

Assuming you're using an *NTFS*-formatted external hard drive, you need to install some NTFS software. This part's super easy:

1. Go to your command line tab, and type in `apt-get install ntfs-3g`.

2. Press **Enter**.

Wait for it to download and install everything. It'll take a little while.

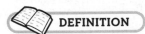 **DEFINITION**

New technology file system (NTFS) is a file system originally developed for Windows but that's now supported by every operating system. Out of the box, many hard drives are already formatted as NTFS, but you can check yours by typing `sudo blkid` into the command line.

Mounting Your Hard Drive

Next, you need to mount your hard drive so Webmin knows where it is. Typically, you'd do this from the command line, but Webmin has a simpler method built into it. Here's what to do:

1. Back on the Webmin configuration screen, click **System**.

2. Select **Disk and Network Filesystems**.

3. From the drop-down menu, select **Windows NT Filesystem (ntfs)**.

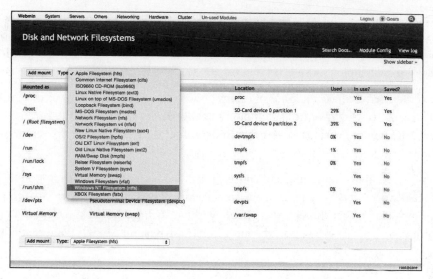

If you have a hard drive connected to your Raspberry Pi, mounting it in Webmin is just a click away.

4. Under **Mounted as,** type in `media/hdd`.

5. Be sure **Save and mount on boot** and **Mount** are both selected.

6. Under **Disk,** select your hard drive. There should be only one option.

7. Under **Read only,** choose **No.** Leave the rest of the settings as they are.

8. Click **Create.**

Now your hard drive is mounted and useable by your server. You should see it listed on the Disk and Network Filesystems page.

Installing MySQL

Next you need to download and configure MySQL. MySQL is database software that provides the back end for a lot of modern websites. "Database software" might sound pretty boring, and at a glance, MySQL isn't exactly the most exciting piece of software you'll install. However, it is very necessary.

In order to add, access, and process data stored on your server, you need database management software. That's exactly what MySQL is. It takes a look at the massive amounts of tables, stats, and details on your server and turns them into useable information. If all your data is a spreadsheet, for example, MySQL is your Excel.

MySQL is required to make all kinds of things on websites. The most obvious is login information, but it's also used to store specifics about picture galleries, lists, and even the basic structure of a website. If your site has various folders that link to other ones, MySQL is there to understand that relationship.

MySQL is incredibly complicated, and entire careers are built around managing MySQL databases. Don't let that worry you, though. It's good to have an understanding of how MySQL works and what it is, but you can get through this project without such extensive knowledge. The more you tinker with your private web server, the more you'll learn about MySQL, and that'll be enough knowledge for you.

 PI POINTER

MySQL is one of the most popular and widely used pieces of database software. It's second only to SQLite (sqlite.org), which is similar to MySQL but a little more lightweight. Certainly other options are out there, but MySQL is the industry standard for nearly every website.

Downloading and Installing MySQL

Next, it's time to install MySQL because without it, you won't be able to use any of the advanced features like ownCloud or WordPress featured later in this chapter.

Here's how to download and install MySQL:

1. On the Webmin page, click **Un-used modules**.

2. Select **MySQL Database Server**.

3. Click on **Click here** to download and install MySQL. You'll see a bunch of text on the screen, so wait until it all downloads and everything installs.

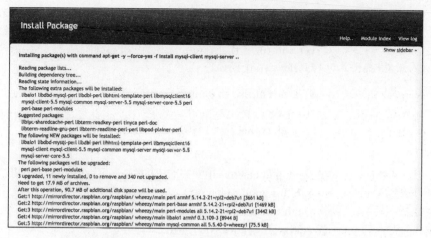

The MySQL install page will take a little while to install everything.

This process might take some time, so let it do its thing and don't close your browser window. When it's finished, you'll see a message on the bottom saying Return to MySQL Database Server. Click that message to head back to the main page.

Setting Up a Database

Now MySQL is installed, but it's not really doing anything. In order to actually use it for something, you'll need to set up a database for your various web applications to use. In this case, you'll set one up for OwnCloud.

Setting up a new database in MySQL is very quick and easy.

1. In Webmin, click **Servers**.

2. Select **MySQL Database Server**.

3. Click **Create New Database**.

4. Name your database here. Because this one's for ownCloud, let's just call it `owncloud`.

5. Leave all the other fields here blank. Click **Create** at the bottom of the page to make the database.

That's all it takes to create a database. Now you'll establish a user so you can actually access your database.

Adding a New User to MySQL

For security, it's good to create a new user for your database. This way, all your data is secured behind a username and password. When you create a user, the web application attached to that database only has access to the database you give the user, so if it's ever compromised, the user can't access the rest of the database. Plus, it just makes things a little neater and easier to understand if you ever do a server overhaul.

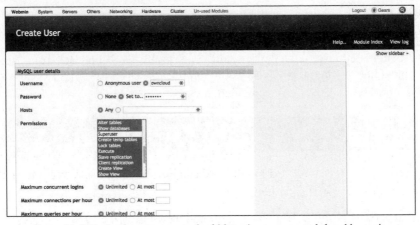

Every MySQL database you create should have its own user to help add security.

Here's what to do:

1. In Webmin, click **Servers**.

2. Select **MySQL Database Server**.

3. Select **User Permissions**.

4. Click on **Create new user**.

5. Create a username. For consistency's sake, I'll use owncloud, but you can make yours whatever you want.

6. Create a password. Be sure it's something you can remember!

7. Leave the **Hosts** section blank.

8. Under **Permissions**, select everything except Superuser.

9. Leave everything else how it is. Click **Create** when you're done.

Now you've created a user for your ownCloud install, which we'll get to later in this chapter.

 PI POINTER

If you want different databases, you can add as many users as you want here. Besides ownCloud, you'll also need one if you decide to install WordPress. You can share databases among web applications, but it's not a good idea. It's better if you set up a new database for each application. That way, if something goes wrong with one of them, it doesn't affect the entire database.

Installing PHP

Next you need to install PHP. Like MySQL, PHP is required for just about all web applications, so this is a must if you plan on doing anything interesting with your server. In this project, it's necessary for both WordPress and ownCloud.

PHP is a scripting language used in web development and works as the back end for many websites. It provides the scripts for sites that perform calculations, process user input, read files, and more. It works with HTML to provide information that's displayed on the site. Like a lot of things in this chapter, a full explanation of PHP can be a book in itself, but you won't be messing around with it beyond installing it here.

Downloading and installing PHP is super easy and works just like installing any other software:

1. Open your command line tab, and type in `apt-get install php5 php-pear php5-mysql`.

2. Press **Enter**.

This process might take a little while.

Installing FTP Software

You also need FTP software. FTP is a file transferring protocol that allows you to move files between computers on a network. With FTP software installed, you can dial in to your web server from any computer, no matter where you are in the world.

You'll be setting up your web server in your home on your own Raspberry Pi, so you might need to connect to it remotely at some point to upload files. For example, maybe you're on vacation and realize the main web page has a typo on it. FTP makes this super easy to access and update.

FTP is also helpful if you decide you want to store some files on your server. Let's say you have a big presentation to give at work but you can't seem to find a thumb drive to put it on as you're getting ready that morning. With FTP, you can upload the presentation file to your private server and then download it to your office computer when you get to work. It's simple, secure, and typically pretty fast.

Downloading FTP Software

First, you need to download some FTP software and configure it:

1. At the command line, type in `apt-get install proftpd`, and press **Enter**.

2. Wait for the software to download and install. When it's finished, type in `echo "/bin/false" >> /etc/shells`, and press **Enter**.

Once that's finished, your next task is in the Webmin panel.

Configuring Webmin

Now you're going to tell Webmin that you installed FTP access. That way, it knows what it's supposed to do when you try to connect over FTP.

Here's what to do:

1. Click on **Webmin**.

2. Select **Webmin Configuration**.

3. Select **Webmin Modules**.

4. Click the box next to **Standard module from www.webmin.com.**

5. Click the ... button to the right of that.

6. Select **proftpd** from the list.

7. Click **Install Module**. Wait for everything to install.

8. When it's finished installing, click **Systems** at the top of the page.

9. Select **Users and Groups**.

10. Select **Create User**.

11. Under **Username**, type in a username. For consistency, I'll use PiFTP.

12. Leave everything else blank. Under **Shell**, select **/bin/false**.

13. Select **Normal Password**, and type in a password.

14. Select **New Group with the same name as user**.

15. Leave everything else how it is, and select **Create** at the bottom of the page.

You've now added FTP to your web server and created a login to use with it. When you're totally finished with this project, you'll be able to log in remotely to your web server and access your files via FTP.

PI POINTER

You can access your FTP server from either special software on your computer or just through your web browser by typing in ftp://*yoursite*.com. This won't be useful until you get your server online in the later section of this chapter, though.

Installing Samba (Optional)

FTP is great for remote file management, but chances are, you'll be managing most of that stuff locally on a computer that's on the same network as your Raspberry Pi server. For that, you'll want to install Samba.

Like FTP, Samba is a file sharing protocol. The difference here is that Samba is for sharing files *inside* a network. So if you have your home computer connected to the same network as your Raspberry Pi web server, you can easily transfer files between the two. Considering you'll likely do most of your web site management this way, Samba makes things a lot easier to use.

Downloading and Installing Samba

Installing Samba from Webmin is super easy and only requires a few clicks to complete:

1. In Webmin, click on **Un-used Modules**.

2. Select **Samba Windows File Sharing**.

3. Click on **Click here** to download and install Samba.

Again, this will take a little while to download and install, so give it some time. When you see *Return to Samba Windows File Sharing,* the install is done.

Setting Up Samba

Samba's an easy way to share files between your server and a computer on the same network, but it needs a little help understanding what's going on before it'll work. Here's what you need to do:

1. Back in the Webmin, select **Servers**.

2. Select **Samba**.

3. Select all the checkboxes next to the different directories.

4. Click on **Delete Selected Drives**. Don't worry; nothing's getting deleted. This is just part of the setup process.

5. Click on **Create a New File Share**.

6. Fill in the following information:

    Share name: Type any name you want here

    Directory to share: /media/hdd/share

    Automatically create directory? Yes

    Create with owner: root

    Create with permissions: 755

    Create with group: root

    Available? Yes

    Browseable? Yes

    When you're done, click **Create**.

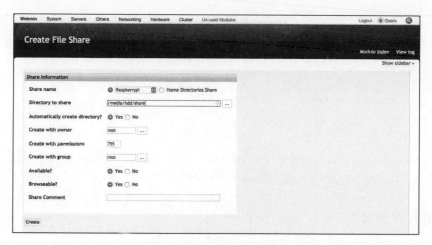

When Samba file sharing is set up, you can easily move files between your home computer and your server.

7. You'll now see your mounted drive. Click on it.

8. Click the **Security and Access Control** option.

9. Change **Writable** to Yes.

10. Click **Save**.

Now, the folder you mounted will be shared locally on your network. You can do this with any other folders you want to share individually by following these instructions and changing the **Directory to share** option to another folder.

 PI POINTER

> You might see Samba called Samba Windows File Sharing in the menu. That's okay. You'll be able to access your Raspberry Pi web server's Samba shares from Windows, Mac, and Linux.

Creating a New Samba User

Now you need to add a little security to your Samba share. This is done by creating a user and a password. Here's how:

1. Open the command line in Shell in a Box.

2. Type in `pbdedit -a -u root`, and press **Enter**.

3. Enter a password for Samba.

That's it. You now should have access to your server from your Windows or Mac computer. Just click on the server in Explorer in Windows or Finder in Mac to access it.

Installing ownCloud (Optional)

Next, you'll install ownCloud. ownCloud is free and open-source software that enables you to sync data across computers using your own server. It's easy to install on your home server.

ownCloud was originally created as a private alternative to services like Dropbox and iCloud, and it works similarly. Out of the box, you can store files on ownCloud that you can access from other computers or mobile apps. It also has a built-in media player, a variety of tools, and more. With ownCloud, you can install the software on your own server, which means you don't have to pay monthly fees for extra storage like you would with some other similar services.

Let's take a look at a few of the bigger features included with ownCloud to get an idea of how it works:

File syncing and storage: ownCloud works exactly like Dropbox in that you create a folder on your computer and everything you do in that folder automatically synchs to your server and any other computer attached to the same account. So if you save a text file in your computer's ownCloud folder, it's automatically uploaded to ownCloud as a backup. If you make any edits, the new file is uploaded as well. It's great for backups.

Calendar: ownCloud includes a basic calendar you can sync across your various devices. If you've ever used Google Calendar, it works similarly.

Music streaming: Want to have access to your music library from anywhere in the world? ownCloud features music playing software. Just upload your MP3 files to your server, and you can play them in any web browser from the ownCloud page.

Photo gallery, video viewing, and PDF viewing: ownCloud includes software to view all the types of files you could possible need it to. So if you upload all your photos, you can easily access them in a slideshow view. If you want to watch some videos stored on your server, you can. In addition, you can open basic documents like PDFs.

Apps: ownCloud isn't limited to what's in the box. If you need more features, you can install third-party apps to get a little more functionality. These apps range from file editing software to games.

If you want, you can set up ownCloud on your server and never actually host a website. This is ideal if you're tired of paying fees for online storage or you'd prefer to keep your private data off third-party services.

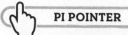

PI POINTER

ownCloud mobile apps are available for Android and iOS. With these apps, you can access your server's file easily while you're on the go. You also can play music, so if you're storing your music library on your server, you can get to it no matter where you are. Likewise, there are apps for Windows, Mac, and Linux that add syncing capability so it's easy to upload files. You can grab all of them at owncloud.org.

Installing ownCloud

You can install ownCloud from the Webmin screen, which makes things pretty easy:

1. In Webmin, click on **System**.

2. Select **Software Packages**.

3. Click the button next to **Package from APT**.

4. Type in ownCloud, and click **Install**.

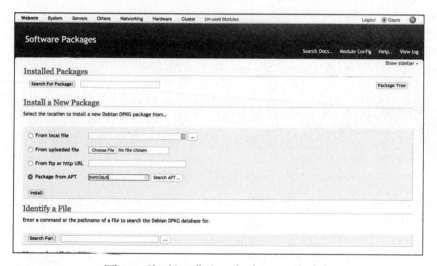

The ownCloud installation takes just a couple clicks.

Like pretty much everything else so far, it'll take a little while for ownCloud to download and install, so sit back and relax while it does its thing. When it's finished, it'll say *Return to module index.*

You'll need to finish with a bit of work in the command line:

1. Open Shell in a Box.

2. Type in `cd /media/hdd`, and press **Enter**.

3. Type in `mkdir cloud`, and press **Enter** to create a directory for the ownCloud installation.

4. Type in `chmod 750 /media/hdd/cloud`, and press **Enter** to change the permissions of the folder.

That's it for the back end portion of setting up ownCloud. Now it's time to configure it.

Configuring ownCloud

You'll configure OwnCloud using a web address. Here's how:

1. Navigate to *YourPisIPAddress*/**owncloud** from your browser. It should be something like *192.168.1.112/owncloud*.

2. At the login screen, you'll create a new user account. Pick a username and password, and type them into the appropriate boxes.

3. Click the **Advanced** button. Change **Data folder:** to `/media/hdd/cloud`.

When you finish the installation, you can set up ownCloud in a variety of ways.

4. Select **MySQL**.

5. Enter in the MySQL info you made before. Our example was ownCloud.

6. Type in the database name.

7. Select **Finish**.

Now ownCloud is all set up. It's time to start using it.

PI POINTER

Your ownCloud installation is locked away behind a password, but be just as careful with your login information as you would be with any other public service. This might be hosted on your own server, but that doesn't mean somebody's won't happen upon it randomly. Use a good, strong password, and don't share it with anyone.

Using ownCloud

As you've already learned, ownCloud is packed with quite a bit of stuff. Thankfully, most of it's pretty self-explanatory to use, but let's make a quick run through the menus.

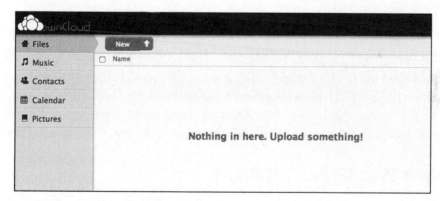

You can access all your files from the main ownCloud screen.

Files: Here is where all the files you've uploaded into ownCloud will reside. This is a pretty basic file browser, but it's easy to navigate and use. You also can share files from here if you need to send something to a friend or colleague.

Music: If you've uploaded any MP3 files to ownCloud, you can play them here. The music player's not going to blow iTunes out of the water, but it gets the job done and gives you access to all your music, regardless of where you are.

Contacts: If you want to sync your address book with ownCloud, this is where you do it. After you've uploaded your contacts, you can easily access them from anywhere.

Calendar: ownCloud makes a handy calendar. You can sync your desktop and mobile calendars with ownCloud so they all match.

Pictures: This is where your photos are stored. Just click the tab and then a picture, and you'll be able to start a slideshow of everything included here. This is an easy and inexpensive way to back up all your photos to any external hard drive without a lot of hassle.

That's the basics of ownCloud. There's a lot more tucked away inside of it, but this is plenty to get you started.

Installing WordPress (Optional)

If you're interested in running a blog on your web server, you'll need to install some blogging software. WordPress is free, open source, and easy to use, so it's a great addition to your Raspberry Pi web server.

WordPress is a content management system (CMS), which is really just a fancy way of saying it's a back end for a blog. Once you have WordPress installed, you can create new blog posts, post your favorite pictures, and run any type of blog you want.

The nice thing about WordPress is how extensible it is. It's not just a boring old blog. You can alter it in countless ways, change the look, change how it functions, and so much more.

Running a WordPress blog and customizing it to suit your content can be a full-time job, but you don't have to take it that far. It's actually pretty easy to learn the basics. Once you get it installed, things like posting a new blog post or changing the theme are all pretty self-explanatory, so even if you have no experience running a blog, you'll be able to figure out what you need to get it online.

Setting Up a WordPress Database

You'll need to give WordPress its own MySQL database. This is where it'll store all kinds of basic information so it can work properly. Here's how it's done:

1. In Webmin, click on **Servers**.

2. Select **MySQL Database Server.**

3. Click on **Create new database**.

4. Give the database the name wordpress.

5. Click **Create**.

Now you need to set up a user for the WordPress database.

1. Back at the MySQL Database Server screen, select **User Permissions**.

2. Click **User Permissions**.

3. Select **Create New User**.

4. Under **Username**, type in wordpress.

5. Give your database a password under **Password**.

6. Under **Permissions,** pick **Select table data, Insert table data, Update table data, Delete table data**, and **Create tables**.

7. Click **Create**.

 PI POINTER

> If it's just you running the blog, you can safely select everything under permissions if you really want to tinker with things. The Permissions settings in step 6 are really the bare minimum for WordPress to work, but it keeps things locked down so nobody messes with something you don't want them to access.

Now your MySQL database is all set up. Let's get WordPress installed.

Downloading and Installing WordPress

You can download and install WordPress from the command line:

1. Open Shell in a Box.

2. Type in wget http://WordPress.org/latest.tar.gz, and press **Enter**. Wait for WordPress to download.

3. Type in tar xzf latest.tar.gz /var/www/, and press **Enter**. This unpacks the WordPress file into your server's website folder.

4. Head back to your computer's browser, and type in RaspberryPiIPaddress/wordpress. It should read something like 192.168.1.112/wordPress.

Next, you'll configure WordPress with the databases you set up earlier.

Creating a WordPress Configuration File

Now that WordPress is installed, it's time to get it set up.

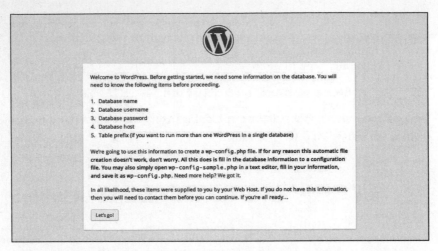

Before you can use it, you need to configure WordPress to work with your database.

Here's what to do:

1. From your main WordPress page, click on **Let's go!**

2. Enter in your database name, your user name, and the password you created in the previous step for MySQL.

3. Under **Database Host**, type in `localhost`. Leave the Table Prefix setting alone.

4. Click **Submit**.

You're almost there. Now you need to install WordPress on your web server.

Installing WordPress

Previously, you downloaded and installed what's basically an installer for WordPress. Now it's time to get it actually working:

1. Click the **Run the Install** button.

2. Now you'll create a special user for WordPress and WordPress alone. This is different from the MySQL user you set up before. Give your website a title, create a username for yourself, type in a password, and enter your email address.

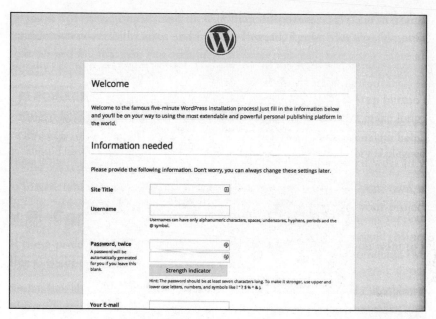

Now it's time to actually install the WordPress front end you'll use.

3. Click **Install WordPress**.

4. When it's finished, click **Log In**.

Congratulations! WordPress is now installed. Go ahead and log in with your username and password.

 SOFTWARE SOLUTION

Besides WordPress, you can install countless other content management systems on your blog. If you don't end up liking WordPress, you might also want to check out Drupal (drupal.org), Ghost (ghost.org), or Plone (plone.org). Each has its strengths and weaknesses, but they're all free and pretty easy to get up and running on your web server if you want to use one of them instead of WordPress.

A Quick Tour of WordPress

As mentioned earlier, running a WordPress blog can be a full-time job, so don't worry if you think it looks a little overwhelming. In this section, let's look at the main Dashboard screen so you're more familiar with how it works.

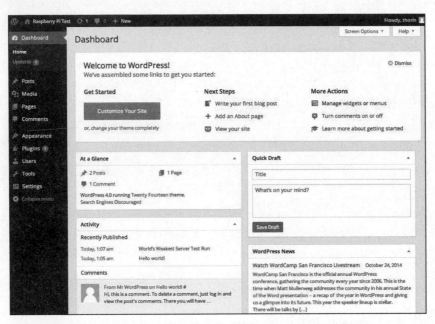

If you've ever used a blog before, the WordPress Dashboard should be familiar to you.

Dashboard: This is the main landing page you come to when you log in to your WordPress site. Here you'll find a menu screen that gets you to other settings, a Quick Draft area where you can quickly type up a blog post, and a link to customizing your blog. This might look a little overwhelming, but click around on the Dashboard to figure out what everything does.

Posts: This is where you can look at all your existing posts, write new posts, and edit old posts. If you're looking to write your first blog post for your new site, this is where to start.

Media: The media section is where you'll find any videos, sound files, or images you've uploaded to your site.

Pages: In WordPress, you get a blog post that's simply part of your blog, and pages, which are separate and static. For example, if you wanted to include an "About Us" section on your blog, you'd make a new page. You can do that here.

Comments: If someone comments on one of your blog posts, you'll find their note here. You can dismiss comments, get rid of spam, and ensure nobody's being a jerk on your blog in this section.

Appearance: This is where you'll make the big changes to your WordPress blog. You can alter little things like font and colors, or you can change the entire appearance of the whole site with different themes. Themes are basically design overhauls for your WordPress blog. You can choose from a variety of free themes from this page or upload and create some yourself.

Plugins: Plugins let you alter how things work on your blog. Think of them like little micro apps. Say you don't like the WordPress comment system. If that's the case, you can find a plugin that changes how it works. Plugins range from altering where a title is located to creating a giant calendar, so mess around in this section to find some cool stuff to customize how your site works.

Users: You don't have to be the only one contributing to your WordPress blog. If you want to invite friends along to blog with you, you can do so by giving them a user account here.

Tools: This includes a bunch of advanced tools for moving blogs between different accounts. You probably won't need to do much here.

Settings: This page handles just about every single setting imaginable on your WordPress blog. You can change the name, alter how links work, change the time, and so much more. It's worth spending a bit of time poking around here to see exactly what you can do.

That's a very brief overview of WordPress. WordPress is an incredibly powerful blogging platform with entire books dedicated to how to use it, so don't be surprised if there's a bit of a learning curve here.

Still, if you just want to post some blog posts and have some fun, you can get to using WordPress right away. Just click that **New Post** button, and you're on your way.

 PI POINTER

WordPress might seem like it has a billion and one options, but don't let that discourage you from poking around. Start by just making a few blog posts and then move on to customization. Using free themes online is a really easy way to set your site apart from the rest without knowing a bit of code, so that's a good place to start.

Assigning Your Raspberry Pi an IP Address

Now you're running your very own web server in your home, and it's packed with a ton of cool features. The only problem is that it's only accessible to computers on your home network. To fix this, you need to open your server to the internet so you can access it while you're out and about.

You have a range of options for doing this. We worked with dynamic DNS in Chapters 13 and 16. Let's use a different service this time around. In this case, No-IP.

Getting an External IP Address with No-IP

Before you can set up and install No-IP on your server, you need to sign up for an account. Here's what to do:

1. Head to noip.com/sign-up.

2. Fill in the form to create an account, being sure to click the **Free Sign Up** button for a free account.

Your resulting address will be *yourname*.ddns.net.

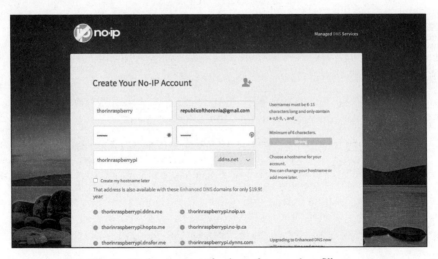

The No-IP sign-up page takes just a few seconds to fill out.

Installing No-IP

Next, you need to install the No-IP server. That means one last job in the command line. Here's what to do:

1. Open Shell in a Box in your browser.

2. Type in cd /usr/local/src, and press **Enter** to change to this directly.

3. Type in wget http://www.no-ip.com/client/linux/noip-duc-linux.tar.gz, and press **Enter** to download and install No-IP. Give it a little bit of time to download and install.

4. Type in tar -zxvf noip-duc-linux.tar.gz, and press **Enter**.

5. Type in cd no-ip-2.1.9-1, and press **Enter**.

6. Type make, and press **Enter** to create the file.

7. Type in make install to start the installation.

8. When prompted, enter in your No-IP email address and password you registered earlier.

9. When prompted, leave the update interval at 30.

10. When prompted to **Do you wish to run something at successful update**, press N.

With that, you're registered online and your website has an address. Now it's time to tell your home router it's okay for your server to be on the internet.

 PI POINTER

If you want a "real" web address like *yourname*.com, you'll need to pay for it through a domain registration site. Countless options exist. Namecheap (namecheap.com), Hover (hover.com), and Dreamhost (dreamhost.com) are all reliable and relatively affordable.

Setting Up Port Forwarding on Your Router

This last step is one of the more difficult ones because all routers are different. However, once you find the setting you're looking for, the rest is super easy.

Here's what to do:

1. Log in to your home router from your web browser. It's usually something like *192.168.1.1*. If you don't know your router's address, refer to your owner's manual.

2. Find the section for port forwarding. It's usually under the **NAT/QoS** menu, but again, all routers are a little different.

3. Next, you need to set up port forwarding for each of the services on your web browser. That means Webmin, Shell, ownCloud, and your WordPress installation. Use the following table to set up everything, substituting your IP where applicable.

Application	Protocol	Port from	IP Address	Port to	Enable
Webmin	TCP	12321	192.168.1.112	12321	X
ownCloud	TCP	80	192.168.1.112	80	X
WordPress	TCP	80	192.168.1.112	80	X
Shell	TCP	12320	192.168.1.112	12320	X

Again, every router's a little different, so you might need to play around and tweak these settings some.

When you're set up, you'll be able to access your server from anywhere in the world. If you used the examples in the preceding table, you'll be able to access them like so:

- **Webmin panel:** *yourserveraddress*.ddns.net:12321

- **WordPress:** *yourserveraddress*.ddns.net/wordpress

- **ownCloud:** *yourserveraddress*.ddns.net/owncloud

- **Shell:** *yourserveraddress*.ddns.net:12320

With that, your server is online and ready to host your website.

The Least You Need to Know

- Setting up your Raspberry Pi as a web server takes about a day's worth of work.

- When you're finished with the setup, you'll have a web server that hosts your private files, a website, a blog, and more.

- Running a server can be tough and take a lot of effort, but it's a great skill to have.

- You'll be able to create any type of website you want, and your Raspberry Pi will host it for you, so anyone in the world can see it.

Building a Network Storage Device

Unless you're deep into data backup and networking solutions, you've probably never heard of a *network storage device* (*NAS*). As the name suggests, a NAS is a hard drive that's accessible on a network. In the case of a home network, this means you can access a hard drive from any computer on the network.

This is useful for a variety of reasons. If you have a lot of computers in your home, you can set up a NAS so they can all access and share data on one hard drive. This is great for media and any other files you need to get to in your home.

Beyond just accessing files remotely, a NAS is great for creating a backup of your home computer. You can set it up so your primary computer automatically backs up everything on your hard drive to the NAS once a day. This way, no matter what happens to your computer's hard drive, you'll always have a backup of all your important data. What's more, you can automate this whole process so once it's set up, you don't even have to think about it.

This might sound complicated, but the setup process is actually pretty simple. In this chapter, you learn to build your NAS, connect your external hard drive to your Raspberry Pi, share folders with your primary computer, and establish a daily backup system.

In This Chapter

- Making your Raspberry Pi a network storage device

- Accessing your hard drives from any network computer

- Creating a daily backup solution

- Automating the whole process

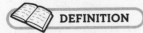

> **DEFINITION**
>
> A **network storage device** (**NAS**) is an external hard drive you can access from any computer on your home network.

Getting Started with Your NAS

A NAS operates as a file server, so everything you store on the NAS is accessible from any computer on your network. Most often, a NAS is run on a computer where nothing else is running. Typically a stripped-down operating system is used because there's really no reason for anything else to be going on.

For that reason, a Raspberry Pi is a fantastic device to turn into a NAS. It doesn't consume a lot of power, it has a very small footprint, and it's easy to tuck away under a shelf somewhere. It's also simple to set up and use, so once you get it working, you'll rarely notice it's there.

In this project, you'll set up your own NAS system for about $120 or so. Commercial solutions tend to retail for anywhere between $300 and $400, so doing this yourself is a great way to save a bit of cash.

> **SOFTWARE SOLUTION**
>
> Technically, you can run a NAS on just about any computer you have. A number of different operating systems exist to turn your computer into a NAS, and the route in this chapter certainly isn't your only option. You'll be doing a bit of a DIY method by setting up a sharing service called Samba, but there are other options available if you'd prefer something else.

The Benefits of a NAS

Having a hard drive that's accessible on your home network is useful on its own. You can store whatever you want on this drive. For example, if you want to make your home movies accessible from any computer in your house, you can store them on your NAS. The same goes for photos or whatever else you want.

Likewise, let's say you set up the XBMC media center in Chapter 12. You could point that media center to your NAS, drop a bunch of video files on there, and play those videos from any computer. It's a pretty slick little system.

Media storage of all kind is a great usage for a Raspberry Pi–powered NAS. If you have a massive music library, you can store all your MP3 files on it, and everyone in your household can access your music library.

Properly set up, having a backup service you don't have to think about can save you if your hard drive ever fails. Using your NAS to essentially make a clone of your computer's hard drive once a day is a simple, effective way to keep a backup of your important data.

The good news is that you can do both of these things. You can use your NAS to store specific files you want to access from your network, and you also can use it to back up your computer. You just need a hard drive big enough to handle both.

What Else You Need

In addition to your Raspberry Pi and its usual components, you'll need a USB external hard drive for this project. Any USB external hard drive will work, so grab whatever's cheap.

If you plan on backing up your entire primary computer, you'll want to grab a hard drive that's at least as big as your primary computer's hard drive. If your hard drive is 1 terabyte (TB) in size, get an external hard drive that's at least that big. If you want to do both a backup and store additional files on the NAS, get a hard drive that's bigger than the one you want to back up. For example, if you're backing up a computer with a 1TB hard drive, you should get a 2TB external drive so you have plenty of room to store both the backup and the additional files you want to access.

External hard drives are really affordable these days. If you hit up the right sales, you can usually find a 2TB external hard drive for about $80. Just be sure you buy one with its own power supply so you don't have to rely on the Raspberry Pi for power.

 HARDWARE HELPER

One hard drive is great and technically all you need for this project, but if you want to practice good backup behavior, you should grab a second one as well. This way, you end up having two backups of all your data, so if something goes wrong and one hard drive fails, you'll have a second one available.

Mounting the External Drive

When you have your external hard drive in hand, all you need to do for setup is plug it in to your Raspberry Pi. Then you'll get the hard drive mounted and formatted so you can start the installation process.

Essentially, you need to add support to your Raspberry Pi to read a specific drive structure, format your hard drive to match that structure, and tell your Raspberry Pi where the hard drive is. This is usually automatic on an operating system like Windows or Mac, but you'll need to do this manually on your Raspberry Pi.

Installing Raspbian

You need Raspbian installed for this project. Refer to Chapter 8 if you don't have an SD card with Raspbian installed already.

Adding NTFS Support for Raspbian

In order to use an external hard drive with your Raspberry Pi, you need to install NTFS support. This is the file system most hard drives use, and the Raspberry Pi needs a little help before it can read them. Here's what to do, working from the command line:

1. Type in `sudo apt-get install ntfs-3g`, and press **Enter**.

2. Wait for everything to download and install.

That's it for NTFS support. Next, you need to get your hard drive mounted on your Raspberry Pi.

Creating Mounting Directories

Unlike a hard drive on your personal computer, your Raspberry Pi doesn't immediately recognize and mount an external hard drive when it's attached to it. You need to do that manually for your Raspberry Pi.

Here's what to do:

1. Type in `sudo fdisk -l`, and press **Enter**. You'll see a display of your hard drives alongside your SD card. The first disk you see, */dev/mmcblk0,* is your SD card. The second disk should read something like */dev/sdb1* or */dev/sda1.* (If you're using two hard drives, you'll see both.) Make a note of the *sdb* or *sda* addresses. You'll need this information later.

2. Now you need to format the external hard drive. This will erase everything on the drive, so only do this if you're using a brand-new hard drive or you can do without the files on the older drive. Replace /dev/sda1 with the information you gathered earlier. Type in `sudo mkfs.ntfs /dev/sda1 -f -v -I -L untitled`, and press **Enter**. Wait for the hard drive to finish formatting.

Be sure you pick the right drive before you format it.

3. Before you can mount the drives, you need to create a directory to which to mount the drives. The Raspberry Pi works a little differently from a Windows PC or Mac here. It can't just automatically create an external hard drive and directory for you, so you need to do it manually. Type in `sudo mkdir /media/hdd1`, and press **Enter**. If you're using two hard drives, also type in `sudo mkdir /media/hdd2`, and press **Enter**.

4. Now that you have the directories, it's time to mount them. Type in `sudo mount -t auto /dev/yourharddrivename /media/USBHDD1`, and press **Enter**. For example, it should read *sudo mount -t auto /dev/sda1 /media/hdd1*. If you're using two hard drives, you'll need to type in the command again with the second hard drive; for example, `sudo mount -t auto /dev/sdb1 /media/hdd2`.

5. Your hard drive is now mounted, but you'll now need to make directories so it can share folders. Type in `sudo mkdir /media/hdd1/shares`, and press **Enter**. If you have a second hard drive, type in `sudo mkdir /media/hdd2/shares`, and press **Enter**.

With that, your hard drives are mounted and ready for sharing. Now you just need to set up the software so your Raspberry Pi can actually share those folders.

Installing Samba

Before you can set up your NAS, you need to get some software that can share your Raspberry Pi's hard drive with other computers on your network. You're going to use Samba to do this.

Samba is free software that was originally developed in 1992 by computer programmer Andrew Tridgell. It's a file-sharing service that enables computers to share data easily over a network.

You'll use Samba in this project because it supports Windows, OS X, and Linux. So no matter what type of computers you have on your home network, they'll be able to access your NAS and save files to it.

SOFTWARE SOLUTION

Originally, each operating system had its own file-sharing system. If you wanted to share a folder on a network, you needed to ensure it was compatible among the different computers. That's still the case, but fortunately, nearly every modern operating system supports a variety of file sharing protocols. Samba was originally just for Windows, but it works perfectly fine on Linux and Mac these days.

Downloading Samba

First things first, you'll need to download Samba. Here's what to do:

1. At the command line, type in `sudo apt-get install samba samba-common-bin`.

2. Press **Enter**.

Wait for Samba to download and install.

Backing Up Samba's Configuration Files

You're going to edit the Samba configuration files quite a bit here, so first, make a backup copy just in case things get messed up. Here's how:

1. Type in `sudo cp /etc/samba/smb.conf /etc/samba/smb.conf.backup`.

2. Press **Enter**.

When Samba is set up, you can access your files from any computer on the same network.

This makes a copy of the configuration file so you can restore it later in case something goes wrong.

Editing Samba's Configuration Files

Next, you'll edit the configuration file. You're going to use nano for this one. Here's what to do:

1. Type in sudo nano /etc/samba/smb.conf, and press **Enter**.

2. This opens the text editor. You're going to change a few things in here. Scroll down until you reach the **Authentication** section. Look for the line **# security = user**.

3. Delete the **#** symbol in front of **security = user**. This makes it so you'll need a password to log in to your NAS.

4. Next, you're going to add a new section. You need to tell Samba it's operating as a backup so it behaves correctly. Scroll all the way to the bottom of the configuration file and type in this:

```
[Backups]
comment = Backup Folder
path = /media/hdd1/shares
valid users = @users
force group = users
create mask = 0660
directory mask = 0771
read only = no
```

When you're finished, tap **Ctrl+X** to save and exit.

5. Type in sudo /etc/init.d samba restart, to restart the Samba server with your new settings.

6. Now you need to add users so you can access your shares. Type in sudo useradd backups -m -G users, and press **Enter**.

7. Next, set your password. Type in sudo passwd backups, and press **Enter**. You'll be prompted to type in your password two more times.

8. Finally, you'll add your username to Samba. Type in sudo smbpasswd -a backups, and press **Enter**. Retype your password a couple times when you're prompted to, and you're all set.

With that, the folder should be shared and working.

 PI POINTER

You can swap out much of this information for your own if you want. **[Backups]** is the name of the hard drive. You can call it whatever you want, but be sure you swap out **backups** in steps 6, 7, and 8 with your updated information.

Configuring Your Raspberry Pi to Mount to External Drives on Boot

With the Samba share working and your external hard drive sharing all set up, your NAS should be good to go. However, the Raspberry Pi won't automatically mount your hard drives when it boots up. You need to do a little more work to get that to happen:

1. Type in `sudo nano /etc/fstab`, and press **Enter**. This loads the file systems table that launches on startup.

2. Add these lines to the end of the file, substituting the information you collected earlier:

   `/dev/sda1 /media/hdd1 auto noatime 0 0`

   If you're using two hard drives, also add the second one. For example:

   `/dev/sdb1 /media/hdd2 auto noatime 0 0`

3. When you're done, press **Ctrl+X** to save and exit.

The fstab file enables you to mount your external hard drive automatically.

Your Raspberry Pi will now automatically mount the external hard drive on startup. This is great in case the Raspberry Pi powers off for some reason, or if you need to move it because you can just plug it in and go without worrying about setting up anything again.

Accessing Your NAS from Your Other Computers

Now to test to be sure a computer on your home network can access the Raspberry Pi. You'll test this with your personal computer. The process is a little different on Windows versus Mac, so follow the guide for your operating system.

Windows:

Here's how to be sure you can access your Raspberry Pi and the external hard drive from your Windows computer:

1. Open Windows File Explorer.

2. On Windows, click **Network** and look for **RASPBERRY PI**.

3. Click **RASPBERRY PI**, and click **backups**.

4. Log in with the username and password you created earlier. You should see an empty folder open.

You now have access to your external hard drive over your network.

Mac:

Now, let's access your Raspberry Pi's external hard drive from your Mac:

1. Open Finder on your Mac.

2. Find **RASPBERRY PI** on the left side of Finder, and click it.

3. Double-click the **backups** folder, and click **Connect As**.

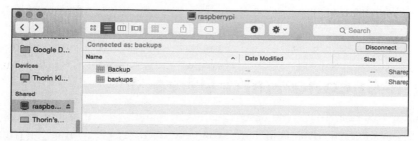

The mounted hard drive works just like it's connected to your computer.

4. Type in your username and password.

You should now have access to your Raspberry Pi's hard drive.

Testing Your Samba Shares

Now that everything appears to be working properly and you can access your Raspberry Pi from other computers on your network, check to be sure it's actually working. Here's how:

1. Navigate to the **Backups** folder from your personal computer.

2. Create a new file, and place it in the **Backups** directory. It can be any type of file you want.

3. Head back to your Raspberry Pi, and type in cd /media/hdd1/shares, and press **Enter**.

4. Type in ls, and press **Enter**.

Create a test file to ensure everything's syncing properly.

You should see the file you just created on your personal computer listed. If it's there, everything's working properly.

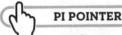 **PI POINTER**

With everything set up, you can now start moving files onto your NAS from your personal computer. Remember that they'll be accessible on the network from any other computer in your house. If your NAS is on Wi-Fi, this process might be a little slow at first, so connect it with an Ethernet cable if you'd like it to move a little faster.

Adding a Second Hard Drive

If you're using two hard drives, you haven't really done anything with the second one yet besides mount it. If you want true data redundancy, you need to ensure everything you put on the first hard drive is copied onto the second one.

The Importance of Data Redundancy

Your Raspberry Pi is hooked up to a network, the hard drives are mounted, file transferring works, and you can now save any file you want to your network hard drive with just a couple clicks. This is great, but if you want a truly bulletproof backup, you also should add a second hard drive that clones the first one.

When you create a backup, you also should make a second backup of your hard drive in case something fails. If anything does go wrong, you'll always have backup. It might sound like overkill, but it's always better to be safe rather than sorry with your data.

This is totally optional, but it's a good idea nonetheless. Hard drives are cheap enough that you can easily add a second one for under $100. If you're storing anything important—like photos, videos, or anything else you find irreplaceable—it's well worth the extra cash to ensure you'll always have your data safe.

To set up extra data redundancy, you'll basically just clone your external hard drive using software called rsync. Your NAS ends up working like this:

1. Drag and save files from your primary home computer to your NAS, or back up your whole computer on your NAS.

2. Your NAS then clones the first drive onto the second drive. Now you have two backups.

All this happens behind the scenes, so once you set it up, you won't have to think about it.

Setting Up rsync Backup

You'll set up your syncing backup using software called rsync. This essentially clones your first external hard drive onto your second one. This is entirely optional, but if you want the data redundancy and three sets of your files, it's a good idea. Hop back to the command line on your Raspberry Pi.

With a schedule, you can ensure you'll always have a recent backup.

Here's what to do next:

1. Type in sudo apt-get install rsync, and press **Enter**. This downloads and installs the rsync software.

2. Type in crontab -e, and press **Enter**. This opens the cron scheduling table. This tells your Raspberry Pi to run something on a schedule.

3. Scroll down to the bottom of the document, and type in this:

   ```
   0 4 * * * rsync -av --delete /media/hdd1/shares /media/hdd2/shares
   ```

   The command tells your Raspberry Pi to run rsync at 4 A.M. every day. You can change the time by changing the **4** in the code.

4. When you're done, press **Ctrl+X** to save and exit.

rsync will now run at 4 every morning. It will compare your first and second hard drives, copy everything from it that's new, and delete anything that doesn't match. It essentially clones the first drive onto the second every morning so you have two backups of all your data all the time.

> **PI POINTER**
>
> You can use crontab to run anything you want on a schedule, not just rsync. The text file makes it look pretty complicated, but all it does is tell your Raspberry Pi to run a specific program at a specific time.

Setting Up Automated Backups

Your Raspberry Pi now has one or two external hard drives mounted, and you can access them from your Windows PC or your Mac. This is great if you just want a hard drive on your network you can access from any computer you own. All you need to do is copy files to your Raspberry Pi's hard drive, and you're all set. For example, you could store all your music and movies on your NAS so you can get to them from any computer in the house. Or you could store photos there so you don't have them spread across multiple computers.

However, if you want, you also can create automated backups of your primary computer. Essentially, you'll use some software to automatically back up your hard drive onto your Raspberry Pi. This is useful if you don't want to worry about backing up specific files. Instead, it happens on a schedule, every day.

So next, you're going to create a system to automatically back up your home computer's hard drive to your NAS. Then you'll have two (or three) hard drives filled with the same data, so if anything goes wrong, you'll have backup copies of everything.

You actually have a variety of options to do this, but for this project, you're going to use backup software called CrashPlan.

Downloading and Installing CrashPlan

CrashPlan is free backup software that works on both Windows and Mac computers. Although both operating systems have built-in backup options, neither works particularly well with the Raspberry Pi's system. CrashPlan is a better alternative and much easier to set up.

CrashPlan is free if you want to just back up to a local hard drive, but it also has paid plans you can use to back up to cloud servers if you're interested. Because you'll have two backups at your home, this probably isn't necessary, but if you're worried about losing your data, it's always better to have backups offsite as well.

Here's how to download and install CrashPlan:

1. From your Windows or Mac computer, head to `code42.com/CrashPlan/download` to download CrashPlan.

2. When it's finished downloading, double-click and run the **Install CrashPlan** file.

3. Follow the on-screen directions to install the software.

Once the installation is complete, it's time to point CrashPlan to your Raspberry Pi and set up a schedule.

SOFTWARE SOLUTION

CrashPlan isn't the only program that does this, but it's the easiest to use and works across multiple platforms. You also can use Time Machine on a Mac or Windows's built-in backup software, but you might need to tweak the settings on your NAS to get them working.

Configuring CrashPlan to Back Up to Your NAS

Once CrashPlan is installed, you need to tell it where to back up your data to. Here's how:

1. Open CrashPlan on your Windows or Mac computer.

2. On the **Backup** tab, find the **Files** section. Click **Change…**, and select the folders you want to back up to your NAS. If your external hard drive is as big as or bigger than your computer's hard drive, select your whole computer. Click **Save** when you're done.

3. Back at the **Backup** tab, find the **Destinations** section and select **Folders**.

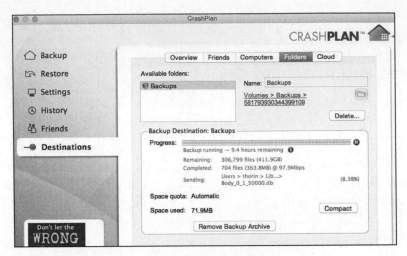

Select your NAS from the CrashPlan menu.

4. Click on **Select…**, and you should see the **Backups** drive listed in the options. Click on it, and select **OK**.

5. Under **Available Folders**, select the **Backups** drive.

6. Click **Start Backup** to begin the backup process. If you have a big hard drive, this might take a few hours or even days.

CrashPlan is now scheduled to automatically back up all the data on your home computer to your NAS.

Scheduling Backups in CrashPlan

By default, CrashPlan automatically backs up all your files whenever it feels like it. If you work on your computer a lot, this can be a bit annoying because it'll slow things down a bit while it runs. It's best to set up a schedule so CrashPlan only backs up when you're probably not using your computer.

1. In CrashPlan, select **Settings**.

2. Click the **Backup** tab.

3. In the **Backup will run** drop-down menu, select **Between specified times**.

4. Choose specific times to run the backups on whatever days you want. You should pick a time when your computer will be on but you won't be using it.

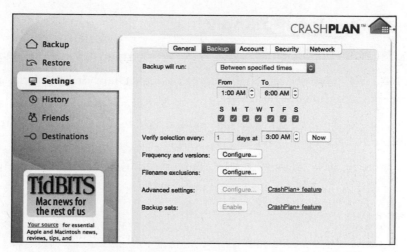

Create a schedule for your backups so you always have access to your newest files.

5. Click **Save** to save all your settings.

Now your backups will only run when you want them to.

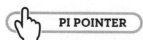

PI POINTER

File sharing tends to take up a lot of bandwidth on your network, so it's best to run your backups when you're not likely to be using your computer. Pick a time in the very early morning or late evening that won't interfere with the rest of your computer use.

Restoring a Backup

If things go bad and you lose all your data on your computer, restoring your CrashPlan backup is quick and easy.

Here's what to do:

1. Click the **Restore** button in CrashPlan.

2. Select your NAS backup, and click **Okay**.

3. Choose the destination computer you want to restore to. Click **Most Recent**.

4. Use the checkboxes to pick specific folders. When everything is set, click **Restore**.

It takes a while for CrashPlan to do its thing, so let it go and eventually all your files will be restored to the same location where they were originally.

The Least You Need to Know

- Backing up your computer regularly ensures you never lose important data.

- A NAS is a network accessible storage device—a hard drive you can access from any computer on your network.

- You can use your NAS as just another hard drive upon which to store files on or as a place to back up all your data.

- It's good practice to back up your computer to two different hard drives.

More Advanced Projects

As you've learned from the preceding chapters, you can do a lot with your Raspberry Pi right out of the box. But you can get even more out of it if you're willing to put in a little extra effort and attach some accessories.

One of the nice things about the Raspberry Pi is how versatile it is. You can hook it up to just about anything, and because of that, people have really pushed what can be done with it to a whole new level.

In this chapter, you learn about a few of these advanced projects, ranging from a retro video game station to a complete home automation solution. Most of these projects require extra parts and a little ingenuity to get them working. Some, like integrating the computer system into your car, can't be made specifically for every single car out there, so you'll have to be willing to improvise to get it working. Others, like the retro game station built into an arcade cabinet, require some woodworking skills. All these projects are doable by anyone; they just require some work.

In This Chapter

- Advanced projects for your Raspberry Pi

- Various video game systems

- Raspberry Pi camera projects

- Projects for your car and home

- Making your Raspberry Pi more portable

To that end, let's take a look at some of the best projects to help get your brain moving to figure out what else you might want to do with your Raspberry Pi.

Retro Game Station Projects

Constructing a retro game station is easily one of the most popular projects for the Raspberry Pi. With just a few clicks, you can play all kinds of old-school video games on your Raspberry Pi using the keyboard and mouse or with a third-party controller.

This works through *emulation*. In order to play games from the Nintendo Entertainment System (NES), Sega Genesis, and countless others, you'll need an *emulator*. This is a simple program that essentially pretends to be a video game console so you can play old games. With a little work, you can play everything from *Doom* to *Duke Nukem* on your Raspberry Pi.

Although it might sound a little shady, emulators are totally legal. However, the games, which are called *ROMs* (for *read-only memory*) in emulation, aren't. That said, a number of ROMs exist for homemade games, older PC games that are no longer copyrighted, shareware, and more, so you'll have plenty of things to play.

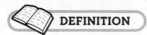 **DEFINITION**

Emulation is when your computer pretends to be another kind of computer. In this case, your Raspberry Pi acts like a game console so it can understand the programming in a game. An **emulator** is the program that does the actual emulation. It duplicates the function of one computer onto another. Here, it makes your Raspberry Pi act like a game console. A **ROM (read-only memory)** is an image of a chip. Games and older computer firmware don't run off software, so ROMs are dumps of everything included on the chip, including the game's code, which makes it possible to run inside an emulator. A ROM is very similar to the ISO files you use to make your Raspberry Pi operating system images.

You learn how to set up the software in a second, but the real appeal of these systems is what other people have done with them. The Raspberry Pi community rarely wants to leave good enough alone, so instead of just setting up a boring emulator on the Raspberry Pi, people have created full arcade systems, tabletop systems, and so much more. How far you want to take your game station is up to you, but you'll find all the resources you need in this chapter.

Retro Game Station Operating Systems

You can install any emulators on your Raspberry Pi, but two of the more popular solutions come in the form of custom operating systems. RetroPie (blog.petrockblock.com/retropie) and PiPlay (pimame.org) are both operating systems that preload your Raspberry Pi with game emulators so you can start playing right away.

RetroPie was one of the first retro game emulator distributions available on the Raspberry Pi, and it's also the one you learn how to set up here. In this project, you basically burn the image just like you would with Raspbian and then run through a simple setup script to get everything working. It's pretty easy to use, but it isn't as intuitive as PiPlay, which we get to in a second. RetroPie comes with a ton of different emulators:

- Amiga
- Amstrad CPC
- Apple II
- Apple Macintosh
- Atari 800
- Atari 2600
- Atari ST/STE/TT/Falcon
- Commodore 64
- Final Burn Alpha
- Game Boy
- Game Boy Advance
- Game Boy Color
- Intellivision
- MAME
- MSX

- Neo Geo
- Nintendo 64
- Nintendo Entertainment System
- PC
- PlayStation 1
- ScummVM
- Sega 32X
- Sega Game Gear
- Sega Master System
- Sega Mega Drive/Genesis
- Sega Mega-CD /CD
- Sinclair ZX Spectrum
- Super Nintendo Entertainment System
- TurboGrafx 16

PiPlay is a little easier for people to use because it uses big, familiar menus to navigate and pick out games. In only supports a few emulators though:

- Atari 2600
- Commodore 64
- Game Boy
- Game Boy Advance
- Genesis
- MAME

- Neo Geo
- Nintendo Entertainment System
- PlayStation
- ScummVM
- Super Nintendo Entertainment System

Really, there's no major difference with performance between RetroPie and PiPlay, so it's mostly about the aesthetics of which you prefer. RetroPie is a little older and has a lot of support, so that's the one you learn how to set up in this project.

PI POINTER

Emulation on the Raspberry Pi is typically pretty good, but you might notice some slow-down with more powerful systems like a PlayStation. The general rule of emulation is that the computer running it needs to be about twice as powerful as the system it's emulating, so PlayStation tends to be a bit sluggish on the Raspberry Pi.

Setting Up RetroPie

I'm not going to guide you through the entire process of building a cabinet for your Raspberry Pi–powered retro game station, but setting up RetroPie is easy enough you can do it in a few minutes. When it's set up, you can easily connect it to your TV and begin gaming.

Here's what to do:

1. Download the RetroPie SD card image from blog.petrockblock.com/retropie.

2. Burn the image onto an SD card using the same methods you used for Raspbian in Chapter 8.

3. Plug your SD card into your Raspberry Pi, and boot it up.

4. You'll be greeted with the raspi-config menu. Select **Expand Filesystem**, and choose **Yes**.

5. Under **Internationalization Options**, set up your location, keyboard, and time zone.

6. Exit the raspi-config screen and wait for your Raspberry Pi to reboot.

7. You'll be greeted by a controller setup screen. If you have a USB controller, plug it in and follow the on-screen prompts. If you're using your keyboard, press **Enter** to get through the prompts. This only sets up your controller to work with the Emulation Station, the RetroPie's navigation screen, not the emulators.

8. Press **Esc** to exit out of RetroPie and get back to the command line.

9. Type in `cd RetroPi-Setup`, and press **Enter**.

10. Type in `sudo ./retropie-setup.sh`, and press **Enter** to load the RetroPie setup screen.

11. Navigate to **Setup**, and choose **Register RetroArch Controller**. Follow the on-screen directions to set up your controller to work with the emulators.

Reboot your Raspberry Pi with `sudo reboot`, and everything should be set up and ready to go. RetroPie comes packed with the emulators to play games, but no actual games outside a few free games and demo versions, so you'll need to track those down yourself.

 **HARDWARE HELPER**

Just about any controller that has a regular USB plug will work with your Raspberry Pi. You can even get drivers so you can play with a PS3 or Xbox 360 controller.

Example Projects

Setting up your Raspberry Pi as a retro game station with software is really only half the battle. It's a fun project, but to take it up a notch, create a whole box and setup for your system. I'm not going to cover all that in this book, but a few guides are available online to get you started if you're looking for ideas:

Build a full-size arcade cabinet: If you're handy with woodworking, you might want to turn your Raspberry Pi into a full-blown arcade cabinet. This project is exactly what it sounds like. You'll make the cabinet, build custom joysticks and buttons, set up the software on your Raspberry Pi, integrate it all with a monitor, and stuff it all inside the cabinet. As you'd expect, you have a ton of different options for doing this.

DIYer Kyle Shipley built one for up to four players. Find the directions at blog.kyleshipley.com/ posts/2013-08-29-raspberry-pi-arcade-cabinet.html. Tested has a large guide for custom making a cabinet from scratch at tested.com/art/makers/463888-tested-projects-building-custom-arcade-cabinet-part-1.

Build a small-scale Raspberry Pi arcade game console: Not everyone has the space to build a massive arcade cabinet in their house, but thankfully, there are plenty of small cases you can build as well.

Adafruit has a kit to build a tiny little machine available at learn.adafruit.com/cupcade-raspberry-pi-micro-mini-arcade-game-cabinet/overview. Instructables shows you how you can make your own with 3D-printed materials at instructables.com/id/Build-your-own-Mini-Arcade-Cabinet-with-Raspberry, and you'll find another guide for an alternate small case on Instructables at instructables.com/id/NaCade-The-Naked-Raspberry-Pi-Arcade-Machine.

Connect official Super Nintendo controllers to your Raspberry Pi: If you really want to live the old-school life, you can connect actual Super Nintendo controllers to your Raspberry Pi with RetroPie. The process is pretty complicated, but you can find how to do it on the RetroPie site at blog.petrockblock.com/2012/10/21/the-retropie-gpio-adapter.

As with most Raspberry Pi projects, you can alter these cases to suit your particular needs. Countless other projects are available online as well, so dig around to see if you find something that'll work for you.

 PI POINTER

Buying an actual arcade machine would cost you upward of $4,000, but with a Raspberry Pi and a lot of spare time, you can build your own for a fraction of that cost. It's not easy by any means, but it could make a great addition to your home or garage.

Raspberry Pi Photography Projects

I walked you through setting up a Raspberry Pi as a home surveillance camera in Chapter 16, but you can do a lot more with Raspberry Pi photography than that.

Using the official Raspberry Pi Camera Module, you can do a variety of projects, including creating a point-and-shoot camera, putting together a time-lapse photography setup, or even integrating your Raspberry Pi with your DSLR camera for a super powerful camera.

Building a Point-and-Shoot Camera

When you look at a point-and-shoot camera, you probably don't think much about what's inside of it. Like any electronic, it's made of a computer. So as you've probably come to expect at this point, you can use a Raspberry Pi to make your own little point-and-shoot camera. It's not going to blow away the competition with image quality, but it will take some pretty good pictures.

Turning your Raspberry Pi into a point-and-shoot camera might sound complicated, but the software portion of it is pretty easy. Beyond that, it's just about building a case and trigger system.

There are a few variations on building this project, but in addition to your Raspberry Pi, you also need a touchscreen, the Raspberry Pi Camera Module, buttons for the trigger, and a battery pack so you don't have to plug it in.

Setting up the camera only takes a few minutes:

1. Install Raspbian (see Chapter 8).

2. Plug in the Raspberry Pi Camera Module and power up your Raspberry Pi.

3. At the command line, type in `sudo raspi-config`, and press **Enter**.

4. Scroll down to **Camera Enable/Disable**, and select **Enable**.

That's it for setting up the camera. Now you need to download a GPIO library so you can actually connect your buttons. Here's how:

1. At the command line, type in `sudo apt-get install python dev`, and press **Enter**.

2. Type in `sudo apt-get install python-rpi.gpio`, and press **Enter**. This downloads all the tools to manage what the GPIO pins are doing.

 HARDWARE HELPER

The camera module is an official Raspberry Pi accessory created by the Raspberry Pi Foundation. It's a very simple, 5-megapixel camera. It doesn't feature zoom or any special filters, but it can take a pretty good picture, especially considering it's only $30. The Pi NoIR is a night vision version that costs the same.

As far as the software setup process is concerned, that's about all you need to do. You can start taking pictures with your Raspberry Pi right now, albeit from the command line and from a nonportable setup. I'm not going to walk you through the whole process of buying and building your camera, but here are a couple great guides to get you started:

Build a simple point-and-shoot camera without a case: DIY magazine *MAKE* has a guide that details all the parts you need, how to set up the GPIO, and how to build your trigger at makezine.com/projects/raspberry-pi-point-and-shoot-camera.

Build a point-and-shoot camera with a case: DIYer Ben Heck built a Raspberry Pi camera using the same basic process as *MAKE,* but with a case and a slimmer construction. You can find his video guide on YouTube at youtube.com/watch?v=iZ3ajIoNIkA.

Really, you can do this in all kinds of ways, so how you decide to build your camera is totally up to you. The important part is getting it working, which is a surprisingly easy process.

Using Your Raspberry Pi for Time-Lapse Photography

Point-and-shoot cameras are pretty cool, but if you really want a project that's above and beyond, a time-lapse photography setup might be just your thing.

Time-lapse photography is a series of pictures taken from the same location at separate times of the day. If you've ever seen one of those videos that turn from morning to night over the course of a few seconds, you've seen time-lapse photography in action.

The software portion of this project is pretty easy. For this one, you need your Raspberry Pi, the Raspberry Pi Camera Module, and Raspbian installed.

Here's what to do:

1. Install Raspbian (see Chapter 8), connect the Camera Module to your Raspberry Pi, and boot it up to the command line.

2. Type in `raspi-still -o cam.jpg`, and press **Enter** to take a picture. If the picture taken is what your camera is pointing at, everything's working as it should be.

Now you need to write a script to tell the camera to take a picture at a set time interval. This is a two-step process. First, you need to write the script to take the picture and save it. Then you need to write the script that tells the first script to run at set times. Here's how:

1. At the command line, type in `sudo nano camera.sh`, and press **Enter**. This creates a new file.

2. To create the script, type in the following:

    ```
    #!/bin/bash
    DATE=$(date +"%Y-%m-%d_%H%M")
    raspistill -o /home/pi/camera/$DATE.jpg
    ```

3. Press **Ctrl+X** to save and exit the file. You've now created a small program that tells your Raspberry Pi to take a picture and save it with the current date and time.

4. Now type in `./camera.sh`, and press **Enter**. You should see a picture taken again. This verifies your program works.

5. To create a schedule to take pictures at set intervals, type in `sudo crontab -e`, and press **Enter**.

6. This is the cron editor. Scroll down to the very bottom until you see this line: **# m h dom mon dow command.** This is the scheduling instructions. *M* stands for "minute," *h* for "hour," *dom* for "day of month," *mon* for "month," and *dow* for "day of the week."

7. Now you just need to schedule the picture. If you want to take a picture every minute, add this line to the file:

```
* * * * * /home/pi/camera.sh 2>&1
```

You can change the timing by substituting numbers in for the asterisks. For example, to run it every 15 minutes, type in:

```
* /15 * * * * /home/pi/camera.sh
```

For every hour, type in the following (hours are listed as 0 through 23, so once an hour is a 0):

```
0 * * * * * /home/pi/camera.sh
```

8. You can alter the script to take pictures at other intervals or even on set days by substituting current information for the asterisks at the beginning of the code. When you're all done, press **Ctrl+X** to save and exit.

9. If everything is working properly, your camera should take pictures at the intervals you select. Type in ~/camera, and press **Enter**. Type in ls, and press **Enter**, and you should see all your pictures appearing in the camera folder.

PI POINTER

As with most of these projects, play around with your setup to get everything working exactly how you want. Change the time intervals, experiment with putting the camera in different places, and spend a little time composing your shot before you start actually recording everything. Time-lapses are very cool, but they're time-consuming to make, so do your best to get it right the first time.

By itself, this is pretty cool. But you also can turn all your single pictures into a time-lapse video if you want. You do this with software called MEncoder.

When you have all the pictures you want, pop back into the command line on your Raspberry Pi and do the following:

1. Type in sudo apt-get install mencoder, and press **Enter**. This downloads and installs the MEncoder software.

2. Type in cd ~/camera, and press **Enter**.

3. Type in ls *.jpg > stills.txt, and press **Enter**. This creates a new text file listing all the pictures you just took so MEncoder knows what to use.

4. Type in the following, and press **Enter**:

```
mencoder -nosound -ovc lavc -lavcopts
    vcodec=mpeg4:aspect=16/9:vbitrate=8000000 -vf scale=1920:1080 -o
    timelapse.avi -mf type=jpeg:fps=24 mf://@stills.txt
```

This tells MEncoder to turn all the images into a video file called *timelapse.avi*.

Congratulations. You just took some time-lapse video.

Now, if you want to use this time-lapse photography setup in the real world, you'll likely want to get a case of some kind for your Raspberry Pi. You don't need to do anything too crazy. Instructables has a guide for building your time-lapse system in a coffee tin at instructables.com/id/Simple-timelapse-camera-using-Raspberry-Pi-and-a-c.

Embedding the Raspberry Pi into a Digital Camera

By itself, a digital SLR (DSLR) camera is already incredibly powerful, but if you want even more power, you can embed your Raspberry Pi into your camera for lots more functionality.

To do this, you need a Raspberry Pi, a battery grip, a power convertor, a short USB cable, and a Wi-Fi adapter. After doing some work to get everything together, you'll end up with a Raspberry Pi hidden inside a battery grip and connected to your DSLR camera. With it, you can set up wireless tethered shooting, USB backups, time-lapse photography, image conversion on remote devices, and so much more.

The process for this is far too complicated to cover in its entirety here, but you can find a large lesson to get you started on photographer David Hunt's website at davidhunt.ie/raspberry-pi-in-a-dslr-camera.

Car-Related Raspberry Pi Projects

Many newer cars have fancy computers with LCD screens built in so you can control music, check out your car's diagnostics, and more. This is a pretty great feature, but it's incredibly expensive to add to an older car. The Raspberry Pi makes an excellent computer to power these types of projects if you want to make one for your vehicle.

When you get everything set up, you can get a camera, on-board diagnostic (OBD) reader, FM radio, media center, and even GPS navigation, all built in to your car, no matter what its age. You also can power a small entertainment system for the backseat using XBMC. This is an incredibly complicated project, but it's also very rewarding once you get it all put together.

Due to the nature of these projects and the fact they differ from car to car, it's hard to write one complete guide that covers all makes and models. Instead, I point you to a few projects online other people have done that you can pick up.

> **PI POINTER**
>
> Working on anything on your car is dangerous if you don't know what you're doing. If you're unsure about any of this, be sure you consult a professional for help. You should never work on your car's electrical system when the battery is plugged in or the car is on.

Raspberry Pi–Compatible LCD Screens

Nearly all these projects require an LCD screen of some kind. And if you want to include features like GPS or cameras, you need a few extra parts as well.

LCD screens: Just about any LCD screen or touchscreen works with the Raspberry Pi, but if you're looking for an inexpensive touchscreen, you have options. Tontec makes one for less than $40 that's available on Amazon (amazon.com/Tontec-Version-240x320-Display-Raspberry/dp/B00GASHVDU), and Adafruit makes one for about $35 (adafruit.com/products/1601). Either option works great on the Raspberry Pi.

GPS screens: To add GPS, you'll need a USB GPS device. Many of these are compatible with the Raspberry Pi, including Garmin's eTrex Vista HCx, Intec's EBT-200, and Bluenext's BN903S. These GPS adapters are pretty expensive though. They usually retail for around $100 to $200.

FM radio: Because you're replacing your car's stereo, you might also want to add a radio to your system. To add an FM radio, you can use a USB FM adapter like the one made by ADS Technologies. You can purchase it at amazon.com/ADS-RDX-155-EF-Instant-FM-Music/dp/B000HNHA12 for about $10.

Of course, what you need really depends on the project you decide to tackle and what you want out of your Raspberry Pi–powered car computer.

Example Projects

These projects are far too complicated to go through in great detail here, and you'll need some technical skill to get them working in your car, especially considering all cars aren't the same. With that in mind, here are a few projects you can track down online to help get you started with a Raspberry Pi–related car project:

Car diagnostics display: If you fancy yourself a stats junkie, you probably already know about your car's built-in diagnostics tool, the OBD. Typically, this is meant for technicians to troubleshoot problems with your car by looking at various readings about the car's speed, temperature, timing, and more. This data is all stored live though, so you can access it in real time pretty easily.

The DIYers at CowFish Studios have made a guide that turns all that data into a heads-up display on your car so you can track your car's real-time engine data. You'll be able to monitor speed, RPM (revolutions per minute), time, intake air temperature, airflow rate, and more. All you need besides the Pi is a Bluetooth adapter, a screen, and a few cables. You can find their guide online at cowfishstudios.com/blog/obd-pi-raspberry-pi-displaying-car-diagnostics-obd-ii-data-on-an-aftermarket-head-unit.

In-car entertainment center: If an entertainment system is more your type of project, it's pretty easy to make one with your Raspberry Pi. The bulk of this project uses the same Raspbmc build you made in Chapter 12 and then wires it through your car. You can set it up with a touchscreen in the front of your car to use for music and then wire everything to the backseat to set up small televisions for people in back.

As you'd expect, you have a ton of different options for building this, but Instructables offers a guide for a single-screen system at instructables.com/id/Raspberry-Pi-Touch-Screen-Car-Computer and *MAKE* has a guide for multiple screens at makezine.com/projects/raspberry-pi-car-computer-2.

Build a complete car computer: If you really want to go all in, you might consider building a full-blown computer car system. You need a GPS for maps, Raspbian for the entertainment system, and a reverse camera so you can see what's happening behind you when you're backing up.

It takes a bit of work to get this set up, but blogger Andrei Istodorescu shows you how on his blog, engineering-diy.blogspot.ro/2013/08/car-pc-projectaugust-2013-update.html.

Really, making your own car computer system with a Raspberry Pi is about what you need, what you want, and what's compatible with your car. Not every car has a place to put in a screen, but if you do, you should be able to do all kinds of great stuff with your Raspberry Pi.

Home-Automation Projects

Another popular project for the Raspberry Pi is home automation. These systems enable you to automate all kinds of things in your home, such as managing the thermostat, playing music in multiple parts of the house, monitoring for leaks, and more.

Essentially, you're creating a house of the future in which you can control various aspects of your dwelling from your computer or smartphone. The Raspberry Pi is a great computer for these projects because it's small and you can connect all types of accessories to it.

Typically, home-automation projects have two parts: the server and the accessories. The server is what's on your Raspberry Pi and gathers information from around the house or tells your house what to do. The accessories connect to your Raspberry Pi to collect that data. To give you a better idea of what you can do with these projects, let's take a look at some of the types of accessories that work with the Raspberry Pi.

PI POINTER

These home-automation projects tend to sound a lot like something out of the *Jetsons*, and for good reason: you can actually do a lot of those "futuristic" types of things with your Raspberry Pi. On the surface, it's about controlling your lights or maybe monitoring some locks, but if you have some ingenuity, you can do so much more.

Raspberry Pi–Compatible Home-Automation Accessories

In the case of home-automation projects, your Raspberry Pi is the brain, and the extra accessories you attach to it handle the actual monitoring. Many options for accessories exist, but let's take a look at a few of the more popular ones to give you an idea of what's possible.

Remote control outlets: Most remote control outlets that come with an infrared (IR) remote work great with the Raspberry Pi. Using these, you can hook anything with a plug to your Raspberry Pi and control it remotely. Typically, this applies to lights, but just about anything works.

Most sensors: If you walk into an electronics store, you'll find all kinds of sensors that can monitor the environment. Most are small, plastic or metal parts you can add to your Raspberry Pi's GPIO. Sensors are available to monitor temperature, sound, distance, motion, light, and so much more. In the case of home automation, you can either use these sensors to trigger an event like turning down a thermostat or to collect data about your home and display it on a screen.

If you're not sure where to start, just about any sensor from Adafruit will work with the Raspberry Pi. You can browse them on Adafruit at adafruit.com/category/35.

Webcams and security cameras: You already learned how to set up a Raspberry Pi–powered home security system in Chapter 16, but that system can work as part of your home-automation system as well. If you don't want to do that, you can use pretty much any webcam on the market. These cameras are a great part of your home-automation setup because they can monitor for movement as well as record anything that happens.

As you'd expect, there are countless other things you can add to your system. You can integrate your home stereo, your lawn sprinklers, or even your pet feeder if you want. If there's a power button on it, chances are, you can connect it to your Raspberry Pi somehow.

Example Projects

Much like the car computer projects, it's hard to really create a guide for home-automation projects because all homes are different. Likewise, not everyone's needs are the same. So to tackle one of these projects, it's best to choose what you want out of a home-automation system and go from there. These tend to be pretty expensive to build, too, but they're still a lot cheaper than retail solutions. To get you started and spark some ideas, here are a few big projects worth tackling.

Monitor your home and play music with BeakPi: If you're interested in doing some lightweight home automation like playing music around the house and controlling lights, BeakPi is a pretty solid solution. It enables you to monitor the temperature in your house, play music from Spotify, and control lights. Find everything you need on GitHub at github.com/beakable/BeakPi.

Track everything with PiDome: If you're looking to track everything going on in your house, connecting several different devices, and creating triggers for different automation tricks, you might want to keep an eye on PiDome. It's an operating system that's currently in alpha, but it promises to do a lot of different home-automation tasks. It works with many sensors alongside various external hardware. The software is still early in development, but if you're curious, you can find it on the PiDome site at pidome.wordpress.com.

Monitor everything in your house: If you're interested more in monitoring what's happening inside your house, you'll likely want to step up your system to also include an Arduino. Instructables user Eric Tsai did, and his system monitors for water leaks, notifies you when the washer is done, tells you if the garage door is open, notifies you when new mail arrives, monitors for dog waste in the yard, keeps an eye on the temperature, monitors the door locks, and even tells you if a fire breaks out.

It's a pretty intense system that'll likely require a few weekends of hard work to put together, but if you're interested, you can find his guide on Instructables at instructables.com/id/Uber-Home-Automation.

 HARDWARE HELPER

The real key with home automation is understanding how sensors work. The best way to learn is to buy a few and give them a try. They're usually very easy to set up, and once you can see the type of data they collect, you can decide what types of uses you might have for them.

With home automation, it's usually best to play around with a few different options, do some research about what's out there, and adapt a project to fit your particular house. The nice thing about most of these projects is that you can easily add accessories and sensors or remove what you don't need without messing up the whole project.

Portable Raspberry Pi Projects

You might not think it when you look at it, but the Raspberry Pi makes a great little portable device, if you know how to use it. Obviously, you need to add a battery pack and a screen of some kind, but from there, your options are just about endless.

In most cases, these portable projects require a lot of work on your part. The software portion is usually easy because it's most often just Raspbian, but building the case can be a tricky task that requires either a 3D printer or an understanding of constructing with plastics.

Still, if you have the resources, you can make some pretty cool portable stuff with your Raspberry Pi, including a tablet, a laptop, and even a handheld gaming system.

Turning Your Raspberry Pi into a Tablet

When you look at your Raspberry Pi, you probably don't think "tablet," but it's completely possible to make one with it. Obviously, it'll be a little thick and require a decent touchscreen, but if you're willing to put in the effort, you can take your Raspberry Pi with you anywhere.

The most elegant solution for a Raspberry Pi tablet was created by DIYer Michael Castor. It comes in a wood case, features a battery pack meant for an Android phone and an LCD touchscreen, and runs Raspbian. It's not nearly as thin and simple to use as an iPad, but the fact you can build it yourself for around $300 is still pretty amazing. You can find the full guide for doing so on *MAKE* at makezine.com/2014/01/07/how-i-built-a-raspberry-pi-tablet.

 PI POINTER

Most of the portable projects require a 3D printer, but if you don't have one, you can check out a local hackerspace to see if you can use one for a specific project.

Turning Your Raspberry Pi into a Tiny Laptop

The Raspberry Pi makes a perfectly good little personal computer, so there's no reason why it wouldn't also work as a laptop. Like the tablet, you need to track down a battery pack, pair it with a screen, and find a way to create a case for the laptop, but it's not as difficult a project as it might seem at first glance.

However, building a full-scale laptop doesn't tend to be very cost-effective. You'll probably want to go for something a little smaller. DIYer Nathan Morgan built a tiny mobile Raspberry Pi computer that includes an LCD screen, a battery pack, a powered USB hub, Wi-Fi, Bluetooth, a keyboard, and a touchpad mouse. It's then packed inside a 3D-printed case. The end result is a pocket-size Raspberry Pi laptop with a 10-hour battery life that you can take with you just about anywhere. It's a bit costly to make at around $300, but it's incredibly useful.

Find the full tutorial to build it on the Parts-People blog at blog.parts-people.com/2012/12/20/mobile-raspberry-pi-computer-build-your-own-portable-rpi-to-go.

Making a Portable Gaming System

If portable computing isn't your thing, perhaps a portable gaming system is. Using the same RetroPie operating system I introduced earlier in the chapter, you can create a powerful little portable gaming machine, if you're willing to put in the effort.

You have a variety of options to do this. One of the best ones is to build your portable gaming system completely from scratch. Adafruit has a guide that walks you through printing out a 3D case, modding an old Super Nintendo controller, adding your own buttons, and attaching your own little screen. The end result is a portable game system that you built yourself entirely from scratch. You can find the guide at learn.adafruit.com/pigrrl-raspberry-pi-gameboy.

If you'd prefer to go more retro, you can build your portable gaming system into an old Game Boy. As you'd expect, this method requires a lot of modification and some serious work on your part to get it working, but the end result is a retro game system inside an old-school case but loaded with the modern conveniences of the Raspberry Pi. Find the instructions for making one on XodusTech at xodustech.com/projects/raspberry-pi-gameboy-pocket.

Making Your Own Mobile Phone

Your smartphone is pretty powerful, and "dumb" phones are pretty inexpensive, but if for some reason you want to turn your Raspberry Pi into a phone, you can. You'll get a large, clunky, and hard-to-use phone out of the project, but it's an interesting idea nonetheless.

Using a Raspberry Pi, a touchscreen, a lithium battery, a GSM module, and some miscellaneous cables, blogger David Hunt built a fully capable little cell phone. It's not pretty by any means, but it makes calls. You can find the lesson for building one for yourself on Hunt's blog at davidhunt. ie/piphone-a-raspberry-pi-based-smartphone.

You can do a ton of stuff with the Raspberry Pi, and not every use is obvious at a glance. The more you dig around online and look at other people's projects, the more ideas you'll have for yourself. Take a look at what's available, and adapt it to suit your needs. Especially with portable projects, what you need and what someone else needs are likely completely different.

The Least You Need to Know

- Beyond what's in this book, you have myriad options for Raspberry Pi projects— seek them out!

- You can turn your Raspberry Pi into a retro game station with just a special SD card image.

- Setting up the camera on your Raspberry Pi is quick and easy—you can do so in less than 10 minutes.

- You can connect your Raspberry Pi to a variety of different screens so you can take it anywhere.

Going Further with Your Raspberry Pi

It's not remotely possible to cover every possible project you could come up with for your Raspberry Pi, so this final part of the book shows you how to take your Raspberry Pi further.

In Part 4, you read about the various ways to learn programming on the Raspberry Pi, exciting peripherals that extend your Raspberry Pi from a small computer into something that can actually interact with the world, and much more.

The projects in this book are just to get you started. The real fun starts when you begin to plan and design projects from your own creativity. This final part helps guide you to that point.

Additional Accessories

As you've seen in preceding chapters, the Raspberry Pi is capable of doing all kinds of things on its own. However, if you really want to make some interesting projects, you can branch out a bit more and take advantage of some of the wide variety of accessories the Raspberry Pi supports.

With the right combination of add-ons, you can turn your Raspberry Pi into a full desktop computer, a camera, and more. You also can connect your Raspberry Pi to additional electronics with breakouts, pinouts, and other accessories. Essentially, you can attach your Pi to just about whatever you want if you have the right accessories.

In this chapter, you discover different pieces you can use with your Raspberry Pi, learn what they do, and take a look at a few examples of how you might use them.

In This Chapter

- Accessories and add-ons for your Raspberry Pi

- Extending functionality of your Pi with cameras, touchscreens, and more

- Using cobbler kits, breakout cables, and prototyping kits

Turning Your Pi Into a Mini Computer

Back in Chapter 10, you set up your Raspberry Pi as a PC, downloaded necessary software, and even gave it a more Windows-like appearance. If you want to really use your Raspberry Pi as your main computer, though, you'll need to add a few accessories.

At this point, let's assume you already have a keyboard, mouse, and Wi-Fi adapter set up on your Raspberry Pi. Now let's take a look at some of the accessories you can add to turn your Raspberry Pi into a self-contained little computer.

Display Adapters and LCD Displays

We've already covered finding a monitor or TV for your Raspberry Pi, but there's also a subset of specialized displays made just for the Raspberry Pi.

These displays tend to fall into two different categories: tiny, text-only LCD screens or small TFT displays.

Alphanumeric LCD displays: LCD displays are small LCD screens that look a lot like a calculator screen. They only have one color and a little bit of text. They connect to the Raspberry Pi's display adapter so you don't need to worry about any crazy wiring. Typically, these are used for projects where you're only displaying a bit of text output, like if you create a weather monitor or a music player.

Small LCD displays: You don't have to go out and buy a full-size monitor for your Raspberry Pi. Retailers like Adafruit and SparkFun have smaller, 7- or 10-inch displays you can use for your Raspberry Pi projects. Likewise, if you're building a computer all your own, you can purchase a display without the casing so you can stuff the display into whatever kind of case you build yourself.

Regardless of what you're looking for, there's probably a display that works for your project, so look online. When you're building something with a Raspberry Pi, think outside the box and consider alternatives to standard monitors. For example, if you want to build one of the retro game arcade machines mentioned in Chapter 20, you can buy a display without a case and then build it into the cabinet yourself. If you're building a little computer, get a little display to go along with it.

 HARDWARE HELPER

> When you're shopping for displays, look for ones that are compatible with the Raspberry Pi. This will make hooking up the display a lot easier, and you'll likely be able to find technical support online if you need it. You can almost always alter a display to work with your Raspberry Pi, but it might take some technical troubleshooting to get it working.

Touchscreen Kits

Beyond regular displays, you also can add a touchscreen display pretty easily. Retailers like Adafruit make special touchscreen kits that work with the Raspberry Pi so you can connect a touchscreen to any project with very little effort.

One such touchscreen kit, the PiTFT, retails for just $35. It's a tiny display, measuring in at just 2.8 inches with a resolution of 320×240, but it's plenty capable of displaying what you need out of Raspbian.

Of course, if you need something a bit bigger, you can go up from there. Tontec makes a 7-inch display for just $48 as well as a 9-inch display for $55. These larger displays typically come with a driver board controller that handles power and any other settings you might need.

With any of these displays, you'll need to know a little about soldering, but it's nothing too complicated. If you're not comfortable with soldering, you can usually find prebuilt kits online.

Why would you need a touchscreen for a Raspberry Pi? If you don't feel like dealing with a mouse, touchscreens are a great alternative. They're also ideal when you want to make a small-scale project that needs a screen but doesn't need a whole computer backing it, such as a miniature tablet. But just about anything you make could benefit from a small screen. If you want your Raspberry Pi to act like a self-contained unit, this is a perfect way to do it.

And if you did get one of these touchscreens, you can skip the keyboard altogether and install a touchscreen keyboard. It takes a little bit of work, but it's nothing too difficult. Here's how to do it:

1. Open the command line on your Raspberry Pi. Type in `sudo apt-get install libfakekey-dev libpng-dev libxft-dev autoconf libtool -y`, and press **Enter**. This downloads some required files.

2. When that's finished downloading, you need to download, compile, and install the keyboard software. You'll use a bit of software called Matchbox for this. Type in `git clone https://github.com/mwilliams03/matchbox-keyboard.git`, and press **Enter**.

3. Type in `cd matchbox-keyboard`, and press **Enter**.

4. Type in `./autogen.sh`, and press **Enter**.

5. Type in `make`, and press **Enter**.

6. Type in `sudo make install`, and press **Enter**.

7. Wait for Matchbox to compile. When it's done, you need to install some libraries. Type in `sudo apt-get install libmatchbox1 -y`, and press **Enter**.

Now, your Raspberry Pi has the required software to power the keyboard. You also can make things a little easier on yourself by adding a toggle to turn the keyboard on and off. Here's how:

1. For this, you'll create a simple little program. Type in `sudo nano /usr/bin/ toggle-matchbox.sh`, and press **Enter** to get into the text editor.

2. Now you need to make a little program. Type this into the text editor:

```
#!/bin/bash
PID='pidof matchbox-keyboard'
if [ ! -e $PID ]; then
killall matchbox-keyboard
else
matchbox-keyboard&
fi
```

   When you're done, press **Ctrl+X** to save and exit the text editor.

3. Now you need to make your program executable. Type in `sudo chmod +x /usr/bin/toggle-matchbox.sh`, and press **Enter**.

4. Finally, you need to add it to the menu in Raspbian. Type in `sudo nano /usr/local/share/applications/toggle-matchbox.desktop`, and press **Enter**.

5. When the text editor opens, type this:

```
[Desktop Entry]
Name=Toggle Matchbox Keyboard
Comment=Toggle Matchbox
Keyboard Exec=toggle-matchbox.sh
Type=Application
Icon=matchbox-keyboard.png
Categories=Panel;Utility;MB
X-MB-INPUT-MECHANSIM=True
```

   When you're done, press **Ctrl+X** to save and exit.

6. Now it's time to add a little icon to the taskbar so your toggle is easily accessible. Type in `nano ~/.config/lxpanel/LXDE/panels/panel`, and press **Enter**.

7. Look for this section of the configuration file:

```
Plugin {
type = launchbar
Config {
Button {
id=lxde-screenlock.desktop
}
Button {
id=lxde-logout.desktop
}
}
Change it to read:
Plugin {
type = launchbar
Config {
Button {
id=toggle-matchbox.desktop
}
Button {
id=lxde-screenlock.desktop
}
Button {
id=lxde-logout.desktop
}
}
```

When you're done, press **Ctrl+X** to save and exit.

You now have a touchscreen on your Raspberry Pi and a touchscreen keyboard upon which to do all your typing. It's not as easy to type on as a real keyboard, but it'll certainly get you by for shorter tasks.

 PI POINTER

If you've never soldered before, adding a touchscreen can be a bit intimidating. But don't worry. Even if you've never soldered anything, what you need to do here is very simple and only takes a couple seconds. You can find a full guide to attaching a screen to your Raspberry Pi on Adafruit at learn.adafruit.com/ adafruit-pitft-28-inch-resistive-touchscreen-display-raspberry-pi.

Miniature Keyboard and Mouse Combos

If you need to do a bit more typing than a touchscreen keyboard will allow but you still don't want a full-size keyboard, a mini keyboard and mouse combination accessory might be what you need.

You have a few different options for these types of keyboard-mouse combos. If you're looking for something very small, Adafruit sells a 6-inch keyboard and touchpad for $50 you can order from adafruit.com/product/922. It uses USB, so it's fully compatible with the Raspberry Pi. You also can find less-expensive models made by FAVI and Rii on Amazon. These are great for projects where you need a keyboard but don't want something full-size, like if you're building a media center or a tiny portable Raspberry Pi.

If you need something a little bigger, any USB keyboard/touchpad combo will work. Logitech and Rosewill both make full-size keyboards that work with the Raspberry Pi out of the box.

Powered USB Hubs

Depending on which model of the Raspberry Pi you have, you have a set number of USB ports. If you need more, a powered USB hub is an easy way to add them.

Any powered USB hub will work with the Raspberry Pi, so you can expand the ports as much as you want. Powered USB hubs slot right into a USB port and easily expand your ports. They don't need special drivers or anything else.

External Hard Drives

One of the big downsides with the Raspberry Pi is the lack of a hard drive. SD cards can only hold so much data, and if you want to do something like run a server or store media, you're kind of out of luck. Fortunately, external hard drives are easy to add to your Raspberry Pi.

You can format a hard drive on your Raspberry Pi in a number of ways, including NTFS (Windows NT File System) and FAT (File Allocation Table). NTFS is typically the best for the Raspberry Pi because it supports large file size and volume size.

 **HARDWARE HELPER**

An external hard drive is useful for a number of projects in this book. If you do any project that needs a lot of extra storage, an external hard drive is helpful. You can use one hard drive for multiple projects though, so don't feel like you have to buy a new one every time.

Any external hard drive will work, but most require a USB hub to run because they need the extra power. When you have everything in hand, setting it up takes just a few steps:

1. From the command line, type in `sudo blkid`, and press **Enter**. This checks to see if the hard drive is recognized. You should see your hard drive make and model listed on the screen.

2. Now you need to ensure it's partitioned. Type in `sudo fdisk -l`, and press **Enter**. You'll see your hard drive listed with information that reads something like */dev/sda1*. Make a note of the name.

3. Type in `sudo mount /devicenamefromstep2 /mount`, and press **Enter**. It should read something like *sudo mount /dev/sda1 /mount*. Your drive is now mounted.

4. You might need to change the permissions on your external hard drive to actually write to it. If that's the case, type in `sudo chmod 775 /mnt`, and press **Enter**. This enables you to read and write to the drive.

That's all it takes to mount an external hard drive. If you want to mount it automatically on boot, you'll need to take an additional step:

1. Type in `sudo nano /etc/fstab`, and press **Enter**. This opens the text editor.

2. Add a line to the end of the file to mount the hard drive, replacing your information for **/dev/sda1** with `/dev/sda1 /mnt ntfs defaults 0 0`. When you're done, press **Ctrl+X** to save and exit.

Now, your external hard drive will mount every time you plug in your Raspberry Pi. If you ever need to unmount it, just type in `sudo unmounts /mnt` and press **Enter**.

Adding a Camera to Your Raspberry Pi

We've already talked a little bit about the camera module in Chapters 16 and 20, but let's talk a little bit more about it alongside other camera solutions like webcams.

What the Camera Module Can Do

As the name implies, the Raspberry Pi Camera Module adds a camera to the Raspberry Pi. You can use it to take pictures or record video. Two different versions of the Raspberry Pi Camera Module exist: the standard one that takes pictures in normal light, and the Pi NoIR, which is meant for nighttime photography.

The camera is pretty simple. It's only a fixed focus lens, so you can't zoom. It's also not particularly powerful, so although it takes decent pictures, it doesn't have a ton of features for exposure control, white balance, or anything similar.

 ## Support for Webcams and External Video Cameras

Beyond the officially supported camera module, the Raspberry Pi works with pretty much any USB webcam or external video camera. You can find a full list of compatible webcams at elinux.org/RPi_USB_Webcams. To use one, you need to install some software. Here's what to do:

1. Open the command line and type in `sudo apt-get install fswebcam`, and press **Enter**. This installs the fswebcam package.

2. Test out the webcam by typing in `fswebcam test.jpg`, and pressing **Enter**. You should see a still image from your webcam.

3. To specify the resolution at which the picture is shot, type in `fswebcam -r 1280x720 test.jpg`, and press **Enter** to take a picture with a 1280×720 resolution.

Sure, this works, but it's kind of a pain to remember all the commands to type in just to take a single picture. It's easier to make a bash script that automatically saves the image with the current date. Here's how:

1. At the command line, type in `sudo nano webcam.sh`, and press **Enter** to get into the text editor.

2. Type in the following:

```
#!/bin/bash
DATE=$(date +"%Y-%m-%d_%H%M")
fswebcam -r 1280x720 -no-banner /home/pi/webcam/$DATE.jpg
```

   Press **Ctrl+X** to save and exit.

3. Back at the command line, type in `chmod +x webcam.sh`, and press **Enter**.

4. Run your program by typing in `./webcam.sh`, and pressing **Enter**. This should snap a picture from your webcam and save it with the current date.

Once your webcam software is installed, you can manipulate it from the command line. It also should show up in Raspbian when you need it.

PI POINTER

If you wanted, you could follow the project in Chapter 16 for creating a surveillance camera using a webcam instead of the Raspberry Pi Camera Module. It doesn't really matter what type of camera you use; you just need something with a lens. The camera module is the easiest and least expensive solution.

Breakouts and Pinouts for Embedded/ Advanced Projects

You've likely noticed that your Raspberry Pi has numerous places to connect peripherals through the GPIO. To use those, you can always connect your accessories straight to the GPIO, or you can use kits and cables to make things a bit easier on yourself (and avoid soldering directly onto your Raspberry Pi).

Cobbler Kits

A cobbler kit is an easy way to plug your GPIO into a solderless breadboard. Basically, it uses a ribbon cable to connect the pins on the GPIO to a breakout that attaches to a solderless bread-board. From there, you can cobble together different wires without having to solder anything.

These aren't meant for a permanent solution; they're meant for testing. But such kits make things a little easier during that testing phase. Most electronics stores sell cobbler kits for les than $10.

Pinouts

Pinouts are overlays that sit on top of your Raspberry Pi's GPIO pins so you don't have to remember what each and every one does. You can typically find printable versions online pretty easily. Here are a few you can print yourself:

Raspberry Pi pinout for Model B: Find a simple little printable pinout that works with the Raspberry Pi Model B at doctormonk.com/2013/02/raspberry-pi-and-breadboard-raspberry.html.

Raspberry Pi pinout for Models A+, B+, and 2: Find a printable pinout for Models A+, B+, and 2 at sander.grids.be/raspberry-pi-b-printable-pinout.

Interactive Pinout Site: If you want a little extra info, Pinout is a simple site that works on computers and smartphones and provides a little more interaction. Just click the pin you're interested in, and you'll get a bunch more info about it. Find it at pi.gadgetoid.com/pinout.

After you printed your guide, place it on top of the GPIO pins and push them through. Then you'll have an at-a-glance guide to what's what.

Breadboards and Prototyping Kits

To prototype your electronics projects, you need a system that doesn't require soldering. This reduces the chances of you getting something wrong, especially if you're not used to soldering. If you're connecting the Raspberry Pi to other devices through the GPIO pins, you can run them through a breadboard or a prototyping board.

A breadboard is pretty straightforward. It features terminals that connect one row to another. So if you want to connect two wires, you simply push them into the breadboard at select points to connect them instead of soldering them together. For example, if you hook a light to one end of the breadboard and a power cable to another, the light will glow.

A breadboard enables you to build complex electronics but still maintain the mobility of moving things around for troubleshooting. Breadboards are inexpensive, usually coming in at less than $5 at your electronics shop of choice.

Prototyping kits operate on a principle similar to breadboards, except they're slightly more permanent. Typically, you'll solder the prototyping kit on top of your Raspberry Pi. From there, you get access to a breadboardlike prototyping area where you can plug in whatever you need. Prototyping boards are modular and easy to mess around with, but they're more permanently attached to the Raspberry Pi.

 PI POINTER

Breadboards are one of those things that are a lot easier to understand once you're actually using one. If you're curious, go to an electronics shop and play around with one. It'll make sense pretty quickly when you see it in action.

Which of these you prefer is really up to you and the project you're working on. For especially intense projects, you can use both, so keep that in mind.

Other Accessories for the Raspberry Pi

A variety of accessories are available to attach to your Raspberry Pi. Let's take a look at just a few more popular ones you might find useful in your upcoming projects.

GPS Modules

You can add a GPS module, much like the one you have in your phone, to your Raspberry Pi. These usually plug in to one of the GPIO ports or a USB port. The initial setup depends on what type of device you have (it should come with instructions), but after that, you'll just need to type in a few commands to get the GPS module working.

Here's what to do:

1. In order for your Raspberry Pi to use the GPS data, it needs to know how to understand it, so you need some software. At the command line, type in `sudo apt-get install gpsd gpsd-clients python-gps`, and press **Enter.**

2. After that, you need to point the software to your GPS module. If you're using a USB module, type in `sudo gpsd /dev/USB0 -F /var/run/gpsd.sock` and press **Enter.** Substitute your device address in for */dev/USB0*.

3. Next you need to test it. To be sure it's working, type in `cgps -s` and press **Enter.** You should see your location displayed in your command line window.

Once it's up and running, you've got GPS on your Raspberry Pi.

Accelerometer Modules

An accelerometer is a simple module that adds motion control to your Raspberry Pi. This is the same type of thing that's in your smartphone that enables it to know whether you're holding it in landscape or portrait mode.

Accelerometers can tell if you're speeding up or slowing down as well as sense tilting. It can sense any type of motion, so it's also the crux of what's inside Nintendo's Wiimote.

 PI POINTER

> Accelerometers are handy in robotics as well as anything else you might want to create that requires a little balance. You could even use it in your home automation setup to detect whether something gets moved around.

Most of us don't have a lot of use for an accelerometer on our Raspberry Pi's, but if you're interested in building something like a robot, an accelerometer is a must. Setup for each is a little different and depends on what you want to do with it, so be sure to hold on to your manual when you order one. Adafruit and Sparkfun both carry accelerometers.

Real-Time Clocks

The Raspberry Pi doesn't include an internal clock, which means it can't keep track of time when it's powered off. Oftentimes, this is totally fine, but it can be problematic when you need your Raspberry Pi to keep precise time and you don't have an internet connection.

Real-time clocks add time-keeping functionality to your Raspberry Pi and keep track of that time using a battery. You need to connect your clock to your Raspberry Pi's GPIO pins. After that, you just need to update a couple things on your Raspberry Pi.

This process might be slightly different for your clock, so double-check with the manufacturer before you run anything.

Here's what to do:

1. At the command line, type in `sudo modprobe rtc-ds1307`, and press **Enter**.

2. Type in `sudo echo ds1307 0x68 > /sys/class/i2c-adapter/i2c-1/new_device`, and press **Enter**.

3. Type in `sudo hwclock -r`, and press **Enter** to see the time. If you're connected to the internet, you should see the correct time. If not, connect to the internet and run the command again.

4. Now you need to ensure your clock starts on boot. Type in `sudo nano /etc/modules`, and press **Enter**.

5. Add `rtc-ds1307` to the end of the file, and press **Ctrl+X** to save and exit.

6. Type in `sudo nano /etc/rc.local`, and press **Enter**. Add these lines to the file:

```
echo ds1307 0x68 > /sys/class/i2c-adapter/i2c-1/new_device
sudo hwclock -s
```

7. Press **Ctrl+X** to save and exit.

Now your Raspberry Pi will load the hardware clock by default and you don't have to worry about being connected to the internet all the time just get the right date and time.

Computer Modules

The Raspberry Pi Computer Module was created by the Raspberry Pi Foundation and released in 2014. It's not exactly an accessory so much as another Raspberry Pi.

On the module are all the guts of the Raspberry Pi, including the processor and RAM, as well as a flash device in place of the SD card. This is all slimmed down to fit onto a tiny, RAM-size board.

The Computer Module is designed for people who want to create their own circuit boards, so it's not really meant for beginners, but it's good to know that it exists if you want to check it out after you've gained some experience working with your Raspberry Pi.

The Least You Need to Know

- The Raspberry Pi supports a variety of accessories that enable you to extend the functionality of your Raspberry Pi.

- Installing software and setting up accessories is usually pretty easy. Once you're set up, what you can do with these accessories is just about endless.

- Many electronics retailers stock accessories for your Raspberry Pi, and most are compatible with other DIY electronics projects.

- You'll need some basic soldering skills to attach many of these accessories, so keep that in mind before you start on a project.

Learning to Code on Your Raspberry Pi

If you pay attention to the tech industry at all, you know there's a big push to teach people how to program. Many jobs today require at least a basic understanding of coding, and plenty of jobs require advanced coding skills.

The Raspberry Pi was initially created to teach kids basic programming skills, and that remains a goal today. You don't have to be a kid to take advantage of this though. Even adults can learn plenty about programming using the Raspberry Pi. In fact, because you can't really multitask much on the Pi, it's a great way to learn how to code without distractions.

Countless programming languages exist, and you can learn just about any of them on your Raspberry Pi. Programming is a book in and of itself though, so let's just take a look at a couple of the simpler tools available on the Raspberry Pi.

In this chapter, you learn how to set up and use Google Coder to teach yourself how to code websites. It might sound tough, but it's a pretty straightforward tool and works great. You also learn about Scratch, the special programming language meant to teach kids the basics of how coding works.

In This Chapter

- The basics of programming on your Raspberry Pi

- Setting up and using Google Coder

- The basics of using Scratch

- More programming skills you can learn

Why Learn to Code?

Learning to code might sound intimidating, but it's not nearly as difficult as it seems if you're willing to put the time in to it. However, when you learn how to code, you're teaching yourself a skillset that's widely applicable in a variety of fields in today's job market.

It's not just about the career opportunities, though. It's also about gaining a new appreciation for technology as a whole. When you start to peek behind the curtain of how software works, you get a better understanding of how to manipulate it to do what you want. In the case of the Raspberry Pi, this means you're preparing yourself to not only write your own programs, but also to change how existing programs work.

Don't let this scare you. You've already done a lot of this in the course of this book. You've changed configuration files, altered boot sequences, and even made a few tiny programs already. Sure, you're not quite prepared to create the next best-selling iPhone app, but you already have a pretty good understanding of how coding works and are familiar with the toolset.

Coding is one of the most rewarding skills for anyone who loves troubleshooting. Nothing you make will work perfectly the first time, so you'll always need to troubleshoot to correct any issues. Sound tedious? It is, but coding teaches you basic problem-solving skills you can use in any number of jobs. You'll iterate on each problem until you get it, and that's a skillset you won't develop with many other jobs.

PI POINTER

Learning to code is a hot topic these days, and a number of schools have created coding classes starting as early as elementary school. Thousands of resources are available for learning to code online, and you can do many of them for free. Sites like Khan Academy (khanacademy.org) and Codecademy (codecademy.com) are excellent resources for learning how to code in a variety of languages.

Apple founder Steve Jobs famously said, "I think everybody in this country should learn how to program a computer because it teaches you how to think." His view provides a great justification for learning how to code, and many in the industry share his opinion.

What Basic Coding Can Teach You

The Raspberry Pi can teach you all kinds of things, but you're going to learn mostly about basic code literacy in this chapter. Again, learning programming is a book (or many books) in itself, so you're just going to get a grasp on the basics here.

First off, you'll learn the basics of the web. Using Google Coder, you'll learn about *HTML, JavaScript,* and *CSS,* which are the primary skills you need to have to do anything online. This isn't just about operating your own website, though. HTML and CSS are great when you're trying to write a complex email or working on a blog post. Google Coder will set you up with the vocabulary and skillset to do all of that.

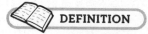 **DEFINITION**

> **HTML** (HyperText Markup Language) is the standard language used on the internet to render web pages. HTML uses tags to tell a web browser how to render elements. For example, <h1> designates a header, and <img> designates an image. **CSS** (Cascading Style Sheets) is a style sheet language that tells a web browser how to render the look and formatting of a website. It's usually used in conjunction with HTML. Whereas HTML covers the basics of a web page, CSS goes into the presentation and can change colors, layout, and fonts. **JavaScript** is a computer programming language commonly used in web pages to create dynamic content. CSS and HTML are typically static and unchanging; JavaScript allows for animations, widgets, and rendering of more complex miniature programs on web pages.

Scratch is more about teaching you the basics of how programming works and getting you familiar with the language. Boiled down to its simplest form, coding is just a series of if … then statements. If one thing happens … then another thing happens. This is the type of logic that rules all programs, and Scratch gets you familiar with how it works.

By the end of this chapter, and after a few weeks of playing around with Google Coder and Scratch, you'll understand the basics. You'll also be familiar enough with your skills and have a better idea if coding is something you want to pursue.

How Coding Can Help You Every Day

Let's say you're an accountant, or a school teacher, or a janitor—it doesn't really matter. Let's just say you're *not* a programmer by trade. Why would you want to learn any of this?

It's mostly about logic. Even if you don't go on to become the world's next great programmer, learning coding teaches you about logic and structure, and that's easily applicable in nearly every job out there.

Coding also teaches you how to work with the technology you already have. We all carry around electronic devices, and most of us don't even begin to utilize all they can do. The more you learn about coding, the more sharpened your sense of technology in general gets. This means you'll breeze through setting up that new printer at the office, installing an operating system on your computer, or even repairing major problems with your home PC. It sounds far-fetched, but coding really does provide the building blocks for dealing with all kinds of real-world problems.

The important thing isn't making your own computer software; it's training your brain to understand how to think. To that end, everyone can benefit from learning the basics, so let's get to it.

Learning Basic Coding with Google Coder

Google Coder teaches you three primary coding languages: HTML, CSS, and JavaScript. These are the main languages you need to know to program for the internet. Once you get everything set up, you'll go through a series of tutorials that teach you how to code in these languages.

Instead of giving you a blank page and a book to build a website, Coder operates in the other direction. It gives you a web page and allows you to jump in and alter whatever you want. This helps you learn what a good web page looks like and reverse-engineer it to do whatever you want. It's a nontraditional approach, but it works really well with web design.

Google Coder works a little differently from how you might expect, and it uses your Raspberry Pi in a rather interesting way. Instead of actually coding on your Raspberry Pi, you'll turn your Raspberry Pi into a mini server using the Google Coder image and then hop over to your personal computer to complete the project. This gives you a private server in your house that you can use to learn how to code from any computer you want.

 PI POINTER

Coding for the web is probably the most applicable type of programming for most of us. You can use HTML to write complex emails and having a basic understanding of HTML and CSS is required if you're writing just about anything online.

Projects and Guides

Google Coder includes a series of projects and guides for you to complete. When you're done, you'll have a basic understanding of the basic web programming languages.

The nice thing here is that you won't be building boring old web pages. Instead, you learn how to manipulate web pages and programs using just a few edits.

Out of the box, Coder contains three different projects:

Hello Coder: Hello Coder is an introduction to Coder and the first place you should start when you get everything working. It familiarizes you with Coder, HTML, JavaScript, and CSS. All the tutorials are built into the code itself, so you'll just follow the instructions on the screen.

```
Hello Coder                          HTML    CSS    JS    NODE   📁  👁  ⚙
29        <h1>Hello Coder</h1>
30        <p>Get started with Coder by exploring this app.</p>
31        <p>Click the edit button "&lt;/&gt;" to dive in.</p>
32        <p>It's at the top right.</p>
33      </div>
34    </body>
35  </html>
36
37
38  <!--
39
40  Hello Coder!
41
42  If this is your first time here, you're now looking at the
43  inside of a program. In here, in the source code, is where
44  you can make anything you can imagine.
45
46  Every app that you install on Coder has different code behind
47  it. You can use that code to learn how the app's author made
48  it. You can change the code to make the app work a little
49  differently. You can even copy the code and use it in your
50  own programs.
51
52  PREVIEW WINDOW
53    To see what your program looks like while you are coding,
54    click on that eyeball icon at the top right.
```

The Hello Coder main screen is a colorful introduction to the software.

Eyeball: Eyeball is mostly about JavaScript and CSS. When you load the guide, you're greeted by an eyeball that tracks your mouse movement around the screen. From there, you can pop into the code and manipulate it to do whatever you want.

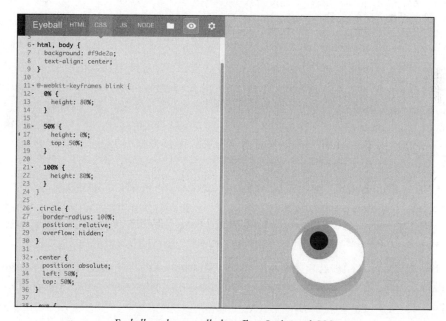

Eyeball teaches you all about JavaScript and CSS.

Space Rocks! Space Rocks! is an Asteroids-esque game built in such a way that you can hack it. In Coder, you can change all types of parameters to alter how the game works.

```
1
2   // Try changing the variables below and see how they
3   SpaceRocks.projectileColor = "#C3FF68";
4   SpaceRocks.projectileSpeed = 400;
5   SpaceRocks.enemyColors = ["#FF4E50","#E32551","#FFC2
6   SpaceRocks.shipColor = "#00CDAC";
7   SpaceRocks.lineThickness = 2;
8   SpaceRocks.outlineShapes = true;
9   SpaceRocks.fillShapes = true;
10
11  // The 3 letter name for your ship and high scores
12  SpaceRocks.ship.name = "You";
13
14  // Ship properties
15  SpaceRocks.ship.speed = 3;
16  SpaceRocks.ship.size = 1;
17  SpaceRocks.ship.drag = 0;
```

Space Rocks! shows you how to alter small bits of code in a game.

That's it for the startup projects. They should keep you busy for a little while. When you finish with those, you can download more at googlecreativelab.github.io/coder-projects.

Learning Basic Web Development Skills

Google Coder teaches you the basics of web development with three languages—HTML, CSS, and JavaScript. Let's take a closer look at exactly what that means.

HTML: When you're using Coder, you can pop over to the HTML section of a page and edit whatever you like. You can change what the text says, move where it is, and alter some basic elements of the web page. HTML is the backbone of just about every website, so it's good to know how to manipulate it to do whatever you want. With Coder, you learn how to alter all these elements.

CSS: CSS and Coder work really well together. CSS is all about changing the overall look of a web page, which includes the colors, fonts, and layout. With Coder, you can pop into any of the premade pages and change all those elements to whatever you want. You can change basic colors, move things around, and update the fonts.

JavaScript: JavaScript is a programming language, and because of that, it's a bit harder to manipulate on your own. JavaScript uses the standard if … then formula of programming, so it's much more complex than HTML or CSS. That said, JavaScript is one of the easier programming languages to learn, so it's a good starting point. Coder does a good job of teaching the basics of how it works. You'll be able to alter the behavior of a web page in Coder, make a game work a little differently, and change how certain elements on a page work.

When you have a good understanding of these three languages, you'll be able to do just about anything online.

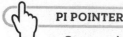

PI POINTER

Once you have a grip on HTML, CSS, and JavaScript, you can start making your own websites. It takes a while to master, but it doesn't take long to get a working knowledge to start making stuff with.

Coder

Coder is pretty easy to set up, but Windows users have to set up a few more things than Mac users.

As mentioned earlier, Coder works a little differently from what you'd expect. You'll burn a custom SD card, but instead of working on the Raspberry Pi, you'll use your Raspberry Pi as a server that you can access from your personal computer, where you'll do most of your work.

Downloading Coder

First, be sure you have a spare 4GB SD card. Coder is its own operating system and image, so you'll burn that onto an SD card much like you did with other operating systems.

Once you have your SD card, download Google Coder. You can get the image from the Google Coder site at googlecreativelab.github.io/coder.

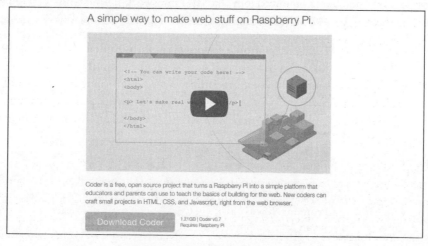

Download Coder just like any other software.

Installing Coder

When the download is complete, unzip the file. What you do next depends on whether you're using a Mac or Windows computer.

Windows:

On Windows, you'll install Coder the same way you installed Raspbian, Raspbmc, and every other operating system so far. Here's a refresher in case you've forgotten how to do that:

1. Download Win32 Disk Imager from launchpad.net/win32-image-writer.

2. Double-click the downloaded file to unzip it. This makes a new folder.

3. Inside that folder is an application called **Win32DiskImager.exe**; double-click it to open it. If you're on Windows 7 or 8, right-click the file and choose **Run as Administrator**.

4. Win32 Disk Imager should automatically choose your SD card, but if it doesn't, click on the drop-down menu and choose your SD card from the list.

5. Click the folder icon, and select the Coder IMG file you downloaded earlier.

6. Click the **Write** button, and wait for Win32 Disk Imager to run.

If your Raspberry Pi is wired through an Ethernet connection, you can insert the SD card into your Raspberry Pi, boot up your Raspberry Pi, and head to coder.local in your personal computer's web browser to load Coder.

If you're on Wi-Fi, you have one more thing to do:

1. From your personal computer, join the Wi-Fi network **CoderConfig**. This is created automatically by the Coder operating system when you have a Wi-Fi card plugged in.

2. From your browser, visit 192.168.0.1 and follow the on-screen instructions to set up your Wi-Fi card.

3. When it's set up, you can get to Coder by pointing your web browser to coder.local.

You're now all set up to use Coder.

 PI POINTER

You can always get into Coder's main settings page by clicking the gear icon in Coder when it's up and running. If you decide you don't want to use Ethernet anymore and prefer Wi-Fi, you can set it up here.

Mac:

If you're on a Mac, Coder comes with an installation program so you don't need to do much work:

1. In the Coder folder you just unzipped, double-click **CoderSetup**. This is the Coder installation program.

2. Remove any SD cards from your computer, and click **Start**.

3. Insert your SD card into your computer, and click **Next**.

Installation of Coder on a Mac is simple.

4. When your card is recognized, click **Next** again and wait for CoderSetup to do its job.

If your Raspberry Pi is wired through an Ethernet connection, you can just insert the SD card into your Raspberry Pi, boot your Raspberry Pi, and head to coder.local in your personal computer's web browser to load Coder.

If you're on Wi-Fi, you need to follow an additional step:

1. From your personal computer, join the Wi-Fi network **CoderConfig**. This is created automatically by the Coder operating system when you have a Wi-Fi card plugged in.

2. From your browser, visit 192.168.0.1 and follow the on-screen instructions to set up your Wi-Fi card.

3. When it's set up, you can get to coder by pointing your web browser to coder.local.

Now Coder is all set and ready to go.

Using Coder

When you first load Coder, you'll need to create a password. Do that first. You might get a warning about Coder's certificate here, too. This is just because Coder is running on your home network and your browser thinks that looks bad. Don't worry about it, and click **Proceed Anyway**. You'll be greeted with Coder's landing page.

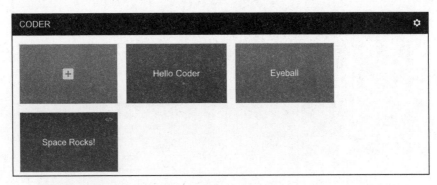

This is the landing page for Coder. It has three projects you can choose from.

Accessing Coder Projects

To open a project, just click on it. When you do, you're taken to a guide that walks you through what you can do with it. To get started, click the **</>** button in the top-right corner of a project.

Unlike a traditional guide, Coder's instructions are all inside the code itself. There are tabs for HTML, CSS, and JavaScript at the top of the page alongside a Node tab. The Node tab is connected to the JavaScript on your site and generates code based on your server. It's meant for more advanced operations.

So to play around with Coder, just pick a tab and start fiddling around with different parameters. Coder has comments designated by lines that start with // that tell you what each section does. Play around and start learning what each thing does. Don't worry about breaking anything; Coder resets to the defaults when you exit the project.

 **PI POINTER**

Seriously, feel free to play around with Coder to your heart's content. You won't mess up anything, and you'll learn more from "breaking" it than you will from making it work properly. Problem-solving is part of the game here, so get your mind ready for it.

After you've messed around with Coder for a while, you'll slowly gain a basic understanding of how to code for the web.

Adding New Projects

Coder comes with just three different projects, but you can add more very easily. Once you get the basics of web design down, you can use Coder to learn all kinds of things.

You can add new projects to Coder with just a couple clicks.

You can find a wide selection of new Coder projects on Google's site at googlecreativelab.github. io/coder-projects, so take some time to browse through them and pick one that looks fun. When you find one, you'll download it and add it to Coder. Here's how:

1. Click the **Download Complete Project** link. This downloads all the files you need for the Coder project onto your computer.

2. In the Coder app, click the **+** button on the landing page.

3. Name your project, pick a color, and click **Create**.

That's it for creating a new project. Each project page has a step-by-step guide for running through the project, so follow the guide to learn everything you need to know.

 PI POINTER

Each project page lists the skills you'll learn, so take some time to decide what you're interested in. Most of these are fun to do, so you'll have a good time making a fun little website regardless. But because they each teach a different skillset, it's worth spending some time picking the right project.

That's it with Coder. After you run through the three basic projects and go through a handful of the additional projects you find online, you'll have a pretty solid understanding of HTML, CSS, and JavaScript.

Bet you didn't think you'd pick up on all this so quickly, huh? It's not as hard as it looks, and the skills you learn are pretty applicable to basic web use.

Scratch

Scratch is a program included with Raspbian you can use to learn basic coding. It's not just in Raspbian though; you can download Scratch for Window or Mac or just use it in your browser. It's included in Raspbian because it's free and open source. It's also one of the best ways to teach kids basic programming skills, so it falls in line with the Raspberry Pi's lineage.

Scratch was created by the Lifelong Kindergarten Group at the MIT Media Lab. It's designed to teach kids aged 8 to 16 core programming principles, but it's great for people of all ages. You'll often find Scratch in elementary and high school computer labs.

 PI POINTER

Because it's free, you'll find Scratch pretty much any place that's teaching programming. Schools of all levels usually have it loaded on their computers, and you can even access it online if you don't feel like downloading software.

Scratch was made so anyone can understand how to make programs. It uses a programming language called *drag-and-drop programming.* Instead of writing out complicated and hard-to-remember lines of syntax, you simply grab a block of programming you want to use and drag it into your program. You connect these blocks until you have a working program. It's meant more for education than it is creating a final sellable product.

Instead of relying on a text editor, Scratch uses a graphical user interface. For people new to programming, this is often easier to understand because you're able to see what you're doing instead of just typing in text.

You're not going to make a massive program with Scratch, but you will learn all about the basics of how programming works. Scratch teaches you core principles like structure, object orientation, and threading. Moving forward, this should help you along the way if you want to take on another programming language.

The History of Scratch

Scratch's initial development at MIT Media Lab was led by Mitchel Resnick, Brian Silverman, and Paula Bonta. It was originally released in 2003. The first web-based version of Scratch was introduced in 2006, and since 2007, users can easily share their projects with other people on the Scratch website. It currently has around 4 million registered users.

According to Mitchell Resnick, the name *Scratch* comes from DJing. "We take the name 'Scratch,' from the way that hip-hop disk jockeys scratch with music. They take pieces of music and then combine them together in unexpected and creative ways," he says. That's the core principle of how Scratch works, too. You're taking bits and pieces of one thing and remixing them into another. It's surprisingly similar to a turntablist's work.

How Scratch Works

Scratch was founded with a simple motto: "Imagine, program, share." This also happens to describe the basic process for how Scratch programs work: first you think of an idea, then you program it, then you share it.

Unlike a traditional coding text editor, Scratch has a graphical user interface. It's divided into several parts that are grouped into three columns. To create a program, you drop blocks onto each other to create a longer script.

The Main Screen

When you first open Scratch, you're greeted with the Project Editor screen. This is the main screen you'll be working in to create your programs.

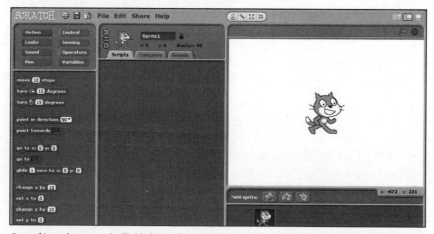

Scratch's main screen is divided into three parts: the palettes (left), the sprites (center), and the stage (left).

This probably looks pretty confusing at first, but it's actually very simple. Spend some time playing around on the main screen. Move stuff around, connect blocks to other blocks, and experiment with what happens.

The basic idea here is pretty simple: you take a block from the block palette, drag it into the scripts, and link them together to form a program that's acted out on the stage.

The Block Palette

The block palette on the left side of the main screen includes all the different operations you can perform. Drag a block from here into the scripting area in the center to add it to your program. This is the coding side of Scratch and where you'll define how your program works.

Let's take a look at each of the different block categories.

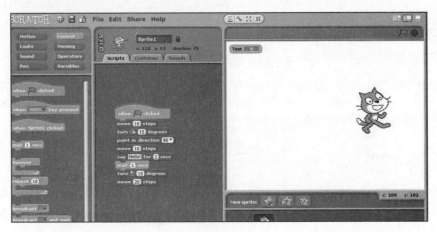

The block pallette is where you'll find the scripts to make your program.

Motion: The motion block moves your sprite around the screen. You have a variety of options here. You can make your sprite move a number of steps, turn, point in a direction, go to a specific point, or even bounce off the edge.

Looks: This is a graphics section. You can make your sprite switch into a costume, say something in text, change color, change size, or hide completely.

Sound: This makes your sprite make a sound effect. You can play a specific sound, play a drum, play an instrument, change volume, or alter the tempo.

Pen: The pen tool enables you to trace the motion of a sprite as it moves.

Control: This section is all about setting up parameters for your program to execute. Regardless of what other blocks you drop into the scripting area, they can't do anything until you add a control. For example, to start a program, you can add the When flag clicked block. This tells the program to start when you click the green flag icon. You can also add blocks for specific *if* variables, make sections repeat or your program repeat, and stop everything altogether. Remember, your program won't work unless you include a control block to start it.

Sensing: Sensing blocks watch for mouse, keyboard, or other sensor signals. For example, you can set your program to perform an action when the mouse is moved to an area, or when you input a specific command into the keyboard.

Operators: These are math, logic, and string functions. It sounds complicated, but it's actually pretty simple. For example, with an operator, you can set it up so math problems pop up on the screen and then have an answer box that needs the correct answer before it can move forward.

Variables: Variables are all about specific operations. These are basically known values. You can set a variable to read a correct answer, a string of text, or nothing at all.

That's all for the block palette. Play around with it for a little while to see what you can make your sprite do.

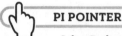

PI POINTER

Like Coder, the best way to learn how to use Scratch is to just mess around with it. You're not going to break anything on your Raspberry Pi, so feel free to try anything that comes to mind.

Sprites and Scripts

The center sprites and scripts section is where you drop your blocks to perform actions. A sprite is a Scratch object that's associated with an image. When you first load Scratch, this is a cat.

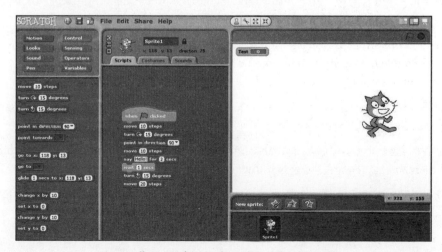

Set up all your actions in the sprites and scripts section.

Essentially, your sprite is the object you're trying to manipulate with your program. You drag the blocks onto the sprite, and it then does whatever you tell it to do.

You can connect these blocks successively by just dragging one block to another. So you could start with the Walk 10 Steps block and add the Turn 15 Degrees block to make your sprite walk 10 steps and turn.

Play around with these for a while. Once you start playing with different variations on your scripts, you'll get a better understanding of how they work.

Also in this section are the Costumes and Sounds tabs. With these, you can change your sprite's costume and record sound effects. With Costumes, you can click the **Paint** button to change the colors, **Import** to bring in your own images, or **Camera** to take a picture from your camera. With Sounds, you can click the **Record** button to record your own voice or the **Import** button to import sounds from your computer.

PI POINTER

You can use the Camera button to take a picture of yourself and insert your likeness into the program. Give it a try if you have the camera module installed on your Raspberry Pi.

The Stage

The stage is where your program executes. When you get everything in order, you can execute your program and you'll see it acted out on the stage.

Depending on what Control block you use, you can trigger it in the stage area. For example, if you used the green flag to start your program, click the green flag on the stage to see it execute.

Below the Stage you'll find the sprite menu. Here you can create new sprites and drag them into the stage so you're not stuck with just the default cat. Click the paint icon to draw your own sprite, and drag and drop it onto the stage when you're done.

Going Further

Scratch might be made for kids, but it's a big program that can do a lot. To really dig in, check out other people's projects, run through a few tutorials, and share your creations with others. Here are a few resources for doing just that:

Scratch Video Tutorials: To learn everything you need to know about programming with Scratch, it's best to start at the source. Scratch hosts a bunch of video tutorials that walk you through everything you need to know about programming with the software. You can find them at scratch.mit.edu/help/videos.

Check out other Scratch programs: Sometimes it's best to see what other people are doing with Scratch to help you with the idea portion. Explore other people's creations at scratch.mit. edu/explore.

Learn to Program with Scratch: This book covers everything you could possible need to know about programming with Scratch. You can make a ton of different programs, learn how Scratch works, and more. Get it from No Starch Press at nostarch.com/learnscratch.

Once you have a grasp on Scratch, you can move on to other programming languages if you're still interested. Scratch provides the mental framework for coding, but you still have so much more to learn if you're interested.

Other Programming Skills You Can Learn on Your Pi

Many different programming languages exist, and your Raspberry Pi is a great place to learn about them.

You'll need to track down books, online guides, and videos to really learn how to code, but the Raspberry Pi is set up to work with a few different programming languages out of the box.

Python

Python is already on your Raspberry Pi if you're using Raspbian. You can program with Python using IDLE or IDLE3; both applications should be on your Raspbian desktop. Whatever programs you create, you'll be able to execute them from your Raspberry Pi.

Python is a general-purpose programming language that works on a wide variety of operating systems. It was conceived in the late 1980s and released in 1991 by Guido van Rossum. Like many programming languages, Python uses standard statements like *if, for, while, try,* and others to designate when things happen. It's far too complicated to cover here, but Python is a great language to learn on the Raspberry Pi because just about everything you make can be executed on your Raspberry Pi.

You can find a lot more information about Python and the Raspberry Pi on the Raspberry Pi site at raspberrypi.org/documentation/usage/python. If you're looking for a fun project, writer Craig Richardson shows you how to use Minecraft to learn Python on the Raspberry Pi at arghbox. files.wordpress.com/2013/06/minecraftbook.pdf.

C++

C++ was created by Bjarne Stroustrup in 1982. It's one of the most popular programming languages today and is compatible with a range of operating systems.

It's known as an object-oriented programming language, which means it works differently from a language like Python. Instead of variables, it uses objects in its language to define characteristics. It'll make sense when you start actually using it.

C++ is a general-purpose programming language designed to work on all types of platforms. It's great for everything from video games to the Raspberry Pi.

In Raspbian, you'll use a program called Geany to write your C++ programs. It's included free in most versions of Raspbian. At a glance, it looks like a regular text editor, but it's made specifically for coding.

If you're looking for a place to get started with C++, element14 has a great guide using the Raspberry Pi at element14.com/community/community/code_exchange/blog/2013/01/02/c-tutorial--hello-raspberry-pi.

Java

Java is a programming language that uses the same object-oriented design as C++. The difference is that once the code is created, it can run on any machine, regardless of what you made it on. In the case of a Raspberry Pi, this means you can make something on your Raspberry Pi and use it on your personal computer running Windows.

Java was created by James Gosling for Sun Microsystems in 1995. Currently, the Oracle Corporation handles development. Java's used for all sorts of programs, but the most popular right now is Minecraft, which was developed in Java.

You can sign up for a free class that teaches you how to develop Java programs using the Raspberry Pi at apex.oracle.com/pls/apex/f?p=44785:145:0::::P145_EVENT_ID,P145_PREV_PAGE:861,143.

 PI POINTER

You can learn these programming languages on any computer you want, but the Raspberry Pi is great because it's packed with everything you need from the start. Plus, if you can get your program working on the Raspberry Pi, there's a pretty good chance it'll work great on every other computer out there.

The Least You Need to Know

- The Raspberry Pi's initial purpose was to teach coding, many programs for learning how to code were made for the Raspberry Pi.

- Learning to code is a great way to flex your mental muscles and learn basic logic and problem-solving skills.

- Google released a special SD card image called Google Coder that's meant to teach basic web programming skills.

- Scratch is free programming software developed by MIT to teach the basics of coding to kids.

The Raspberry Pi Community

Now that you've learned how to use your Raspberry Pi, run through a few projects, and have a good understanding of the hardware, it's time to branch out on your own. A big part of making things with the Raspberry Pi is the community around it, so if you want to continue making projects, it's good to get to know other people who are doing the same thing.

You have a lot of options for doing this. You can make your own Raspberry Pi guides and share them online, talk about the projects you're working on in various forums, meet up with your local hackerspaces to work with other people, or even share your finished projects at larger events.

In this chapter, you learn about all these options and more. By the end of it—and this book, for that matter—you'll be ready to branch out and start making on your own, collaborating with others, and sharing what projects you're working on. This book is just the beginning; the next step pushes you to really venture out and make something on your own.

In This Chapter

- Raspberry Pi communities online and off

- Writing your own Raspberry Pi guides

- Joining hackerspaces and maker groups

The Raspberry Pi Foundation

As you'd probably expect, the Raspberry Pi Foundation provides a lot of community activities to help support its device. In addition to basic tutorials and guides, the foundation's website has a forum for sharing your projects, teacher guides, student guides, and more.

Raspberry Jams

Depending on where you live, you might be able to take part in Raspberry Jams. These community events are organized by the Raspberry Pi Foundation to get people together to meet and talk about their Raspberry Pi projects.

Raspberry Jams vary from country to country and month to month, but the one consistency is the Raspberry Pi. Typically though, these events are pretty focused and easy to figure out. They often include basic open houses, child-learning activities, and even "Pi and Pints" meet-ups.

If you go to one of these jams, you can expect any number of things. At the very least, you'll meet some other Raspberry Pi enthusiasts. Typically, they also have workshops to teach you new skills, demonstrations to show off other people's projects, and speakers who talk more in-depth about all things Raspberry Pi. If you're lucky, they also have pizza.

It might seem strange to attend something like this if you're not a die-hard Raspberry Pi fan, but these events tend to be pretty fun, regardless of your level of interest. When you're at one, you'll meet a lot of likeminded people, learn about cool projects, and walk away a little more inspired than when you walked in.

 PI POINTER

You might not feel like you're expert enough to attend a Raspberry Pi event, but you don't have to be. Most of these events are geared toward people of all ages and skill levels, so go out, have fun, and make some cool stuff.

These events take place all over the world throughout the year. Keep track of them at raspberrypi.org/jam.

Making the Most of the Foundation's Resources

Beyond the Raspberry Jams, the Raspberry Pi Foundation offers a slew of other resources:

Forums: The forums are the most useful section on the Raspberry Pi website and where you'll likely spend the most time. If you're having trouble with a project, trying to brainstorm ideas for something new, or just want to chat about the Raspberry Pi, the forums are the place to do it.

You'll likely spend the bulk of your time in the Troubleshooting section, but the forums also offer areas to discuss programming, different project types, hardware, and plenty more. Chances are, if you Google a problem, the answer that pops up will be from the forums.

Of course, you might run into a brand-new type of problem that's all your own, so it's worth getting an account on the forums so you can ask questions of the community when you need help. Before long, you'll probably be one of the people answering those questions, too. You can find the forums at raspberrypi.org/forums.

Resources: Beyond the forums and everything else the Raspberry Pi Foundation does, it also offers a large selection of resources on its site, including free online classes, video guides, teacher's guides, and more.

You won't be interacting with anyone directly when you explore the resources, but they're a good venue for learning. You can find the resources at raspberrypi.org/resources.

Community: On top of providing plenty of original content and classes, the Raspberry Pi Foundation also curates a list of solid outside sources. Included are Geek Gurl Diaries, a collection of video tutorials from Carrie Anne Philbin; RasPi.TV, a collection of videos from Alex Eames; and countless others.

If you're ever feeling a little stuck on what to do with your Raspberry Pi, the community section on the Raspberry Pi Foundation website is a great place to start. Find it at raspberrypi.org/community.

The Raspberry Pi Foundation website is a fantastic resource for all things related to the Raspberry Pi. The forums alone are well worth your time. They're one of the best resources online for finding help to any Raspberry Pi problems you might have.

Instructables

The Raspberry Pi Foundation certainly isn't the only website talking about the Raspberry Pi. There are countless others, and one of the biggest is Instructables (instructables.com). Instructables is a site where users can share DIY projects of all types.

The Instructables Website

Instructables started in 2005 as an in-house documentation system to keep track of a set of projects happening in SQUID Labs. Eventually, in 2006, SQUID Labs launched Instructables as a public website.

Since then, Instructables has become home to millions of DIY projects ranging from cooking recipes to constructing solar panels. It's one of the biggest sites to share and find DIY projects of all kinds. Anyone can write an instructable guide for just about anything. The only requirement is that it's something you've made.

As you'd probably expect, the Instructables community latched onto the Raspberry Pi the second it was released. Over the last few years, Instructables has hosted hundreds of community-made Raspberry Pi projects—a number of which served as help and inspiration in the writing of this book. Basically, anyone who has an idea for a project can make an Instructables guide. This has made Instructables the go-to spot for community-written guides. You can find a list of all of the Raspberry Pi guides at instructables.com/howto/raspberry+pi.

 PI POINTER

If you're ever short of ideas, Instructables is a great place to visit for all types of DIY projects. The Raspberry Pi stuff is great, but even if you're looking for recipes, a Halloween costume idea, or just about anything else, Instructables is a solid resource.

How to Join

You can look at anything on Instructables for free, but if you want to write your own guide, you need to join the site. Joining Instructables is very easy and, for the most part, it's free. Head to instructables.com and click the **Sign Up** button. A free account is likely all you'll need so click the **Free Account** button, and follow the on-screen instructions to create your account.

After you've created an account, you can start posting comments, participating in the forums, and create your first guide. You can write a how-to Instructable guide for anything you've made, but chances are, after all the work you've put into it, you'll start off with a Raspberry Pi of some kind.

You can make one of three different types of Instructables: a video guide, a photo slideshow, or a step-by-step guide. For most electronics projects, you'll probably want to stick with a step-by-step guide.

Here are a few tips for making your first guide:

Prepare to take photos or screenshots: Your guide will be pretty similar to what you've seen in this book, so screenshots and photos are pretty helpful. Even if it's just a shot of the command line, a screenshot can help readers know they're on the right track.

If you're making something that does require photos, be sure they're clear and the subject is the focus. If you're taking pictures of the GPIO on your Raspberry Pi, for example, ensure that's the main focus of the shot.

Provide a good introduction: Writing an introduction can be tough, but what readers want from an Instructables introduction is very simple. They want to know what they'll get from doing your project, about how long it'll take to complete, and what materials you used. State all that up front, and you'll easily hook readers.

Clear steps: After your introduction, you just need to click the **Next Step** button to add new steps to your guide. Break up your steps as cohesively as you can. Don't make long steps; instead, go for shorter steps, even if that means you have more.

When you're done with your guide, click the **Publish** button and share it with all your friends.

The more Instructables guides you read, the better you'll be at writing your own, so spend some time on the site before you write your own. It's a fantastic way to share your projects with the public at large, so get used to spending a lot of time on the site.

 PI POINTER

Remember that anything published on Instructables is written by amateurs like you. This is awesome, but it also means you should be careful about what you're doing. If an instruction doesn't seem right or if you're not sure if you should be doing something, consult another site or an expert before you proceed.

Maker Media

Maker Media is a four-pronged DIY company that covers a ton of stuff with the Raspberry Pi. The company's facets are: *MAKE* magazine; Makezine.com; the Maker Faire; and the store, the Maker Shed.

The company started in 2005 as *MAKE* magazine, a bi-monthly DIY magazine that features how-to guides for all types of projects ranging from welding to electronics. The magazine spun off to the website, Makezine.com, which has since become an excellent resource for community and professionally made DIY projects. As you'd expect, the Raspberry Pi has become a favorite at *MAKE*.

MAKE, as well as the other Maker ventures, are all huge players in the DIY electronics industry. Countless Raspberry Pi projects have been created by the writers at *MAKE* and the entire community.

Maker Faires

Beyond the magazine, Maker Media also sponsors the Maker Faire. The Maker Faire is a family-friendly event that showcases DIY projects, crafts, engineering, and more in a variety of cities around the world. The first Maker Faire was in 2006 in the Bay Area and hosted around 22,000 people. The most recent Faires took place in the Bay Area, New York, Austin, Detroit, Kansas City, Tokyo, and Rome and totaled around 455,000 visitors.

Typically, these events have exhibitors showing off their projects, hands-on workshops, demonstrations, and vendors. When you walk in, you'll see people in costumes, vendors showing off fun DIY projects, and kids playing with a variety of electronics.

Aside from the larger Maker Faires, countless U.S. cities also host smaller events, called Mini Maker Faires. As the name implies, these are smaller versions of the larger Maker Faires. They operate on the same basic premise and have the same types of events; there's just less of them. If you live in a major U.S. city, there's probably a Mini Maker Faire near you. Go to makerfaire.com/map to find your closest faire.

The Raspberry Pi tends to be a big feature at these events. The very idea of the Raspberry Pi—an inexpensive, open-source computer designed for prototyping—is in line with what the Maker Faire is all about. If you go to one, you'll see many Raspberry Pi–inspired projects, demos, and workshops. If you get the chance, they're well worth attending and often a lot of fun. Plus, you'll probably meet some other Raspberry Pi hobbyists while you're there.

Aside from the faires, Maker Media also hosts MakerCon, a convention with a focus on engineering; Maker Camp, a summer camp for kids that's all about DIYing; and the Hardware Innovation Workshop, a workshop that focuses on the tools needed to manufacture your projects.

MAKE Magazine

The Maker Faires are awesome and a lot of fun to attend, but *MAKE* magazine and its website are where you'll find most of the Raspberry Pi community involvement.

The magazine's website, makezine.com, is host to a blog and a large projects page that are both great for inspiration on projects. The *MAKE* projects page isn't nearly as big as Instructables, but it tends to be a bit more focused and better written. The projects are similar, and the Raspberry Pi shows up regularly. Browse the projects at makezine.com/projects.

The printed version of *MAKE* magazine is also an excellent resource for tutorials, and the Raspberry Pi is often the focus of projects in the magazine. If you're interested in learning more about DIY electronics beyond the Raspberry Pi, *MAKE* is the best place to start.

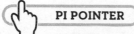 **PI POINTER**

MAKE magazine is one of the only magazines of its kind, and it's always a good place for inspiration. You might not find a new Raspberry Pi project in every issue, but you'll probably find another DIY project to tackle.

Getting Involved

Makezine.com isn't nearly as open as Instructables, but you can participate in the community pretty easily.

If you're interested in contributing to the magazine or its guides, you can do so by filling out a simple form at makezine.com/contribute. If you want to take a look at some of the Raspberry Pi projects that have been featured in the past, you can do so at makezine.com/category/electronics/raspberry-pi/?post_type=projects.

But getting involved isn't just about making projects with your Raspberry Pi. It's also about showing up to events. If you have a Maker Faire or Mini Maker Faire in your city, there's a really good chance they need volunteers. Giving your time not only gets you into the event for free, it also puts you in touch with other DIYers like you. This is a great way to meet other Raspberry Pi enthusiasts.

There's no dedicated landing page for volunteers, but each city has its own Maker Faire page. When you find yours, you'll usually find a section about volunteers. Just fill out the form, and you'll hear back from someone about whether or not you can join in the fun. It's a rewarding experience and well worth your time. Plus, you usually get a cool shirt.

Hackerspaces

Unless you're already involved in the DIY community, you've probably never heard of a hackerspace before. Hackerspaces are community workspaces where DIYers can get together and work on projects together, use equipment, and host workshops. They exist in most major cities and typically require a monthly fee.

You can think of a hackerspace as a community center for DIYers. They're typically in large buildings or warehouses, and inside is usually a DIYer's dream. You'll find tons of expensive equipment like 3D printers, CNC machines, and laser cutters along with large tables to work on whatever you want. It's basically a public garage where you can work on your projects with other likeminded people.

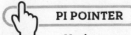

Hackerspaces are also sometimes known as *hacklabs, hackspaces,* or *makerspaces.* Regardless of the name, the premise behind each is fundamentally the same.

In addition to being loaded with tools, hackerspaces often have training classes, workshops, and community events where you can meet other members. They're usually very inclusive, welcome newcomers and experts alike, and thrive on a culture of sharing knowledge and tools.

Hackerspaces tend to be most prevalent in larger cities, partially because there are simply more people there, but also because many of the people who live in cities don't have access to a garage in which to work. Hackerspaces provide the space and freedom to work on your project when you don't have your own space.

They're also about community. If you join a hackerspace, you're immediately part of a community of likeminded people who are also making things. This is great for friendships and collaborations. Remember earlier in this book when I discussed building things like arcade cabinets and 3D molds? That's the kind of stuff you can do at a hackerspace. If you don't have the skills to do it yourself, you can find someone else who can and collaborate with that person. You can share your newfound knowledge of the Raspberry Pi and learn something new about woodworking or whatever else.

With respect to the Raspberry Pi, most hackerspaces are well versed in using the little computer and should have plenty of resources for you. They probably also have some classes you can take to extend your experience a little further. If nothing else, you can always volunteer your skills.

Finding a Hackerspace Near You

If you've never heard of a hackerspace, trying to find one probably sounds like some type of crazy underground research project. Thankfully, it's a lot easier than that.

You'll find a worldwide list of hackerspaces at hackerspaces.org/wiki/List_of_Hacker_Spaces. Just search for your city, and you'll find any hackerspaces near you.

You also could search online for "hackerspaces *yourcity*" to see if any others come up. It's really that simple.

If you don't have a hackerspace in your own town or close by, Adafruit has a great guide for starting one yourself at adafruit.com/blog/2012/11/12/how-to-start-a-hackerspace.

How to Join

Once you find a hackerspace you're interested in, you need to join before you can participate. Typically, you'll find a website listing on hackerspaces.org that tells you about the process.

In most cases, joining depends on what you need and want. Most hackerspaces offer a variety of membership packages at different rates. For example, Metrix in Seattle has a bottomless toolbox walk-in rate for $5 an hour and a soldering room for $15 an hour. It also has a basic membership for $50 a month that includes discounts on the toolbox, soldering room, textiles machines, and more.

It's not just monthly memberships and subscriptions, though. Most hackerspaces also have classes and workshops you can take priced at a set rate.

Joining is just as easy as joining any club. The website will likely tell you what you need to do, you'll pay a fee, and you'll be all set. Oftentimes, you'll need to go through a quick class to learn about the equipment in the space so you don't mess up anything, but it's pretty much a free-for-all after that.

The Least You Need to Know

- After you're finished with all the projects in this book, you can find lots more online.
- A massive community of other Raspberry Pi hobbyists are out there to help you with your own projects.
- Sharing projects online is easy with sites like Instructables.
- Getting involved with your local community through hackerspaces is a great way to learn more about the Raspberry Pi and meet likeminded people.

Glossary

access point (AP) mode   A mode in which a wireless adapter can act as an interface for a router or server.

AirPlay   An Apple software that enables your Raspberry Pi to receive a music signal from your home computer. With it, you can stream music from software like iTunes right to your Raspberry Pi without the need for cables.

amperage   The amount of ampere (usually shortened to *amp* or abbreviated *A*), the unit used to measure electric current. For power adapters, it's used to gauge the maximum number of power the adapter can send from an outlet to the device.

Arduino   A family of single-board microcontrollers similar to the Raspberry Pi but much more simple. A variety of different models of Arduino exist, and most are capable of running single programs that you create yourself. Like the Raspberry Pi, there's a massive community of DIYers who use the Arduino for their own electronics projects.

ARM processor   A type of processor architecture made to use fewer transistors than other processors. This means they're usually less expensive, use less power, and don't create as much heat. They're often the choice for processors in smartphones, tablets, laptops, and set-top boxes. The Raspberry Pi uses an ARM processor to keep costs down and power consumption low.

BeagleBoard   The BeagleBoard is incredibly similar to the Raspberry Pi, but it's a bit more powerful. Like the Raspberry Pi, it's an open-source single-board computer. The BeagleBoard is developed by Texas Instruments but was created to be used in schools to teach programming, much like the Raspberry Pi. The processor is a bit more powerful than the Raspberry Pi, it includes Flash memory on the board, but it has less RAM than the Raspberry Pi. It can also run a variety of different distributions of Linux.

breadboard   A board for making a model of an electronic circuit without the need for soldering.

cascading style sheets (CSS)   CSS is a special language used for web design that changes the look and formatting of a website. It's a little different from HTML because you can apply changes made in CSS to a variety of HTML pages at once instead of making individual changes on each page. Nowadays, it's used mostly to quickly change the look of a web page.

central processing unit (CPU)   The "brains" of a computer.

codec   The software that enables compression and decompression of a digital video.

command line   A way to interact with a computer program using typed commands as text instead of a mouse. Rather than clicking on something with your mouse, you tell your computer to perform an action using a simple string of text.

domain name server (DNS)   A directory of domain names on the internet. Like a phone book, it takes an IP address and translates it into a domain name that's easy to remember.

driver   A small bit of software that tells your computer how to interact with hardware. Without a driver, the computer doesn't understand that a new piece of hardware is connected and can't use it.

emulation   Emulation is when a computer mimics the behavior of another computer. For example, a Windows machine could emulate a Mac, or a Linux machine could emulate a Nintendo Entertainment System.

emulator   The program that does the actual emulation. It duplicates the function of one computer onto another.

encoding   Refers to the video codec, the software that enables compression and decompression of a digital video, with which a file is saved. Different types of software save using different codecs, and codecs can change the quality of a video.

encryption   Encryption is when information is encoded in such a way that nobody without the key can read it. When you send data, it's sent through a cypher so anyone who intercepts it can't read it. This is helpful when you're sending things like passwords or personally identifiable information.

Ethernet   Ethernet is a cable and port used in local area networks (LAN). An Ethernet cable looks like a larger phone cable.

file transfer protocol (FTP)   A network protocol used to transfer files between computers. In most cases, it's used to transfer files onto a web server.

firewall   A security system that protects your computer from the outside network. A firewall controls the incoming and outgoing connections of your computer and establishes a barrier that protects it from another network.

general-purpose input/output (GPIO)   A generic pin connector that enables you to connect your Raspberry Pi to other computers for more advanced projects. GPIOs can be used for just about anything because they don't have a dedicated purpose.

graphics processing unit (GPU)   An electronic circuit made to control and manipulate the visual processing on a computer. The better the GPU, the more complicated graphics it can process at once.

headless machine   Running your Raspberry Pi without a monitor.

high-definition multimedia interface (HDMI)   An audio/video interface that sends an uncompressed signal so it doesn't lose quality in the transfer. Because of this, it's typically used for high-definition signals so the video and audio quality remains high.

HyperText Markup Language (HTML)   The standard markup language on web pages. HTML uses tags enclosed by angle brackets to instruct a web browser how to display a page. For example, <h1> tells the browser to render text as a header.

Java   The programming language Minecraft was written in, universal across a variety of platforms. Java was originally released in 1995 by Sun Microsystems. Because Java is made to run on every platform imaginable, its original promise was to enable programmers to "write once, run anywhere."

JavaScript   JavaScript is a computer programming language typically used client-side on websites. Generally, it's used to create scripts so a user can interact with a website in interesting ways.

Linux   A free, open-source operating system that works on a wide range of computers. Because it's open source, anyone can make their own version of Linux, called a *distribution*. The most popular Raspberry Pi operating system, Raspbian, is a Linux distribution.

media center   A computer that hosts your media. You can set up a media center to stream content from an external hard drive, another computer in your house, or online sources. It's basically a DIY set-top box.

megabit   1 million bits, or 1,000 kilobits—the equivalent of about 100 pages of plain text. This measurement is usually used when talking about data transfer, so you'll see it places like your internet service provider bills. For context, a megabyte—the word we use to describe data storage—is 8 megabits combined.

microprocessor   Also known as the central processing unit (CPU), a microprocessor is essentially the heart of a computer. It processes instructions from code, executes that code, and sends the information where it needs to go.

MySQL   MySQL is database software used on web servers. It keeps track of data in tables so a website can easily access that information later.

network accessible storage (NAS)   A setup that enables a hard drive to be accessible by multiple computers attached to a router.

network address translation (NAT)   A setup that enables your computer to communicate with the internet via an internal IP address and a second group of IP addresses for external traffic.

new technology file system (NTFS)   A file system originally developed for Windows but that's now supported by every operating system. Out of the box, many hard drives are already formatted as NTFS, but you can check yours by typing `sudo blkid` into the command line.

open-source software   Computer software whose source code is available publically. Anyone can alter the code without worrying about copyright. Because of this, open-source software is often developed in collaboration among a large team of people.

overclocking   The act of making your CPU work harder than it's supposed to. The Raspberry Pi has a 700MHz processor, but you can overclock it up to 900MHz for speed increases. You can overclock your Raspberry Pi with any operating system, including Raspbian.

personal video recorder (PVR)   The device you often get with a cable package to record live video from your TV. It's also used in camcorders. With Raspbmc, you can access the video saved on your PVR so you don't have to go through your cable box.

PHP (PHP: Hypertext Preprocessor)   PHP is an open-source scripting language that can be embedded into HTML and is often used to run the back end of web servers so small scripts can run on websites.

port forwarding   A setup that enables your router to communicate with the internet. It translates the address online into a packet of information. A port is a number that makes it possible for your internal IP address to communicate with the outside internet.

Python   A programming language with an emphasis on syntax and readability. Unlike other programming languages, Python programmers can create expressions in just a few lines, which makes it easier to use for beginners.

random access memory (RAM)   A form of computer storage that allows data to be read and written at the same speed regardless of the order the information is accessed. Unlike traditional data storage, RAM isn't stored permanently.

Raspberry Pi   A small, credit card-size single-purpose board. It was created by the Raspberry Pi Foundation as an affordable means to get computers into schools. It runs Linux as its main operating system.

Raspberry Pi Foundation   The foundation responsible for creating the Raspberry Pi. The goal of the foundation is to provide affordable, programmable computers to everyone in the world.

RCA connector   A type of electrical connector that sends low-quality audio and video signals between devices through a coaxial cable.

read-only memory (ROM)   An image of a chip, or a computer file that contains a direct copy of a read-only memory chip like you'd find on a video game cartridge, an arcade game board, or a computer firmware.

Scratch   Scratch is a computer program built by MIT meant to teach people programming. Instead of using a specialized syntax to code software, Scratch uses event-driven, visual sprites that are easy to understand. It doesn't look like a typical program or block of code, but it works the same way and teaches the same principles.

secure digital (SD) card   A memory card typically used in portable devices. They're small cards that can store data that's accessible on a wide variety of devices.

Secure Shell (SSH)   A network protocol that allows for a secure connection between two computers on a network. In the case of the Raspberry Pi, it's a means for you to interact with the command line on the Raspberry Pi remotely from your desktop computer.

security certificate   Information that allows another computer to decrypt an encrypted message you send. Without the certificate, the two computers can't understand each other.

solderless breadboard   A prototyping board that allows you to make connections between cables without soldering or securing them together. Because it doesn't require soldering, it's reusable and easy for anyone to use. With the Raspberry Pi, you'd most likely use a solderless breadboard when you're working with anything involving the GPIO.

`sudo`   An abbreviation for *superuser do* that indicates you're running a command as a root user. This is essentially the same as running a command as an administrator. As a superuser, you can access files that wouldn't normally be available to all users and delete system files you might need, so be careful when you run anything as `sudo`.

synchronous dynamic random access memory (SDRAM)   RAM that can run at higher clock speeds than other types of RAM. The speed is synchronized with the system speed.

system on chip (SOC)   A system on a chip integrates all the components of a computer into a single chip. This typically means the CPU, GPU, and even the RAM are all on one chip. This is often used in mobile devices to keep costs down and sizes small.

virtual private network (VPN)   A network that shares a smaller local network over a larger network, like the internet. It's also a means to encrypt and secure any information that's sent over the network. VPNs are often used by remote workers to give them access to a company's private network from anywhere in the world.

web server   A computer that's accessible online. Typically, it's used to host the files and data needed to operate a website.

Wi-Fi adapter   A small USB device that adds Wi-Fi capability to any device that uses it. They come in small, nano-size kits hardly bigger than the USB port itself as well as larger versions with antennas that can help extend the signal.

XBMC   Media center software initially made for the Xbox but now available for many different operating systems—the Raspberry Pi included. It's basically a media player and streams software so you can turn a computer into a media device to play videos and music and display photos. Originally, XBMC stood for Xbox Media Center, but in 2014, the team announced the software name would change to Kodi.

Resources

You can do so many things with your Raspberry Pi, and there's no single right way to do things. This list of resources can help you troubleshoot problems, find new projects to work on, and try out alternate ways to take on some of the very same projects in this book.

Must-Reads

These books are some of the best for general Raspberry Pi information.

Bradbury, Alex, and Ben Everard. *Learning Python with Raspberry Pi*. Wiley, 2014.
If you're interested in learning Python, this is the place to start.

Girling, Gary. *Raspberry Pi: A Practical Guide to the Revolutionary Small Computer*. Owners' Workshop Manual, 2013.
This is a solid beginner's book with loads of projects to take on.

Richardson, Matt, and Shawn Wallace. *Getting Started with Raspberry Pi: Electronic Projects with the Low-Cost Pocket-Sized Computer*. Maker Media, 2014.
Another great beginner's book packed with all kinds of projects.

Upton, Eben, and Gareth Halfacree. *Raspberry Pi User Guide*. Wiley Press, 2014.
This was written by Raspberry Pi Foundation founder Eben Upton and is a great resource of all things Raspberry Pi related.

Raspberry Pi Resources

Websites

Adafruit
adafruit.com
Adafruit is not only a great store, it also has a ton of guides, tutorials, and other project ideas.

Building a Raspberry Pi VPN by Lauren Orsini
readwrite.com/2014/04/10/raspberry-pi-vpn-tutorial-server-secure-web-browsing
If you're interested in more information about building a VPN, this is a great place to start.

Getting Started with Sonic Pi V2.0
raspberrypi.org/learning/sonic-pi-2-taster
Curious about making some music on your Pi? This guide gets you started.

How to Host a Website with Raspberry Pi by Lauren Orsini
readwrite.com/2014/06/27/raspberry-pi-web-server-website-hosting
The guide in this book isn't the only way to create a server. This is another method.

How to Run a Low-Cost Minecraft Server on a Raspberry Pi for Block Building on the Cheap
howtogeek.com/173044/how-to-run-low-cost-minecraft-on-a-raspberry-pi-for-block-building-on-the-cheap
If you're looking for an alternate way to set up a Minecraft server, this guide will get you there.

IPSEC/L2TP VPN on Arch Linux on Raspberry Pi by Ray Mii
raymii.org/s/tutorials/IPSEC_L2TP_vpn_on_a_Raspberry_Pi_with_Arch_Linux.html
Another resource for another method to set up a VPN.

Raspberry Pi as a Low-Cost HD Surveillance Camera by Scavix
instructables.com/id/Raspberry-Pi-as-low-cost-HD-surveillance-camera
Another resource for building a low-cost camera with your Pi.

Raspberry Pi Foundation
raspberrypi.org
The Raspberry Pi Foundation started it all, so be sure you visit its site.

Raspberry Pi Web Server by Drcurzon
instructables.com/id/Raspberry-Pi-Web-Server
Yet another way to build a web server with your Raspberry Pi.

Turn Your Raspberry Pi into a Wireless Router by Jacob Salmela
jacobsalmela.com/raspberry-pi-and-routing-turning-a-pi-into-a-router
Another way to turn your Raspberry Pi into a router.

Ultimate Pi Home Server by DrWilson
instructables.com/id/Ultimate-Pi-Based-Home-Server
A similar web server to the one in this book but packed with even more applications.

Web Server Setup and WordPress
raspberrypi.org/learning/web-server-wordpress
Just looking to set up WordPress on your blog? Here's a good place to start.

Books

Karvinen, Tero, Kimmo Karvinen, and Ville Valtokari. *Make: Sensors: A Hands-On Primer for Monitoring the Real World with Arduino and Raspberry Pi*. Maker Media, 2014.
Interested in extending your Raspberry Pi into the real world? This book will get you there.

Monk, Simon. *Raspberry Pi Cook Book*. O'Reilly Media, 2014.
You can make all kinds of great new projects with this book.

Raspberry Pi Cookbook for Python Programmers. Packt Publishing, 2014.
If you're interested in learning Python on your Raspberry Pi, here's a great place to start.

General Linux Resources

Websites

Advanced Bash-Scripting Guide by Mendel Cooper
tldp.org/LDP/abs/html
If you're interested in learning how to write your own bash scripts, this is the place to start.

Bash Guide for Beginners by Machtelt Garrels
tldp.org/LDP/Bash-Beginners-Guide/html/index.html
Another great guide for learning bash scripts.

Learn Python the Hard Way
learnpythonthehardway.org
If you want to learn how to program in Python, this is a fantastic resource.

Linux.org
linux.org
A great landing site for all things Linux.

Linuxtopia
linuxtopia.org
Like Linux.org, this is a great resource for Linux guides and information.

Books

Cannon, Jason. *Linux for Beginners*. CreateSpace, 2013.
   A nice beginner's guide for all things Linux.

Negus, Christopher, and Christine Bresnahan. *Linux Bible*. Wiley, 2012.
   As the name suggests, you'll learn pretty much everything there is to know about Linux here.

Programming Resources

Websites

Code School
codeschool.com
Like Codecademy, Code School is a great place to learn how to code all types of language.

Codecademy
codecademy.com
If you want to learn programming, Codecademy is a great place to start.

JSDares
jsdares.com
If you're interested in JavaScript, JSDares is a fun place to learn it.

Khan Academy
khanacademy.org
Khan Academy has a ton of guides on just about everything you can imagine, including coding.

Udemy
udemy.com
Udemy is a great online class for learning programming.

W3Schools
w3schools.com
W3Schools will teach you everything there is to know about coding for the web.

Books

Briggs, Jason R. *Python for Kids: A Playful Introduction to Programming.* No Starch Press, 2012.
Learning to code when you're young makes things a lot easier, and this book gets you going at a young age.

Downey, Allen. *Think Python.* O'Reilly Media, 2012.
Python is complicated; this book breaks it down.

LEAD Project. *Super Scratch Programming Adventure!* No Starch Press, 2012.
Meant for children, this book is fun for anyone, of any age, learning Scratch.

Marji, Majed. *Learning to Program with Scratch.* No Starch Press, 2014.
If you want to learn more about Scratch, this is a solid starting place.

Index

B

C

Q-R

X-Y-Z

WITHDRAWN